Malaysia

WORLD BIBLIOGRAPHICAL SERIES

General Editors:
Robert L. Collison (Editor-in-chief)
Sheila R. Herstein
Louis J. Reith
Hans H. Wellisch

VOLUMES IN THE SERIES

VOLUME 12

Malaysia

Ian Brown
Rajeswary Ampalavanar
Compilers

CLIO PRESS

OXFORD, ENGLAND · SANTA BARBARA, CALIFORNIA
DENVER, COLORADO

220536

R
016.9595
B 878

© Copyright 1986 by Clio Press Ltd.

All rights reserved. No part of this publication may be reproduced, stored in any retrieval system, or transmitted in any form or by any means, electronic, mechanical, photocopying or otherwise, without the prior permission in writing of the publishers.

British Library Cataloguing in Publication Data

Brown, Ian, 1947–
Malaysia. – (World bibliographical series; v. 12)
1. Malaysia – Bibliography
I. Title   II. Ampalavanar, Rajeswary   III.   Series
016.9595   Z3246

ISBN 0–903450–23–2

Clio Press Ltd.,
55 St. Thomas' Street,
Oxford OX1 1JG, England.

ABC-Clio Information Services,
Riviera Campus, 2040 Alameda Padre Serra,
Santa Barbara, Ca. 93103, USA

Designed by Bernard Crossland
Typeset by Columns Design and Production Services, Reading, England
Printed and bound in Great Britain by
Billing and Sons Ltd., Worcester

THE WORLD BIBLIOGRAPHICAL SERIES

This series will eventually cover every country in the world, each in a separate volume comprising annotated entries on works dealing with its history, geography, economy and politics; and with its people, their culture, customs, religion and social organization. Attention will also be paid to current living conditions – housing, education, newspapers, clothing, etc. – that are all too often ignored in standard bibliographies; and to those particular aspects relevant to individual countries. Each volume seeks to achieve, by use of careful selectivity and critical assessment of the literature, an expression of the country and an appreciation of its nature and national aspirations, to guide the reader towards an understanding of its importance. The keynote of the series is to provide, in a uniform format, an interpretation of each country that will express its culture, its place in the world, and the qualities and background that make it unique.

SERIES EDITORS

Robert L. Collison (Editor-in-chief) is Professor Emeritus, Library and Information Studies, University of California, Los Angeles, and is currently the President of the Society of Indexers. Following the war, he served as Reference Librarian for the City of Westminster and later became Librarian to the BBC. During his fifty years as a professional librarian in England and the USA, he has written more than twenty works on bibliography, librarianship, indexing and related subjects.

Sheila R. Herstein is Reference Librarian and Library Instruction Coordinator at the City College of the City University of New York. She has extensive bibliographic experience and has described her innovations in the field of bibliographic instruction in 'Team teaching and bibliographic instruction', *The Bookmark*, Autumn 1979. In addition, Doctor Herstein coauthored a basic annotated bibliography in history for Funk & Wagnalls *New encyclopedia*, and for several years reviewed books for *Library Journal*.

Louis J. Reith is librarian with the Franciscan Institute, St. Bonaventure University, New York. He received his PhD from Stanford University, California, and later studied at Eberhard-Karls-Universität, Tübingen. In addition to his activities as a librarian, Dr. Reith is a specialist on 16th-century German history and the Reformation and has published many articles and papers in both German and English. He was also editor of the *American Society for Reformation Research Newsletter*.

Hans H. Wellisch is a Professor at the College of Library and Information Services, University of Maryland, and a member of the American Society of Indexers and the International Federation for Documentation. He is the author of numerous articles and several books on indexing and abstracting, and has also published *Indexing and abstracting: an international bibliography*. He also contributes frequently to *Journal of the American Society for Information Science, Library Quarterly*, and *The Indexer*.

For Andrew and Alasdair

Contents

Contents

Contents

Introduction

Malaysia came into existence on 16 September 1963, formed by the union of the Federation of Malaya which had achieved independence from Britain in August 1957, the island of Singapore which had been given internal self-government by Britain in 1958, and the two Borneo territories of North Borneo (henceforth Sabah) and Sarawak which had been British crown colonies since July 1946. On 9 August 1965 Singapore was expelled from the new Federation and became a separate independent state. Present-day Malaysia therefore comprises two territories separated by the South China Sea. West Malaysia (Peninsular Malaysia) forms the southern projection from the Asian mainland, with Thailand immediately to its north and the island of Singapore to the south. It has an area of 50,806 square miles and a population at the June 1980 census of 11,426,613. East Malaysia, occupying the northern part of the island of Kalimantan (Borneo), comprises the state of Sarawak, with an area of 48,050 square miles and a 1980 population of 1,307,582, and the state of Sabah, with an area of 28,725 square miles and a 1980 population of 1,011,046. As there are very considerable differences between West Malaysia and East Malaysia in terms of ethnic composition, forms of economic activity, history, and cultural traditions, this introductory essay will consider separately these two components of the modern state.

West Malaysia
The creation of a unitary polity in the Malay peninsula was not achieved until the establishment of British colonial administration, and even then not until the final decade of colonial rule. Historically the peninsula was occupied by a number of distinct states of varying territorial extent and political influence. By far the most prominent in the pre-colonial period was Melaka (Malacca). Founded in c. 1400, Melaka rapidly rose to become

the dominant entrepôt in the archipelago, indeed probably the greatest emporium in the Asia of that period, as well as a vigorous centre of Malay culture. In the early 15th century Melaka embraced Islam, as Muslim traders, principally from India, brought their religion into the region. Although the Melaka sultanate fell to the Portuguese in 1511, its institutions and cultural traditions continued to exert a powerful influence in the peninsula down to the modern period.

In the three centuries from the first establishment of a European territorial presence in the peninsula, no Malay state rose to match the former commercial strength and cultural splendour of Melaka. The most powerful peninsular Malay polity in this later period was Johor, her position being secured in part through her alliance with the Dutch who had taken Melaka from the Portuguese in 1641. Yet although the Dutch, and the Portuguese before them, sought political and commercial hegemony in the peninsula, neither power could be said to have seriously influenced the emerging pattern of Malay polities. In terms of commercial acumen, administrative strength, and military might, neither the European outposts nor the indigenous states could achieve sustained pre-eminence over the other. However, with the acquisition of Penang by Britain in 1786, her seizure of Melaka in 1795, and the founding of Singapore by Sir Stamford Raffles in 1819 (these three acquisitions being brought together into one administrative unit, the Straits Settlements, in 1826), the political structures, and the economic and social character of the peninsula came increasingly to be shaped by the European presence.

By the middle of the 19th century, the British possession of Singapore had emerged as the pre-eminent entrepôt in South East Asia, and one of the major trading ports in the East. Inevitably, therefore, the states particularly on the western side of the peninsula, the immediate hinterland of the Straits Settlements, became drawn into an increasingly dependent commercial relationship with the British ports. The relationship was based primarily on the exploitation of tin, as major deposits, notably in Larut (Perak), began to be worked out from the 1840s. Mining was financed in large part by Chinese Straits merchants, the labour force was predominantly immigrant Chinese coolie labour, and the extracted tin ore was exported principally through Penang and Singapore. However, by the 1860s the exploitation of tin had begun seriously to undermine the political structures and social order of the western peninsular states. As rival factions within the Malay political élite, frequently in alliance with rival Chinese secret societies, fought for control of an increasingly important new source of wealth, a severe breakdown in the established order threatened. In these circumstances the pressure for formal British intervention, notably but not exclusively from mercantile interests in the Straits, sharply increased. The precise reasons which led Britain to extend its political authority into the Malay states has long been the subject of academic controversy (see Cowan [154], Parkinson [166], Khoo [160], SarDesai [170], MacIntyre [164]), but it can be argued that the two crucial considerations were a determination to protect Britain's domination of the strategically important Straits of Malacca, and a more generally expressed wish to secure for Britain access to markets and to sources of raw materials in a period when rival European empires were capable of restricting commercial opportunities in other parts of South East Asia. By the terms of the Pangkor Treaty of January 1874, the Sultan of Perak agreed to accept a British Resident whose advice 'must be asked and acted upon on all questions other than those touching Malay religion and custom'. Later that year British authority was extended to Selangor and Sungai Ujung, and in 1888 to Pahang. In 1896 these four states (with Sungai Ujung part of a wider confederacy of Negeri Sembilan) were brought into a Federation of Malay States [FMS] with the federal capital at Kuala Lumpur. In 1909 the four northern Malay states of Kedah, Perlis, Kelantan, and Trengganu, long within Siamese suzerainty, were transferred to British authority: and in 1914 the southern state of Johor was required to accept a British Adviser. These five states, however, declined to enter the Federation, and were therefore collectively known as the Unfederated Malay States [UMS]. In brief, by 1914 British authority extended throughout the peninsula, but it was exercised through three distinct constitutional arrangements – in the Federated Malay States, the Unfederated Malay States, and the Straits Settlements. Although the inter-war years saw a vigorous consideration of constitutional reform, it was not until the 1940s that the British moved decisively towards the creation of a single, unified administration.

Three particular aspects of British rule in the peninsula should be noted for the important implications which they have had for contemporary Malaysia. The first concerns the political and social status of the Malay élite within the Malay community. In a formal sense government in the Malay states was conducted in the name of the sultans, acting on the advice of the British

Residents. In reality executive authority lay very firmly with the British officials. This was certainly the case in the FMS, occasionally less so in the UMS where the sultans could develop a small measure of independence from British advice. In order to sustain the fiction of government by the sultans, the British authorities in Malaya took meticulous care to treat the former with the full deference and ceremony due to royalty. In addition junior members of the Malay ruling houses and aristocracy, after acquiring an élite English-language education, were recruited into a distinct Malay Administrative Service. The effect of British administration in this respect was to enhance the political and social authority of the traditional Malay élite, and this class has succeeded in maintaining a powerful position in the Malay community well into the independence period. A further consequence of this aspect of British rule was that it laid the basis for a political tenet which has had a most powerful influence on the political, economic and social structures of the peninsula through to the present – the principle that the Malays occupy a privileged position in the country. Second, it was during the colonial period that Malaya emerged as the principal world producer of both tin and rubber. In the early decades of British rule, tin dominated the export economy. As the tin seams were concentrated in the west coast states it was inevitable that the peninsula's modern economic infrastructure – its railways, international ports, financial and trading agencies – came to be located predominantly in those same states. Consequently, with the rapid emergence of rubber as Malaya's principal commercial crop in the opening years of the 20th century, the plantations and smallholdings too were located overwhelmingly on the west coast of the peninsula. Thus to this day there is a clear distinction in the character of the west and east coast states. The west of the peninsula is more urbanized, export orientated, and economically sophisticated: the east coast states are overwhelmingly rural, less densely populated, and orientated towards subsistence agricultural production. Finally, it was during British rule that the Malay states experienced a major immigration of Chinese and, to a lesser extent, Indians, as well as the emergence of a distinct division of economic roles and occupational patterns along ethnic lines. In broad terms, Chinese coolie immigrants were found in tin mining; the rubber plantations were tapped by Indian labour; whilst the Malays remained predominantly subsistence padi cultivators. As a result the Malays found not only that their numerical superiority was threatened (the 1931 census showed that Chinese constituted 39 per cent of the population of 'British Malaya' compared with 44.7 per cent for Malays, and that Chinese outnumbered Malays in all states except the four northern UMS), but also that economic power was largely and increasingly concentrated in non-Malay hands. This close balance between the size of the Malay and non-Malay communities, allied to the serious imbalances in their relative economic strengths, remains the fundamental issue for the contemporary Malaysian polity.

The invasion of Malaya by Japanese forces on 8 December 1941, the surrender of the 'impregnable' fortress of Singapore in mid-February 1942, and the subsequent Japanese occupation of the peninsula until August 1945 constitutes a major turning point in the modern political history of the country. Britain's humiliating defeat finally destroyed the myth of white superiority which had been important in sustaining colonial rule in Malaya, as elsewhere; whilst the collaboration of the Malay sultans with the Japanese, the fierce anti-Japanese resistance of major sections of the Chinese community, and the harsh treatment of many Indians at the hands of the Japanese, very considerably heightened political awareness and communal antagonisms among the Malayan peoples. Major constitutional reform proposed by the British soon after their return to Malaya in September 1945 inadvertently raised still further political and communal sensibilities. In the post-war period the re-established colonial administration was repeatedly forced to confront a major dilemma. On the one hand the colonial power's treaties with the sultans which had introduced British administration to the Malay states from the 1870s and the subsequent public deference shown to the Malay rulers, constituted an explicit recognition of the privileged political position of the Malays among the peoples of Malaya. On the other hand, by the post-war period both the Chinese and Indian populations had taken on the demographic patterns of permanently-settled communities and thus were increasingly seeking equal citizenship rights in their adopted country. The dilemma was aggravated by economic considerations. Whilst there was unease among British officials that colonial administration had in effect allowed the Malays to be out-run by two economically aggressive immigrant races, there was also a realization that the very major contribution of the Chinese and Indians to the creation of the export economy of Malaya had to be recognized.

Post-war British policy in Malaya first came to grief over this dilemma when, in January 1946, the colonial power announced proposals for the creation of a Malayan Union which would include within a single, unitary state, the FMS, the UMS, Penang, and Melaka. All citizens of the Malayan Union would have equal rights, and citizenship was to be extended to all without discrimination as to race. These provisions provoked such extreme anger among the Malays, (it led to the formation of the major Malay political party, the United Malays National Organization [UMNO] in May 1946), that the Malayan Union proposals could not be brought into effect. In February 1948 the colonial administration secured the inauguration of an alternative constitutional arrangement, the Federation of Malaya. The Federation maintained the earlier proposal for a single, unitary state (with Singapore withdrawn from the Straits Settlements to form a separate crown colony), but its provisions for the acquisition of citizenship were considerably more restrictive for the non-Malays than those contained in the abortive Malayan Union.

Four months later, in June 1948, the Malayan Communist Party [MCP] launched an armed struggle against British rule. Formally organized in 1930, the MCP had provided the most formidable opposition to the Japanese during their war-time occupation, and had constituted the sole organized political and military force in Malaya in the brief period between Japan's surrender and the landing of British troops to restore colonial rule. Even so, in August-September 1945 the MCP felt itself to be insufficiently prepared and armed to seize and hold power by force, and consequently in the immediate post-war years it engaged in an 'open and legal' struggle, principally by strengthening and politicizing the labour movement. However, by the early months of 1948, strongly-restrictive trade union legislation, introduced by the British administration in order to weaken the authority of the MCP over the labour movement, allied with a change in international communist strategy, led the Party to embark on an armed revolt. A series of murders of European rubber estate managers in June 1948 signalled to the colonial authorities the changed direction in communist strategy, and on the 18th of that month the government proclaimed a state of emergency throughout Malaya.

In its opening years the communist insurrection severely stretched the British and Commonwealth forces which were brought into Malaya. Moreover, in October 1951 the communists delivered a stunning blow to the British by assassinating the High

Commissioner, Sir Henry Gurney. Yet despite these advances, the MCP failed to disrupt seriously the export economy of Malaya: more importantly, from the outset, a decisive military-political victory lay beyond the communists. The MCP's most severe disadvantage lay in the fact that it drew its membership almost exclusively from among the economically deprived Chinese. It found little support, indeed very considerable hostility, both in the Malay community and among the wealthy, influential Chinese élite. The principal anti-communist strategy, employed by the British from 1950, was the resettlement of the Chinese squatter communities which had supplied the guerrillas with food, information and recruits, into militarily enclosed 'New Villages'. It is estimated that by 1952, some 423,000 Chinese squatters had been resettled in 410 such compounds. By the mid-1950s the communist insurrection had been effectively broken, although the 'Emergency' was not officially ended until July 1960.

The communist insurrection was also undermined from the early 1950s by increasingly clear evidence that Malaya was being moved towards political independence. This process first involved the British in an attempt, from the end of the 1940s, to encourage discussion between the Malay, Chinese, and Indian élites. Partly as a result of these initial discussions, the President of UMNO, Dato Onn Ja'afar, sought to persuade his party to adopt a less communal position, specifically to open its ranks to all, irrespective of race. When Dato Onn failed in this attempt, he left the UMNO and founded the non-communal Independence of Malaya Party [IMP]. But the IMP's interests, although non-communal, were primarily élite-centred, and as a result the party failed at the polls in the early 1950s. With the IMP's electoral failure, British hopes of seeing the emergence of a non-communal party to dominate Malayan political life, collapsed.

In the event the political reconciliation of Malay interests and non-Malay aspirations arose not from the prompting of the colonial administration but from within Malayan political life itself. In early 1952 the Selangor branches of the UMNO and of the MCA [Malayan Chinese Association, formed in 1949] agreed to contest the Kuala Lumpur municipal elections as a united front. From this successful local alignment grew a national alliance in which both parties retained their separate identities and policies whilst acting as a single unit in selecting the candidates who would contest each seat. The MIC [Malayan Indian Congress, formed in 1946] entered the Alliance in 1954.

Introduction

The following year the UMNO-MCA-MIC alliance demonstrated its domination of Malayan politics by securing 81 per cent of the vote and all but one of the 52 contested seats in the first federal elections. The colonial administration then turned to framing a constitution for an independent Malaya. In this the British again faced the critical dilemma of securing the privileged position of the Malays whilst satisfying the aspirations of the now permanently-settled Chinese and Indians. The independence constitution sought to resolve that dilemma, first by providing for a single Malayan nationality in which all persons in the Federation could qualify as citizens either by birth, or by meeting requirements of residence, language and loyalty; and second, by charging the Yang Di-pertuan Agung [the King] with responsibility for protecting the privileged position of the Malays, as well as the 'legitimate interests' of the other races. With the ratification of that constitution, Malaya moved to independence [Merdeka] on 31 August 1957.

Independence for the Federation left British rule in the peninsula limited to Singapore. In 1958 the island was given internal self-government under an interim constitution that was to expire in 1963. The prospect of a fully-independent Singapore caused considerable concern in Kuala Lumpur, primarily because it was feared that the left-wing elements then dominant in the island's politics would seek to aid their counterparts on the mainland. From this emerged the proposal, vigorously pursued by the Federation's Prime Minister, Tunku Abdul Rahman, from 1961, that an independent Singapore be incorporated in a wider Malayan federation. Such a merger would also secure the economic and commercial ties between the mainland and the island which had developed so strongly during the colonial period. But merger also carried a serious disadvantage for Kuala Lumpur, in that the inclusion of Singapore's overwhelmingly Chinese population would threaten the slim numerical superiority of the Malays in the Federation. The solution to this problem was sought in the further inclusion of the territories of North Borneo and Sarawak within the new grouping, for it was argued that their populations would restore Malay dominance. Despite initial reluctance, North Borneo [Sabah] and Sarawak joined with Singapore and the Federation of Malaya in the creation of the Federation of Malaysia, inaugurated on 16 September 1963.

The Malaysian federation was soon under strain, from both external and internal forces. Driven primarily by domestic political tensions, the Indonesian government under Sukarno declared its strong opposition to the new Federation. Diplomatic links between Jakarta and Kuala Lumpur were severed, military incursions into Sarawak and Sabah were conducted across the border from Indonesian Borneo, and saboteurs were infiltrated into Peninsular Malaysia and Singapore. However, these military threats were contained without serious difficulty by Malaysian and Commonwealth forces, and with the abortive coup in Indonesia in October 1965 and the subsequent fall of Sukarno from power, Indonesian opposition to the Federation faded. External opposition had also come from the Philippines, which from early 1962 had pursued through diplomacy territorial claims to Sabah. But by 1966 the Philippines too extended recognition to the Malaysian federation, although her claim to Sabah remained, and indeed to this day the issue is not fully resolved. The reconciliation of the Philippines and Indonesia with Malaysia was crucially reinforced when, in August 1967, those three states joined with Thailand and Singapore in the creation of the Association of Southeast Asian Nations [ASEAN]. The internal strains of the Malaysian federation arose primarily from the ambitions of Singapore's Peoples Action Party [PAP] under Lee Kuan Yew to extend its political influence into the mainland and to secure representation in the Kuala Lumpur parliament. In effect the PAP sought to challenge the MCA for the Chinese vote on the mainland, a challenge which if successful would have broken the Alliance. For its part, the PAP saw in some of the economic and political measures being pursued by the Kuala Lumpur administration an attempt to remove it from power. As the political conflict between the Alliance and the PAP threatened to provoke serious communal violence, in August 1965 Singapore was, in effect, expelled from the Federation.

The federal elections of May 1969 and their immediate aftermath, have proved to be the crucial turning point in the history of independent Malaysia, for the consequences of those events continue to dominate the character of the modern Malaysian state. The elections left the Alliance with less than 50 per cent of the popular vote and a substantially reduced majority in the federal parliament: electoral support had swung dramatically in favour of Chinese-dominated opposition parties, notably the Gerakan and the Democratic Action Party [DAP]. The day following the elections, 13 May, Gerakan and DAP supporters held victory celebrations in Kuala Lumpur: a counter-demonstration by UMNO supporters then rapidly led to severe racial violence. It was four days before civil order was restored to the capital, and fully two months before all inter-communal violence came to an end. The official death toll arising from the initial riots was 178, but in reality the number of dead may well have been much higher.

The May 1969 riots, in exposing the tense fragility of communal relations in Malaysia, until then largely masked by the communal bargaining which had taken place within the Alliance, provoked a decisive refashioning of Malaysian political life and economic structures. In essence this refashioning, which took place in the opening years of the 1970s, involved the removal from open public discussion of major contentious issues thought likely to incite communal discord, and the emergence of a firm commitment not simply to protect, but to *advance* Malay interests. Three aspects of this realignment were particularly important. First was the formulation of a national ideology, *Rukunegara*, formally promulgated in August 1970. The principles of *Rukunegara* were, *inter alia*, that Islam is the official religion of the Federation (although no citizen would be discriminated against on religious grounds), and that the powers and position of the Malay rulers and the privileged rights of the Malays, as stipulated in the Constitution, were inviolable. With the declaration of these principles, the government then sought, primarily through use of the Sedition Ordinance, to prohibit any public questioning or criticism of those sections of the Constitution covered by *Rukunegara*. Second, beginning in 1971 the UMNO secured the expansion of the Alliance coalition into the much broader alignment of the Barisan Nasional [National Front], within which were included former opposition parties, notably Gerakan and, for a time, Parti Islam [PAS], as well as political parties from East Malaysia. This major expansion of the ruling coalition had the effect of bringing the potentially discordant processes of communal bargaining still further within the secluded confines of government itself. Moreover, those processes of communal bargaining within the Barisan Nasional were primarily influenced by the UMNO which had a clear domination of the government coalition not matched during the Alliance years. Most notably, through the 1970s UMNO ministers came to hold an increasingly large majority of important government portfolios. Third, again in 1971 the government inaugurated a New Economic Policy [NEP] to be implemented over the period to 1990. The two principal objectives of the NEP were the reduction and eventual eradication of poverty irrespective of race, and, perhaps more notably, the reduction and eventual elimination of the identification of race with economic function. This second objective primarily implied reducing the concentration of the Malays in subsistence agriculture, and increasing their employment in the modern rural and urban sectors of the economy; and increasing the proportion of Malay ownership of industrial and commercial share capital. The government held that this restructuring would be secured not through a redistribution of existing resources away from the non-Malay communities but through the proceeds of sustained economic growth. In detail, from the early 1970s the Malaysian administration pursued with gathering rigour and comprehensiveness a major programme of positive discrimination in favour of the Malay population. It involved, for example, the creation of a number of public enterprises which would provide assistance to Malay entre-preneurs, establish business concerns which in time could be transferred to private Malay interests, and purchase shares in established companies on behalf of the Malay community; the introduction of Malay as the medium of instruction at all levels of education; and the institutionalization of privileged access for Malays in such crucial areas as the allocation of public sector housing, university entrance, civil service employment, and in the allocation of commercial licences.

Through the 1970s and into the 1980s, therefore, the society and institutions of Peninsular Malaysia have taken on an increasingly distinct Malay dominance. This process has been encouraged by the growing influence of Islamic fundamentalism particularly among young urban Malays, although it should be emphasized that senior Malay government ministers and the UMNO as a whole, aware of the need to maintain the accommodation between the Malay and non-Malay communities even within the context of a rigorously pursued Malayization, have firmly sought to curb the demands and ambitions of the more fundamental Islamic groups. Yet increasing Malay domin-ance, and the related characterization of open discussion of 'sensitive issues' as sedition, has clearly placed a major strain on the non-Malay communities and on the non-Malay components of the Barisan Nasional – notably the MCA, which in the mid-1980s has come close to disintegration. It might be added that unease with, and frequently opposition to, the objectives and strategy of the UMNO-dominated ruling coalition can also be found among significantly large segments of the Malay community where it is argued that, despite declared government ambitions and rhetoric, there has in fact emerged an alliance between the

Introduction

Malay administrative élite and Chinese capital which stands in opposition to the interests of the Malay poor, indeed all the poor irrespective of race. To this the Malaysian government would argue, with some justification, that its firm intent to secure a full Malay participation in the ownership and control of the modern Malaysian economy, and the removal of 'sensitive issues' from public debate provides the only viable path for Malaysia (given its finely balanced communal interests and ambitions) to achieve political and social stability with economic advance.

East Malaysia

As was noted in the opening paragraph of this essay, the two states of East Malaysia provide a strong contrast with the peninsula in terms of historical experience, patterns of economic activity, and ethnic composition. In particular the populations of Sabah and Sarawak have an ethnic variety and richness that has made the area a major focus of anthropological research for a century and more. Many of the indigenous peoples here number only a few hundred, but among the numerically more important are, in Sarawak, the Iban ['Sea Dayak'], the Land Dayak, and the Melanau; and in Sabah, the Kadazan [Dusun], the Bajau, and the Murut. Both states also have substantial Malay and, in particular, Chinese populations, the latter having arrived in the area in numbers from the mid-19th century. It might be added here that these territories also possess an exceptionally rich flora and fauna which have long attracted the interest of naturalists.

This area of Borneo has seen, particularly in recent decades, important archaeological work. Perhaps most notable has been the discovery at Niah [Sarawak] of one of the oldest finds of modern man, dating from some 35,000 years ago. There have also been important excavations of trading polities in this area dating from the early centuries of the second millennium AD. Yet it must be said that in the absence of indigenous texts and with the paucity of European trading contacts and thus records, the early history of this area – the rise and collapse of trading communities, the internal migrations of the indigenous peoples – remains frustratingly inadequate, although recently historians have begun to use indigenous oral sources to reclaim the early historical record (Sandin [327]). With the first establishment of European administration in north-west Borneo in the middle of the 19th century, the history of the area comes more fully into view. In 1840 an English adventurer, James Brooke, came to the aid of the Raja Muda of Brunei (then the dominant polity in that area) in his suppression of an uprising of Malay chiefs in the area of the Sarawak River. In return for this assistance and for a modest annual payment, Brooke was granted territory in the western extremity of present-day Sarawak. In 1841 Brooke took the title of Raja of Sarawak, and established a capital at Kuching, hitherto a small Malay village. After consolidating his authority in that initial concession, he rapidly moved to extend the territory under Sarawak control, moving still further into areas nominally under the authority of Brunei. This process involved Brooke in military campaigns against, and political intrigues among, the Iban whose head-hunting culture, warfaring traditions and 'piratical' expeditions stood temporarily against the European advance. In the 1850s and 1860s the weak Brunei sultanate accepted, in return for further annual payments, major Brooke annexations into the principal Iban-occupied districts. The expansion of Sarawak territory continued under James Brooke's nephew, Charles Brooke, who became Raja on the death of his uncle in 1868. Indeed additions to Sarawak territory continued into the opening years of the 20th century, although the last major annexation at the expense of Brunei (the Limbang River) took place in 1890. By this time Sarawak occupied by far the largest territory in north-west Borneo.

Brooke rule had a distinctive character among the western administrations in colonial South East Asia. First the Brookes strongly discouraged the entry of western capital into their territory, fearing that the major economic changes which would follow might irreparably disturb, even destroy, the long-established way of life of the indigenous peoples: possibly there was also fear that those changes might in time undermine Brooke authority itself. Consequently the considerable economic potential of Sarawak remained largely unexploited under Brooke rule, the principal trade of the territory in this period involving the collection of jungle products which were shipped mainly to Singapore. Second the Brookes maintained a strongly exclusive, personal authority over their territory, although that authority was exercised in a firmly paternalistic manner. Yet if Brooke rule left the peoples of Sarawak without significant training for self-government, it did at least encourage in the territory an early acknowledgement of a central authority beyond the traditional allegiance to the longhouse and to the kin group.

European rule came to the northern-most fragment of Borneo (present-day Sabah) at a later date and in a different form than it did in Sarawak. Into the 1870s this territory was under the nominal suzerainty of the Sultan of Sulu, the southernmost islands of the Philippine archipelago. However, from that decade there was growing British apprehension at the possibility of intervention by another European power in northern Borneo, for such an intervention might be said to threaten the security of the trade routes to China from both Australia and India. Towards the end of the 1870s a consortium which included an influential London businessman, Alfred Dent, actively supported by the governor of the British colony of Labuan, William Treacher, negotiated major territorial concessions in north Borneo from first the Sultan of Brunei and then the Sultan of Sulu. Then, having established their position in the territory, in 1881 the concessionaires secured the formation of a chartered company in London, the British North Borneo Company. In 1888, North Borneo, as well as Sarawak and Brunei, was granted protectorate status, under which responsibility for foreign policy was surrendered to the British Government in return for assured protection from external attack.

Under chartered company rule, North Borneo experienced significant economic growth – in the export of timber and tobacco from the 1890s and, in particular, of rubber from the beginning of the new century – although it should be added that that growth fell some considerable way behind the pace of export expansion then being experienced in the peninsula. In contrast, the Company's political administration lacked the coherence and perception of Brooke rule in Sarawak. Perhaps most notably, few Company officials acquired the thorough knowledge of the peoples under their authority that was a feature of later Brooke administration. Neither was the Company able to secure the wider allegiance to central authority then being secured by the strongly personal rule of the Brooke raj.

European rule in North Borneo and Sarawak was swept aside by the Japanese military advance through the region from late 1941. Following the Japanese surrender in August 1945, the effective re-establishment of the Company and Brooke administration proved impossible, primarily because the costs of economic reconstruction in the post-war period lay beyond their resources. In July 1946 Sarawak and North Borneo became crown colonies, so ending more than a century of 'white raja' rule and of chartered company administration from the 1880s. The period of direct colonial administration was very short for both territories, certainly insufficient for any substantial political advance in the direction of responsible and representative government to be initiated. Consequently there was considerable apprehension in North Borneo and Sarawak when, in 1961, the Prime Minister of Malaya, Tunku Abdul Rahman, proposed the incorporation of the independent Borneo territories with Malaya and Singapore to form a Malaysian federation. The prospect of Malaysia brought a proliferation of political parties in both Borneo states, which in time were structured primarily along communal lines, and a wave of political activity which touched even the remote jungle communities. Early opposition to federation on the part of the principal political leaders of North Borneo and Sarawak soon faded, partly because Malaya was prepared to make a number of important concessions to Bornean autonomy in order to entice the two states into federation, partly because Bornean opinion became seriously concerned over the aggressive stance then being adopted towards the territories by both Indonesia and the Philippines. In state elections held in the first half of 1963, pro-Malaysia alliances in both North Borneo and Sarawak won decisively: September 1963 brought independence and merger.

Although there has never been a serious East Malaysian challenge to the unity of the Federation, from 1963 there has been an underlying tension in the relations between the federal government in Kuala Lumpur and the state governments of Sabah and Sarawak. In essence this tension has derived from the notably lower level of economic development and political sophistication in the East Malaysia states, which leaves there a recurring apprehension of peninsular authority. In fact the federal government has shown a notable sensitivity to these fears, not only by allowing Sabah and Sarawak a measure of autonomy denied to the states of the peninsula but also by actively promoting their economic and social development. Yet Kuala Lumpur has also been prepared to intervene in the local politics of East Malaysia to ensure the supremacy of those political leaders who would co-operate more fully with it, to secure the eclipse of those seen to be *too* ambitious in their assertion of state autonomy. Consequently the last decade has seen a perceptible closing of the relations between the states of East Malaysia and the peninsula, although the full economic and social integration of the peoples of Sabah and Sarawak into a unified Malaysian nation still lies some considerable distance in the future.

On the use of this bibliography
The rich variety of human existence and, of course, of animal and plant life found in the territories which constitute present-day

Introduction

Malaysia has engendered a comparably rich literature. Perhaps most notably the distinct racial balances of the peninsula – their full emergence during the period of colonial rule and their contemporary manifestations and implications for the economic and political structures of the modern state – have attracted very considerable attention from historians, political scientists, economists, and sociologists; while the explosive variety of flora and fauna, and the exceptional number of distinct peoples who inhabit the Borneo territories (to a lesser extent the peninsula as well) has made the area a major focus of research by naturalists and anthropologists. It should therefore be emphasized that this bibliography is a selective one, ruthlessly so in certain fields (for example, those referred to immediately above). Yet an attempt has been made to include the important works in all fields, and certainly this bibliography provides the most detailed entrance into the full literature on the country.

The bibliography is divided into thirty-four main subject headings, nine of which are further sub-divided. Within each main subject heading or sub-division, (as the case may be), entries are arranged alphabetically by author. Each entry gives full details of title and author. For books, details are also provided for place of publication, publisher, date of publication, edition (where appropriate), number of pages (or volumes), number of maps, and whether the work contains a bibliography or bibliographical references (denoted by 'bibliog.'). For articles, details are also provided for the name, and volume and part number of the journal in which the article appears, and the precise page references. All entries are fully annotated. The index is a single alphabetical sequence of authors, titles of books and journals (but not of individual journal articles), and subjects. The subject entries are both detailed and comprehensive, and thus make possible the identification of the literature concerned with very discrete subject areas. Title entries are in italics and numeration refers to the entries as numbered.

A brief note on the arrangement of Malaysian names may also be useful at this point. Malays carry only personal names. For bibliographical purposes therefore, Malays are normally indexed by their full personal name: *Husin Ali*; *Shahnon Ahmad*. However some Malays are more usually referred to by the later components of their full personal name: Mohamed *Noordin Sopiee*. Readers seeking a particular Malay author are advised to check all components of that author's name. Note should also be made of two insertions which frequently occur in Malay names:

bin ('son of'); and *haji* (which indicates that that person has made the pilgrimage to Mecca). Prominent Malays may also carry honorifics, notably 'Tunku' and 'Dato'. Indeed Malaysia's independence leader and first prime minister, Tunku Abdul Rahman, is frequently referred to simply as 'Tunku'. Chinese names present less problems. The family name comes first, followed by the given names: thus *Wong* Lin Ken, who is indexed under Wong. Indian names, at least those which appear in this bibliography, are, for bibliographical purposes, arranged in the same form as European names: thus Sinnappah *Arasaratnam*; Jagjit Singh *Sidhu*.

And there must be some reference to the use of the word 'Malaysia' itself. Strictly speaking it should be applied only to the Federation established in September 1963, comprising the peninsula (excluding Singapore) and the two Borneo territories. The use of the name 'Malaya' is riddled with difficulties. Again strictly speaking it should be applied only to the peninsula from the creation of the Federation of 1948 (and thus excluding Singapore) through to 1963. In practice the term 'Malaya' (on occasions 'British Malaya') is also used to refer to the peninsula (*in*cluding Singapore) prior to 1948, when constitutionally it comprised the Federated Malay States, Unfederated Malay States, and the Straits Settlements. The inhabitants of the country are called Malayans (prior to 1963) and Malaysians thereafter. They may then be divided by ethnic community: thus Malaysian Chinese, Malaysian Indian, and simply Malay.

Finally: some confusion may be caused by variations in the spelling of Malay words, for a new spelling system has recently been adopted by Malaysia (and Indonesia): thus 'Malacca' has become 'Melaka', and 'Tunku' has become 'Tengku'. No attempt has been made to impose a uniform spelling on the titles in this bibliography: each entry follows the spelling used in the item being annotated.

Acknowledgements

We are very pleased to acknowledge the assistance of the following good friends who guided us when this bibliography took us beyond our own specialist interests: Peter Ayre, John Bastin, Janice Brownfoot, Lewis Hill, Ulrich Kratz, Robert Taylor and Andrew Turton. There must be a special word of appreciation for Helen Cordell of the Library of the School of Oriental and African Studies, London, for her assistance was

Introduction

simply invaluable. Each of the above will be relieved to read that we remain responsible for all errors and inadequacies.

Ian Brown and Rajeswary Ampalavanar
Hitchin
January 1986

Abbreviations

ASEAN	Association of Southeast Asian Nations
BMA	British Military Administration
DAP	Democratic Action Party
FELDA	[Felda] Federal Land Development Authority
FMS	Federated Malay States
KMT	Kuomintang [Chinese Nationalist Party]
MCA	Malaysian Chinese Association
MCP	Malayan Communist Party
MCS	Malayan Civil Service
MIC	Malaysian Indian Congress
MPAJA	Malayan Peoples Anti-Japanese Army
PAS	Parti Islam Se Malaysia [Pan-Malayan Islamic Party (PMIP)]
PMCJA	Pan-Malayan Council of Joint Action
PUTERA	Pusat Tenaga Ra'ayat [Nucleus of the People's Force]
NEP	New Economic Policy
NUPW	National Union of Plantation Workers
RIDA	Rural and Industrial Development Authority
SNAP	Sarawak National Party
SS	Straits Settlements
UMNO	United Malays National Organization
UMS	Unfederated Malay States
USNO	United Sabah National Organization

Glossary

adat	customs, traditions
amok	frenzied attack
Barisan Nasional	National Front [Government]
bomoh [bomor]	medicine-man, sorcerer, spirit doctor
bumiputra	'sons of the soil': the Malays and all other indigenous peoples
chettiar	Indian money-lending caste
dakwah	[In Malaysia]: primarily urban-based, Islamic revival movements
Dato, Datuk	Malay personal title
desa	village [Indonesian usage]
Dewan Bahasa dan Pustaka	Language and Literature Agency
gamelan	Malay orchestra
haj	pilgrimage to Mecca
haji	pilgrim to Mecca: title used by Malays who have performed the pilgrimage
hantu	ghost, evil spirit
hari raya	festival marking the end of Ramadan, the 'fasting month'.
hikayat	story, narrative, chronicle

Glossary

imam	a mosque official who normally leads the Friday prayer
jawi	Malay language written in a modified Arabic script
kampung	village: compound of houses
Kaum Muda-Kaum Tua	reformist and traditional religious and social elements in conflict in early 20th-century Malay society
Merdeka	Independence: Freedom
mukim	lowest unit of local administration: parish
munshi	language teacher
negeri, negri	state, country
Orang Asli	indigenous peoples of the peninsula, excluding the Malays
padah	omen, premonition
pawang	sorcerer
penghulu	headman (usually of a group of *mukim*)
Persatuan	association
ra'ayat	the subjects of a ruler, specifically the peasants
Raja Muda	heir-apparent
Rukunegara	Articles of Faith of the State [promulgated 1970]
sarong	long, lower garment, tucked round the waist
shaman	spirit medium
silat	traditional Malay martial arts
towkay	wealthy Chinese employer
Tunku, Tengku	title for Malay princes
ulama	Muslim religious teacher

Glossary

wayang	shadow play
Yang Di-pertuan Agung	Paramount Ruler, King

The Country and Its People

1 **Silent invasion. The Chinese in Southeast Asia.**
Garth Alexander.   London: Macdonald, 1973. 274p. map. bibliog.
The author's main purpose is to demonstrate that 'a racial fear of the Chinese has
. . . played a predominant role in starting and keeping alive the Cold War in the
Pacific; . . . that anti-Sinitic fears have played, and continue to play, a far more
important role in Southeast Asian politics than any historian or commentator on
Asia has so far credited'. His analysis includes consideration of: the business
practices of the overseas Chinese; the origins of the Chinese expansionist myth;
the Kuala Lumpur riots of May 1969; and, most prominently, anti-Sinicism in the
region in the later 20th century. Alexander argues, from the perspective of the
early 1970s, that when Western and Eastern political leaders have claimed that
there exists an imminent and belligerent expansionist threat from China, 'they
have driven the region and the world horribly close to a war which is not in fact
directed against *communist China* but against the entire Chinese race'.

2 **Threatened paradise. North Borneo and its peoples.**
Cyril Alliston.   London: Robert Hale, 1966. 208p. map. bibliog.
This is essentially a popular, well-informed introduction to the territory of North
Borneo, mainly concerned with the lives, beliefs and activities of the indigenous
peoples of that area. There are a considerable number of black-and-white
photographs.

3 **Indians in Malaysia and Singapore.**
Sinnappah Arasaratnam.   Kuala Lumpur: Oxford University Press,
1979. rev. ed. 239p. 2 maps. bibliog.
A succinct account is provided of the settlement and naturalization of Indians in
Peninsular Malaya and Singapore from the early 19th century through to the late
1970s. There is consideration of: Indian immigration and settlement from 1800;
Indian society in Malaya in the period 1880-1945; political developments after

1

1945; trade unionism and labour welfare after 1945; religion and social reform; Indian education and its social effects; and the Indians in contemporary Malaysia and Singapore.

4 Malay kinship.
David J. Banks. Philadelphia: Institute for the Study of Human Issues, 1983. 200p. 3 maps. bibliog.

This advanced study of the Malay kinship system draws on fieldwork conducted mainly in 1967-68 in the district of Sik in the hill regions of the state of Kedah. Banks argues notably that 'the Malay conception of spiritual kinship provides the moral basis for the social traditions and institutions which channel kinship in everyday life'. But he also suggests that recent economic and political trends 'may be changing the fundamental ideology upon which Malay kinship in Sik rests'.

5 The Sarawak Chinese.
John M. Chin. Kuala Lumpur: Oxford University Press, 1981. 158p. 5 maps. bibliog.

The development of the Chinese community in Sarawak through to the late 1970s is considered in this study. It discusses, for example, the early Chinese contacts with Borneo; the Chinese rebellion of 1857; Chinese immigration and the development of agriculture over the period 1863-1941; the social and economic organization of the Chinese community in the period prior to 1941; the Japanese occupation; and the Chinese role in Sarawak politics since the 1950s.

6 An introduction to Chinese secret societies in Malaya.
Leon Comber. Singapore: Donald Moore, 1957. 77p. map. bibliog.

A brief introduction is provided to the history, organization, activities and rituals of the Chinese secret societies in Malaya. An appendix provides a list of the societies in the Federation and Singapore as of the mid-1950s, with a description of each of their activities (e.g., 'extortion, intimidation, gang fights, opium smuggling').

7 Culture shock! What not to do in Malaysia and Singapore. How and why not to do it.
Joann Craig. Singapore: Times Books International, 1979. 217p.

This book has two main aims: a] to consider some of the main problems which can confront Western expatriate families living and working in Malaysia/Singapore, and to offer practical guidance with respect to them; b] to provide an introduction to the main social customs and cultural traits of the Chinese, Malay, and Indian communities. Despite a rather jocular title, this book, and particularly those sections concerned with the customs and behaviour of Malaysians, is clearly serious in intent and presentation. It is a valuable introduction to Malaysia/Singapore for the visitor.

8   **The Far East and Australasia 1984-85. Sixteenth edition.**
London: Europa Publications, 1984.
The most recent edition of an annual survey and directory, which was first
published in 1969. The section on Malaysia (p. 568-603) contains articles on
physical and social geography, history, and the economy. There is also a statistical
survey, a directory, and a brief bibliography.

9   **The political economy of Malaysia.**
Edited by E. K. Fisk, H. Osman-Rani.   Kuala Lumpur: Oxford
University Press, 1982. 364p. 7 maps. bibliog.
This work contains fourteen articles which 'examine some of the more important
features of Malaysian development after two and a-half decades of independence'.
The subjects covered are: development in Malaysia; the geographical setting; the
physical infrastructure; the demographic situation; the political structure; the
social structure; the economic structure; development planning; trade and
external relations; agricultural sector; extractive industries; manufacturing
industries; money, banking, and monetary policy; and public finance. Nearly all
the contributors are Malaysians.

10   **The United States and Malaysia.**
James W. Gould.   Cambridge, Massachusetts: Harvard University
Press, 1969. 267p. map. bibliog.
This volume appears in a series entitled 'The American Foreign Policy Library'
which aims to produce 'brief but authoritative handbooks which would enlighten
the public on key countries or areas where the United States faced major foreign
policy problems'. Gould's study considers not only Malaysia but also Brunei and
Singapore. It considers, for example: the Malaysian people; the history of the
Malaysian peoples; government and politics; creating a Malaysian nation; society
and culture; international relations; and American relations with the area. He
argues that 'the most significant thing is that Malaysia has found a way to
encourage three ancient cultures to exist together in peace, and to get them to
cooperate politically and culturally'.

11   **Malaysia: economic expansion and national unity.**
John Gullick.   London: Ernest Benn; Boulder, Colorado:
Westview Press, 1981. 290p. map. bibliog.
Gullick was a member of the Malayan Civil Service from 1945 to 1956. He
subsequently worked for the Guthrie Corporation, one of the major British
business interests in Malaysia, founded in 1821. This book is probably the most
illuminating general introduction to the country, even if it is a little weak on East
Malaysia. There are chapters on: the Melaka sultanate and its successor states,
1400-1786; British rule, 1786-1942; the indigenous communities; the immigrant
communities; the advance to independence, 1941-61; the making of Malaysia;
politics and government from 1957; the management of the economy – including
analysis of the New Economic Policy; agriculture, mining, industry and trade;
defence and foreign policy; education, language and culture. This is a completely
rewritten edition of *Malaysia*, by J. M. Gullick (Ernest Benn, 1969. 304p. map.
bibliog.).

3

12   **Hailam Chinese in Sabah: a study of occupational patterns and changes.**

Han Sin-Fong. *Journal of Southeast Asian Studies*, vol. 6, no. 1 (March 1975), p. 25-37.

The Hailam, one of the least-known overseas Chinese speech groups, migrated solely from the tropical island of Hainan. Han considers 'the Hailam's past and present livelihood activities [in Sabah] as manifested in their occupational patterns: [and] the impact of Western technology and education on their changing occupational patterns and preferences [as well] as the Hailam's general responses to a changing Sabah society'.

13   **The Chinese in Sabah East Malaysia.**

Han Sin-Fong.   Taipei: Orient Culture Service, 1975. 244p. 8 maps. bibliog. (Asian Folklore and Social Life Monograph, no. 67).

This study of the Sabah Chinese has three principal objectives: to examine the community's occupational specialization along speech group lines; to analyse how, and to what extent, the pre-Second World War occupational pattern has been affected by the impact of Western technology and education; and to examine the changing social interactions among different speech groups, (measured principally by the incidence of inter-speech group marriage), arising from the diffusion of Western forms. Particular attention is given to the 'general transformation of the Sabah Chinese community from a speech group oriented, fragmentary society to a modern, more integrated one'. Two opening chapters provide an historical sketch of the Chinese in Sabah, and describe the spatial distribution of overseas Chinese in this area. Field research was undertaken in 1970.

14   **The Malays of south-west Sarawak before Malaysia. A socio-ecological survey.**

Tom Harrisson.   London: Macmillan, 1970. 671p. 8 maps.

This monumental study of the Malays of south-west Sarawak broadly covers the period 1947-63, although it is 'mainly descriptive of the situation as at January 1960'. Harrisson, who was the government ethnologist and curator of the Sarawak Museum from 1947-66, is concerned essentially with the social and economic organization of the south-west Sarawak Malays, in relation to their physical environment. There is discussion of, for example: the topography of the south-west area of Sarawak; Malay identity, beliefs and social organization; Sarawak Malay land usage, cultivation or exploitation in all its forms; and land pioneering and the creation of new settlements. There are some thirty-seven black-and-white photographs.

15   **South Indians on the plantation frontier in Malaya.**

Ravindra K. Jain.   New Haven, Connecticut; London: Yale University Press, 1970. 460p. bibliog.

An examination of the changing structure of Indian social life on one rubber plantation 'about ten miles east of the Strait of Malacca' over a period of some seventy years. The book is divided into two parts: the first primarily describes 'the domestic and economic organization of the estate laborers'. For example, consideration is given to the income and expenditures of labourers; savings and credit; and economic stratification. The second part is concerned principally with 'the interplay between power and authority in the plantation situation' from the late 19th century through to the rise of Asian estate bureaucracy and trade unionism in the 1940s. The final substantive chapter examines 'the nature of social stratification and political processes and . . . their present interrelationship in the social field'. The fieldwork was conducted in 1962-63.

16 **Introduction to the peoples and cultures of Indonesia and Malaysia.**
R. M. Koentjaraningrat. Menlo Park, California: Cummings
Publishing Company, 1975. 193p. 5 maps. bibliog.

The major part of this volume provides an ethnographical introduction to the principal ethnic groups and language communities of the Republic of Indonesia and the Federation of Malaysia – their economy, settlement, social system, and religious beliefs. This discussion is preceded by a very brief historical introduction, from earliest times to the present; and the volume concludes with an examination of the importance of anthropological concepts and methodology for the study of national integration in Indonesia and Malaysia. This basic text is intended for the 'uninitiated student'.

17 **The Chinese community of Sarawak. A study of communal relations.**
Michael B. Leigh. Singapore: Malaysia Publishing House, for the
Department of History, University of Singapore, 1964. 68p. bibliog.

This study, completed as the Federation of Malaysia came into being, seeks to examine the accommodation of the Chinese community in Sarawak with awakening indigenous nationalism, in the context of the ending of colonial rule in the early 1960s. It divides into two main sections: economic development and political aspects.

18 **The Chinese in Southeast Asia.**
Edited by Linda Y. C. Lim, L. A. Peter Gosling. Singapore:
Maruzen Asia, 1983. 2 vols.

A collection of twenty-six papers, most of which were originally presented at a conference, entitled 'The Chinese in Southeast Asia: Ethnicity and Economic Activity', held at the University of Michigan in 1980. Among the large number of contributions on Malaysia are: 'The political economy of a Chinese-Malaysian New Village: highly diversified insecurity' [Judith Strauch]; 'The political economy of urban Chinese squatters in metropolitan Kuala Lumpur' [Paul Chan]; 'Chinese business, multinationals and the state: manufacturing for export in Malaysia and Singapore' [Linda Y.C. Lim]; 'The ownership and control of large corporations in Malaysia: the role of Chinese businessmen' [Lim Mah Hui]; 'Race, income distributions, and development in Malaysia and Singapore' [Pang Eng Fong]; 'The ethnic status of the rural Chinese of the Kelantan plain' [Robert Winzeler]; 'Acculturation and the Chinese in Melaka: the expression of Baba identity today' [Tan Chee-Beng]; 'The problems of ethnic cohesion among the Chinese in Peninsular Malaysia: intraethnic divisions and interethnic accommodation' [Moli Siow]; 'The transformation from class to ethnic politics in an opposition area: a Malaysian case study' [F. Loh Kok-Wah]; 'Chinese and Malay factory workers:

5

desire for harmony and experience of discord' [John Stough]. This is a most valuable collection.

19 **Concept of a hero in Malay society.**
Shaharuddin bin Maaruf. Singapore, Petaling Jaya: Eastern Universities Press, 1984. 140p. bibliog.

This work seeks to examine the Malay conception of the hero as projected by the Malay ruling class. It attempts to understand the Malay élite's ideal of excellence; what they consider as great achievements; what they feel Malays should aspire to; their view of leadership; their attitude towards intellectual achievement or ethical integrity. This inquiry is conducted primarily through an examination of both historical texts (including the *Sejarah Melayu* and the works of Abdullah Munshi), and contemporary newspapers, and through personal conversations and observation. The author's overriding concern is to ascertain whether the contemporary Malay élite can facilitate the social, economic, cultural and political development of the Malays as a whole. In a concluding chapter he argues that in fact the Malay ruling class is an underdeveloped élite: that it lacks 'ethical integrity and standards, intellectual capacity and stamina for productive and creative endeavours'.

20 **The role of Indian minorities in Burma and Malaya.**
Usha Mahajani. Bombay: Vora & Company, 1960. Issued under the auspices of the Institute of Pacific Relations, New York. 344p. bibliog.

This study is primarily concerned with the problems of the Indian minorities in relation to the nationalist movements in Burma and Malaya, the countries of their settlement. It is 'not a study of Burmese and Malay nationalisms in themselves nor of the Indian minorities per se, but of both in relation to each other'. The Burma and Malaya experiences are, in general, considered separately. Those chapters specifically concerned with Malaya consider: the anatomy of the Indian community in Malaya prior to the Pacific War; the Japanese occupation; Indian problems in post-war Malaya; and the triple interaction of minority nationalism in post-war Malaya through to independence.

21 **The sociology of secret societies. A study of Chinese secret societies in Singapore and Peninsular Malaysia.**
Mak Lau Fong. Kuala Lumpur: Oxford University Press, 1981. 178p. 7 maps and diags. bibliog.

The author suggests that there are three circumstances which can account for the emergence and persistence of Chinese secret societies in Singapore and Peninsular Malaysia: the inadequacy of the legal protection given to the general population; the adaptability of secret societies to change; and the existence of a symbiotic relationship between local Chinese secret societies and the larger society, which was an effective means of reducing conflict. The analysis, which covers the period from the early 19th century to the present, draws in part on interviews with secret society members conducted in the years 1971-75.

22 **Malay wedding customs.**
Haji Mohtar bin H. Mohammed Dom. Kuala Lumpur: Federal
Publications, 1979. 80p. (Federal Cultural Series).
This brief volume is intended for the general reader. It considers the customs and
practices followed in Malay society in finding a bride: and the differing forms of
Malay weddings as practised in Melaka, Perak, Kelantan, Johor, and Sarawak.

23 **Kinship and social mobility among the Malays.**
Judith A. Nagata. *Man*, new series, vol. 11, no. 3 (Sept. 1976), p.
400-9.
This is an advanced, theoretical discussion of the perception and practice of kin
relationships among the Malay population in west Malaysia, and how these have
been influenced by a rapid social mobility engendered by a modernizing,
urbanizing environment. Nagata draws out, for example, the general absence of
class consciousness among the Malays, and how this has permitted the
continuation of established forms of patronage, 'particularly under conditions of
differential social mobility'.

24 **Malaysian mosaic. Perspectives from a poly-ethnic society.**
Judith A. Nagata. Vancouver, British Columbia: University of
British Columbia Press, 1979. 316p. 2 maps. bibliog.
A study of ethnicity in Malaysia. In the first half of the book there is: an
account of the historical evolution of the categories that form the basis of
contemporary Malaysian society; an analysis of the impact of urbanism on ethnic
relations in Malaysia; a detailed description of the social ecology and structure of
George Town (Penang) and of a small traditional Malay town in Kedah. In the
second half there is consideration of some 'of the major problems of Malaysian
society for Malaysians, e.g., issues of national unity and integration'. Emphasis is
given to 'the public indecision and ambiguity of the Malaysian government over
the ideal cultural and social foundation of the Malaysian state – Malay
assimilationist, synthetic blend of all groups, pluralist separatism, or "neutral"
westernization'. It is concluded that for Malaysia 'there will be more disunion
than union, at least in the immediate future'.

25 **Perceptions of social inequality in a 'plural society': Malaysia.**
Judith A. Nagata. In: *Sociology of South-East Asia. Readings on
social change and development.* Edited by Hans-Dieter Evers.
Kuala Lumpur: Oxford University Press, 1980. p. 125-39.
Nagata is primarily concerned with the ways in which people in Malaysia perceive
social inequality in their own society. Particular attention is devoted to the
traditional Malay system of ranking and prestige, although there are illustrative
contrasts with the Chinese and Indian systems. Among her conclusions: there is
clearly a trend from 'a Furnivallian type of pluralism with distinct systems of
status ranking for each ethnic section to a form of objective stratification in which
there is increasing competition for the same statuses and resources by members of
all ethnic groups . . . . On the subjective level, however [the perceptions of the
people *themselves* of their society], this process is obscured, with the result that a
form of "subjective pluralism" may be said to exist'. Reprinted from:
Contributions to Asian Studies, vol. 7 (1975), p. 113-36.

7

26 **Treacherous River. A study of rural Chinese in north Malaya.**
William H. Newell. Kuala Lumpur: University of Malaya Press,
1962. 233p. 4 maps.

This volume is primarily 'a fieldwork monograph [of a Teochiu rural community in Province Wellesley, Treacherous River] with an emphasis on those theoretical aspects of Teochiu social organization in this village which [the author considered] to be of the widest possible application'. There are chapters on: the Teochiu family; religion; associations; the organization of work within the village; and disputes among the Chinese villagers. The fieldwork was conducted in the mid-1950s.

27 **Chinese new villages in Malaya. A community study.**
Ray Nyce, edited by Shirle Gordon. Singapore: Malaysian
Sociological Research Institute, 1973. 278p. 3 maps. bibliog.

A major element in the counter-insurgency programme pursued during the Emergency was to move the inhabitants of Chinese squatter communities from the edges of the jungle (where they could easily supply the MCP guerrillas), into tightly protected and supervised new villages. Ray Nyce, a Christian evangelist, worked in and around some of the new villages near Ipoh and Kuala Lumpur between 1957 and 1961. His study considers mainly the social organization of the new village communities – including the family and wider kin groups; relations between dialect groups; informal associations outside the family; and relations with other ethnic groups – although there is also discussion of commercial and political activities within the new villages. There is a lengthy introduction by Kernial Singh Sandhu which describes and analyses the Emergency resettlement programme itself.

28 **Diversity and development in Southeast Asia. The coming decade.**
Guy J. Pauker, Frank H. Golay, Cynthia H. Enloe. New York:
McGraw-Hill, 1977. 1980s Project of the Council on Foreign
Relations. 191p. bibliog.

This book explores 'the likely paths of economic and political development of the nations of Southeast Asia and of the roles that Southeast Asian states might play in world politics' through the 1980s. It is divided into three main parts: national politics and regional powers; national economic priorities and international coalitions; and ethnic diversity – the potential for conflict. There is considerable discussion of Malaysian politics, economics, and ethnic divisions.

29 **The Chinese in Malaya.**
Victor Purcell. Kuala Lumpur: Oxford University Press, 1967. 327p.
6 maps. bibliog.

This is a reprint of a book which was first published in 1948. It divides into three parts: the early history of the Chinese in Malaya, to the later 19th century; social, economic, and political features of the Chinese in Malaya; and developments for the community in the period 1939-46. This is the standard, but now dated, introduction to the subject.

30 **The Chinese in Southeast Asia.**
Victor Purcell. London: Oxford University Press, under the
auspices of the Royal Institute of International Affairs, 1965. 2nd
ed. 623p. 3 maps. bibliog.

The author was in the Malayan Civil Service between 1921 and 1946, principally
as a senior official in the Chinese Protectorate. From 1949 he was a don at Trinity
College, Cambridge. This book, which first appeared in 1951, is the standard
introduction to the overseas Chinese in Southeast Asia. It has been reprinted in
1982 by Oxford University Press in Kuala Lumpur/Singapore. The section on the
Chinese in Malaya and Singapore (p. 223-356), includes consideration of:
demographic features; the Chinese in Penang and Singapore, 1786-1900; Chinese
social life and education in Malaya; the economic position of the Malayan
Chinese; Chinese political societies in Malaya, 1911-41; the post-war constitutional
experiment; the Chinese before and after Malayan independence. The section on
the Chinese in British Borneo (p. 357-81), considers demographic features and
history.

31 **Issues in contemporary Malaysia.**
Chandriah Appa Rao, Bruce Ross-Larson, Noordin Sopiee, Tjoa
Hock Guan. Kuala Lumpur: Heinemann Educational Books
(Asia), 1977. 188p.

This introduction to contemporary Malaysia, intended primarily for the general
reader, divides into two main sections. The first provides a background
discussion, outlining the principal developments in government and politics; the
economy; and in the three main ethnic communities. The second, and major,
section analyses some of the important issues facing modern Malaysia, including:
forging a Malaysian national identity; population growth; rural poverty;
industrialization in development; foreign investment; public enterprises; insurgency and internal security; and the future of ASEAN (Association of South-
East Asian Nations).

32 **British North Borneo. An account of its history, resources and native
tribes.**
Owen Rutter. London: Constable & Company, 1922. 404p.
2 maps. bibliog.

Owen Rutter resided in North Borneo for a number of years in the early 20th
century, first as a government officer and later as a planter. This introduction to
the territory includes consideration of: the geography; native population; early
history; administration by the British North Borneo Company; agriculture;
mineral resources; native customs and folklore; and native affairs. There are a
large number of black-and-white photographs.

33 **Indians in Malaya. Some aspects of their immigration and settlement 1786-1957.**
Kernial Singh Sandhu. Cambridge, England: Cambridge University Press, 1969. 345p. bibliog. 43 illus.

This is an extremely detailed account of Indian immigration and settlement in Malaya during the colonial period. Sandhu's study divides into three parts. The first is concerned with the origins and characteristics of Indian migration to Malaya – the causes of migration, the types of migrant, and the methods of recruitment. The second part is devoted to an analysis of the growth of the Indian population of Malaya from the founding of Penang – notably the pattern of distribution, settlement characteristics, and ethno-linguistic composition. The final part considers the roles of the Indians in the modern Malayan economy – in agriculture and industry, in communications, and in commerce.

34 **Melaka. The transformation of a Malay capital c.1400-1980.**
Edited by Kernial Singh Sandhu, Paul Wheatley. Kuala Lumpur: Oxford University Press, under the auspices of the Institute of Southeast Asian Studies, Singapore, 1983. 2 vols. approximately 150 figs. bibliog.

This collection of forty-six papers is divided into the following principal sections: Melaka in history; the territory of Melaka; Melaka town; ethnic diversity in Melaka; and the modernization of Melaka. There are two lengthy appendixes: a descriptive list of historical maps, prints, and drawings; and a bibliography of Melaka studies.

35 **Malay courtesy. A narrative account of Malay manners and customs in everyday use in Peninsular Malaysia.**
Mubin Sheppard. Kuala Lumpur, Singapore: Eastern Universities Press, 1981. 4th rev. ed. 47p.

A brief introduction to Malay etiquette in the following situations: meeting and greeting; at home; a wedding; the fasting month and *hari raya*; and a birth and a funeral.

36 **Chinese society in rural Malaysia. A local history of the Chinese in Titi, Jelebu.**
Laurence K. L. Siaw. Kuala Lumpur: Oxford University Press, 1983. 197p. map. bibliog.

Jelebu lies about 40 kilometres by road to the north-east of Seremban, the state capital of Negeri Sembilan. It is a district which contains substantial tin deposits; and it was these deposits which attracted increasing numbers of Chinese into the area in the final decades of the 19th century. The author provides an economic, social and political history of that Chinese community from its beginnings (c.1870), through the inter-war decades, the Japanese occupation, the Emergency (when a New Village was established in the Titi area), to 1960. One chapter considers the role of the secret societies in Titi between 1948 and 1955.

37 **Rural Malay women in tradition and transition.**
Heather Strange. New York: Praeger, 1981. 264p. map. bibliog.
'This book is primarily a study of rural Malay women in one village, Rusila [a coastal village south of Kuala Trengganu] and how they are affected by the structure of their society, by the development process, and by changes in the direction of attaining or not attaining equity'. There is consideration of: the life cycle of women; education; mate selection, marriage, and the family; polygyny and divorce; and the economic activities of women in Rusila. The study draws on fieldwork conducted in 1965-66, 1975 and 1978.

38 **Malaysia. A survey.**
Edited by Wang Gungwu. Singapore: Donald Moore Books, 1964. 466p. 20 maps and charts. bibliog.
This volume was compiled as Malaysia came into existence in 1963 and was intended to provide 'the basic data for an understanding of the new country', without, for the most part, attempting to be topical and immediate. There are twenty-six articles, divided under the following headings: natural and human structure; historical background; society and culture; the economy; politics and government.

39 **The Malays. A cultural history.**
R. O. Winstedt, revised and updated by Tham Seong Chee. Singapore: Graham Brash, 1981. rev. ed. 221p. bibliog.
This classic study by probably the most prominent official-scholar of the colonial period was first published in 1947. It considers the origin, migrations and language of the Malay; their beliefs and religion; their literature, arts and crafts; and the social, political, legal and economic systems of the Malay. There is a substantial postscript by Tham Seong Chee which surveys changes in Malay society and culture since 1961, the date at which Winstedt's last (revised) edition had appeared.

Geography

General

40 South-East Asia. A social, economic and political geography.
Charles A. Fisher.   London: Methuen, 1966. 2nd ed. 831p. 110 maps. bibliog.

The most perceptive introduction to the human geography of South East Asia. The first part of the book is concerned with the region as a whole. This is followed by a more detailed examination of the component countries, a consideration of their contemporary social, economic and political problems in the appropriate geographical setting. The section concerned with Malaysia (and also including Singapore and Brunei) is contained within p. 583-688. Inevitably some parts of the analysis have become dated, but this remains the outstanding book in its field.

41 South-East Asia: a systematic geography.
Edited by R. D. Hill.   Kuala Lumpur: Oxford University Press, 1979. 214p. 62 figs. bibliog.

This book was designed specifically to meet the requirements of the syllabus for the Higher School Certificate (the equivalent of A level) in Malaysia and Singapore; more generally it provides a basic geographical introduction to South East Asia. It is organized thematically, with the following chapters: geology, landforms and soils; weather and climate; vegetation; population; tribal and peasant agriculture, fisheries; commercial agriculture; minerals, mining and power; trade, transportation and manufacturing; the changing cities; and politics and problems.

42 **Man in Malaya.**

B. W. Hodder. London: University of London Press, 1959. 144p.
25 maps and diags. bibliog.

Hodder considers 'the characteristics of human settlement and the bio-geographical background to social and economic development in Malaya'. The first part of this study 'describes briefly the physical environment and discusses the life and work of those who live in it'. Included are chapters which consider: the land; the growth of settlement up to 1900; population; economic life; rural settlement; and urban settlement. The second part 'analyses the interactions between the population on the one hand and certain elements of the natural surroundings' – particularly climate; water supply; soil erosion; and health, disease and diet – 'on the other'. Although parts of this account and analysis have inevitably dated, this remains a valuable introduction to the interactions between man and his environment in the peninsula.

43 **Sarawak. A geographical survey of a developing state.**

James C. Jackson. London: University of London Press, 1968.
218p. 34 maps and diags. bibliog.

A comprehensive survey of the geography of Sarawak is provided as at the mid-1960s. There are chapters on: the environmental setting; population and settlement; agriculture and fishing; forest products industries; mining and manufacturing industries; transport; trade and commerce; public utilities and social services; and the challenge of development.

44 **Peninsular Malaysia.**

Ooi Jin-Bee. London: Longman, 1976. new ed. 437p. 77 figs.
bibliog.

This is a new edition of the author's *Land, people and economy in Malaya* (London: Longman, 1963). The volume is divided into three parts. The first provides an introduction to the physical geography of Peninsular Malaysia, with chapters on geological evolution, relief and drainage; climate; soils; vegetation. The second part examines the people – the evolution of the population pattern; the pattern of population distribution; and settlement patterns. The third part includes analysis of the rudimentary economies of the Orang Asli; agriculture; mining; industry; trade; and transport. This is the standard introductory text on the geography of Peninsular Malaysia.

Physical

45 **The rainfall of Malaya, part 1.**

W. L. Dale. *Journal of Tropical Geography*, vol. 13 (Dec. 1959),
p. 23-37.

This article together with the following three articles by W. L. Dale, also in the *Journal of Tropical Geography*, provide a detailed analysis of the rainfall, surface

13

temperatures, and sunshine patterns in Pensinsular Malaysia: 'The rainfall of
Malaya, part 2', vol. 14 (July 1960), p. 11-28; 'Surface temperatures in Malaya',
vol. 17 (May 1963), p. 57-71; and 'Sunshine in Malaya', vol. 19 (Dec. 1964),
p. 20-26.

46 **Geology of the Malay Peninsula (West Malaysia and Singapore).**
Edited by D. J. Gobbett, C. S. Hutchison. New York: Wiley-
Interscience (a division of John Wiley & Sons), 1973. 438p.
approximately 150 figs. bibliog. (Regional Geology Series).
This very substantial volume, which contains 11 chapters and is the work of 7
contributors, presents 'a detailed summary of our present [early 1970s] knowledge
of Malayan geology'. This standard text includes an extensive bibliography.

47 **The climate of West Malaysia and Singapore.**
Edited by Ooi Jin-Bee, Chia Lin Sien. Kuala Lumpur: Oxford
University Press, 1974. 262p. approximately 90 maps. bibliog.
This volume contains nineteen articles reprinted (mainly from the *Journal of
Tropical Geography*), selected to provide a comprehensive survey of the climate
of West Malaysia and Singapore. It is intended not only for the specialist
climatologist, meteorologist and geographer, but also for 'planners, research
workers, agriculturists, architects, engineers, students and the interested public'.
The articles divide under three headings: the upper air; the climatic elements
(sunshine and solar radiation, temperature, cloudiness, rainfall, evaporation); and
applied climatology. There is a comprehensive bibliography for the volume as a
whole, as well as a list of references for the individual articles.

48 **The climate of Kuala Lumpur-Petaling Jaya area Malaysia. A study
of the impact of urbanization on local climate within the humid
tropics.**
Sham Sani. Bangi, Malaysia: Universiti Kebangsaan Malaysia
Press, Department of Geography, 1980. 309p. approximately 18
maps. bibliog. (Monograph no. 1).
This book is concerned with the climate of the Kuala Lumpur-Petaling Jaya area:
it considers 'the nature of the local climate, including the manner and degree to
which this varies, in sympathy with changes in the city's morphology, and studying
in particular the contrasts between the built-up area and the surrounding rural
districts'. A concluding chapter 'considers [briefly] some of the consequences and
implications of an urban climate', in the context of the Kuala Lumpur-Petaling
Jaya area.

49 **Climates of Southern and Western Asia.**
Edited by K. Takahashi, H. Arakawa. Amsterdam; Oxford,
England; New York: Elsevier Scientific Publishing Company, 1981.
333p. maps. bibliog. (World Survey of Climatology, vol. 9).
The opening chapter of this volume, 'The climates of Continental Southeast Asia'
by S. Nieuwolt, contains substantial references to the climate of the West
Malaysia-Singapore area. There is an extensive list of references, and a large

number of statistical tables at the end of the chapter. There is a brief discussion of
the climate of Borneo/Kalimantan in a companion volume: *Climates of Northern
and Eastern Asia*, edited by H. Arakawa (Amsterdam, London, New York:
Elsevier Publishing Company, 1969. 248p. maps. bibliog. [World Survey of
Climatology, vol. 8]).

Economic

50 **Development and environment in Peninsular Malaysia.**
    S. Robert Aiken, Colin H. Leigh, Thomas R. Leinbach, Michael R.
    Moss.   Singapore: McGraw-Hill, 1982. 310p. 46 maps. bibliog.

This work is mainly devoted 'to an examination of the relationships between
specific economic activities [in Peninsular Malaysia] – rubber, oil palm, padi,
timber exploitation, tin mining, industrialization – and their environmental
consequences, both past and present'. The chapters consider, in essence: the
growth of population in the peninsula from prehistoric times to the present; the
components of the biophysical environment; the economic development of
Peninsular Malaysia from the earliest colonial contact to the present; the nature
and extent of environmental change to 1957; the major agents of rural land use
change in the post-independence period; the environmental consequences of
various human activities in recent decades; the growth of the settlement system,
trends in urbanization, and the demographic, economic, and societal components
of urbanization; the rapidly growing environment problems of urban areas – in
the context of Malaysia's largest conurbation, the Klang Valley; and the context
of national development policy, planning, and environmental legislation in
Peninsular Malaysia.

51 **Emerging Southeast Asia. A study in growth and stagnation.**
    Donald W. Fryer.   London: George Philip & Son, 1979. 2nd ed.
    540p. 35 maps and diags. bibliog.

An introductory text on the economic geography of South East Asia, organized
mainly on a country-by-country basis. The section on Malaysia and Singapore
(p. 224-317) includes consideration of: the land and the people; population;
rubber; oil palm; estates in Sabah and Sarawak; rice cultivation; tin; manufacturing;
and transport. Fryer is a strong advocate of the capitalist route to economic
development.

Human settlement

52 **Urban development and landownership in Butterworth, Malaysia.**
Goh Ban Lee, Hans-Dieter Evers. *Journal of Southeast Asian Studies*, vol. 9, no. 1 (March 1978), p. 28-49.

A consideration of the severe pressure on urban land in Butterworth currently being generated by industrialization, increased business activities, and a growing population. The emphasis is on the social factors in this process of rapid urban development. Particular attention is paid to 'the distribution of urban land among members of different ethnic groups and between different categories of owners, like private individuals, companies, religious bodies, and government agencies: [and] the social forces of urban development in relation to the ownership of scarce and valuable urban property'.

53 **The evolution of squatter settlements in Peninsular Malaysian cities.**
Michael Johnstone. *Journal of Southeast Asian Studies*, vol. 12, no. 2 (Sept. 1981), p. 364-80.

This work is concerned with 'the forces that have influenced the character and present distribution of Malaysian [urban] squatter settlements, illustrating how and why this settlement form has evolved'. The paper considers the history of urban squatter settlement in the peninsula from the later 19th century through to the late 1970s, and concentrates in particular on the Kuala Lumpur area.

54 **Malay urbanization and the ethnic profile of urban centres in Peninsular Malaysia.**
Lee Boon Thong. *Journal of Southeast Asian Studies*, vol. 8, no. 2 (Sept. 1977), p. 224-34.

Lee argues that the rapid urbanization of Peninsular Malaysia since independence, and the greater involvement of the Malay population in the urbanization process, 'does not seem to have [had] the effect, so far, of bringing about any substantial change to the basic ethnic structure of urban areas'. In other words, 'the increasing proportion of the Malays in the urban areas are absorbed into Malay-predominated centres. Malay movement into non-Malay areas is only substantially evident in the metropolitan areas'.

55 **North Borneo (Sabah). A study in settlement geography.**
Lee Yong Leng. Singapore: Donald Moore for Eastern Universities Press, 1965. 156p. 36 maps and diags. bibliog.

The opening three chapters of this study provide an introduction to the physical, historical, and economic geography of North Borneo. The remaining five chapters provide a more detailed analysis of the population of North Borneo, land use, rural settlements, land settlement for agriculture, and urban settlements.

56 **The evolution of the urban system in Malaya.**
Lim Heng Kow. Kuala Lumpur: University of Malaya Press, 1978.
229p. 27 maps. bibliog.

The central theme of this study is that the 'present-day urban system [of Malaya]
is the product of the colonial-immigrant complex'. Lim first considers the failure
of traditional society in the peninsula to generate an urban system, and then
discusses traditional settlements and the beginnings of urban growth during the
19th century. This is followed by a lengthy examination of various patterns of
urban development during the colonial period – in Perak, in Selangor (Kuala
Lumpur), in Kelantan and Trengganu, and in Singapore and Penang.

57 **The Southeast Asian city. A social geography of the primate cities of
Southeast Asia.**
T. G. McGee. London: G. Bell & Sons, 1967. 204p. 35 maps and
figs. bibliog.

A study of the growth, characteristics and roles of the primate cities of South East
Asia which includes consideration of: the indigenous cities of the region, and
primary urbanization; the impact of the West and the emergence of the colonial
city; the modern city in South East Asia; the demographic character, economic
patterns, and residential patterns of the modern city; and slums and squatters.
The author draws in part on the primary urban research which he carried out in
Malaysia whilst he was teaching at the University of Malaya. Inevitably some of
the descriptive analysis relating to the modern period has become outdated since
the publication of this book, but it remains a valuable introduction to the subject.

58 **Urbanization and the urban population in Peninsular Malaysia,
1970.**
Ooi Jin-Bee. *Journal of Tropical Geography*, vol. 40 (June 1975),
p. 40-47.

This study is primarily concerned with the markedly rapid rate of urbanization in
Peninsular Malaysia in the post-war inter-censal years 1947-70. He considers the
growth of urban centres, particularly in the post-war period; those factors which
determined urban growth in the pre-war and post-war periods; and the relation of
race to urbanization in the period 1947-70. He concludes that in this period
'urbanization has proceeded more rapidly than economic circumstances
warranted, in the sense that urban economic opportunities have lagged behind
urban population growth, with the result that the urban centres are faced with the
problems of unemployment and underemployment' and the related problems of
'overcrowding, the creation and expansion of slums and squatter settlements, and
the overloading of public infrastructure and utilities'.

59 **The changing settlement system of West Malaysia.**
Robin J. Pryor. *Journal of Tropical Geography*, vol. 37 (Dec.
1973), p. 53-67.

The purpose of this paper is 'to identify changes occurring in West Malaysia's
settlement system at the present transitional phase of that country's development,
and in particular to determine the degree to which a multiplication of points of
population concentration is occurring; the degree to which individual concentra-

tions of population are increasing in size; the changing hierarchical relationships of central places; and other changes in the spatial patterns of settlement which are relevant to an evaluation of the centre-periphery paradigm of regional developmental differentiation'. As part of his conclusion, Pryor argues that 'the settlement system is now relatively stable apart from continued frontier settlement expansion by the Federal Land Development Authority schemes, and the major phase of settlement elaboration was over by the time of the 1957 census'.

60 **Urbanization of the Malays since independence: evidence from West Malaysia 1957 and 1970.**
Peter J. Rimmer, George C. H. Cho. *Journal of Southeast Asian Studies*, vol. 12, no. 2 (Sept. 1981), p. 349-63.

This article is concerned in general with the slackening in the pace of Malay urbanization in the period 1957-70 (compared with the years from the occupation to independence): more specifically it seeks to explain how and why the growth of the Malay urban population between 1957-70 has varied considerably as between the various urban centres in West Malaysia, being most pronounced in Kuala Lumpur, Petaling Jaya and Seremban.

61 **Emergency resettlement in Malaya.**
Kernial Singh Sandhu. *Journal of Tropical Geography*, vol. 18 (Aug. 1964), p. 157-83.

One of the most far-reaching effects of the Emergency was the resettlement of approximately one million rural dwellers in more than 600 'new' settlements. Sandhu brings together the information relating to the Emergency resettlement, and analyses some of its characteristics and consequences. Specifically he considers: the need for resettlement; the resettlement itself (including, of course, an account and analysis of the Briggs Plan); and the consequences of resettlement. The article presents a very considerable volume of statistical data.

62 **Patterns of urbanization in West Malaysia, 1911-1970.**
Saw Swee Hock. *Malayan Economic Review*, vol. 17, no. 2 (Oct. 1972), p. 114-20.

Saw presents a brief account of the urbanization process in West Malaysia during the years 1911-70. There is consideration of the rates of urbanization over that period, the growth of towns, urbanization by state in West Malaysia, and urbanization and race.

63 **Changing South-East Asian cities: readings on urbanization.**
Edited by Y. M. Yeung, C. P. Lo. Singapore: Oxford University Press, 1976. 245p. 36 figs. bibliog.

This collection of readings includes the following papers specifically concerned with Malaysia: 1] 'Contemporary urbanization in Malaysia', by Hamzah Sendut. Reprinted from: *Asian Survey*, vol. 6, no. 9 (Sept. 1966), p. 484-91; 2] 'The port towns of British Borneo', by Y. L. Lee. Reprinted from: *Australian Geographer*, vol. 8 (March 1962), p. 161-72; and 3] 'The spread of modernization in Malaya: 1895-1969', by Thomas R. Leinbach. Reprinted from: *Tijdschrift voor Economische en Sociale Geografie*, vol. 63 (1972), p. 262-77.

The story of Kuala Lumpur (1857-1939).
See item no. 206.

Population and settlement in Sarawak.
See item no. 285.

Travel accounts and travel guides

64   **The golden chersonese and the way thither.**
Isabella L. Bird, with an introduction by Wang Gungwu.   Kuala
Lumpur: Oxford University Press, 1967. (Originally published in
1883.) 384p. 2 maps.
Isabella Bird was a noted traveller and writer of the later 19th century, who made
an 'unexpected and hastily-planned expedition' into the Malay States, in fact to
Sungai Ujong, Selangor and Perak for five weeks in early 1879. This volume
consists primarily of her letters written to her sister whilst she was on her travels,
which provide a vivid description of the peoples and lands she visited. There are
also four, rather less vivid, background chapters which describe and explain the
recently-established British administrative presence in the Malay peninsula.

65   **Fodor's Southeast Asia 1985.**
London: Hodder & Stoughton, 1984. 440p. (Malaysia section;
p. 274-313. 3 maps).
This travel guide follows the standard Fodor format. The publication is revised
annually.

66   **Malaysia and Singapore.**
Gladys Nicol.   London: B. T. Batsford, 1977. 224p. 4 maps.
After an historical opening chapter, this book provides an evocative tour of each
of the main regions of Malaysia, including East Malaysia. The author is a
professional travel writer.

67   **Into the heart of Borneo. An account of a journey made in 1983 to
the mountains of Batu Tiban with James Fenton.**
Redmond O'Hanlon.   Edinburgh: Salamander Press, 1984. 192p. 3
maps. bibliog.
An extremely entertaining account of an expedition through Sarawak to the
mountains of Batu Tiban in Kalimantan. The author's deep professional interest
in natural history is much in evidence, but the main emphasis lies in recounting a
series of startlingly humorous adventures.

68 **Life in the forests of the Far East.**
Spenser St. John, with an introduction by Tom Harrisson. Kuala
Lumpur: Oxford University Press, 1974. 2 vols. 3 maps.

Spenser St. John was a British official stationed in north and west Borneo for
some thirteen years in the mid-19th century. These two volumes, originally
published in 1862, principally recount the expeditions which he undertook during
that period through that part of the island. Of particular value are St. John's
accounts of the indigenous peoples – notably the Sea Dayaks, the Land Dayaks,
and the Kayans; and of contemporary events, including the early years of Brooke
rule, the Chinese insurrection of 1857, and the work of the Christian missionaries.
Of less value are his descriptions of the natural life of Borneo: as Tom Harrisson
notes; 'on the whole [St. John] seems surprisingly insensitive to one of the world's
richest and most varied faunas; and one very largely unknown to science when he
headed inland'.

**Expedition to Borneo. The search for proboscis monkeys and other
creatures.**
See item no. 83.

The Malay archipelago.
See item no. 96.

Ulu. The world's end.
See item no. 305.

Head-hunters. Black, white, and brown.
See item no. 314.

Malaysia. Travel planner '86.
See item no. 627.

Flora and Fauna

69 The amphibian fauna of Peninsular Malaysia.
P. Y. Berry. Kuala Lumpur: Tropical Press, 1975. 130p. bibliog.
The principal aim of this book is to assist naturalists, school-teachers, as well as scientists, in identifying the eighty or more species of amphibian found in Peninsular Malaysia. Where possible the descriptive notes on each species is accompanied by a photograph.

70 The butterflies of the Malay peninsula.
A. Steven Corbet, H. M. Pendlebury. Kuala Lumpur: Malayan Nature Society, 1978. 3rd ed. 649p. bibliog.
This is a completely revised and updated edition of a work which originally appeared in 1934. The revisions – a major achievement in themselves – were undertaken by Lt. Col. J. N. Eliot. Immensely detailed, profusely illustrated, and exhaustively indexed, this finely-produced book is the standard work on the subject.

71 Butterflies of West Malaysia and Singapore.
W. A. Fleming.   Faringdon, England: E. W. Classey; Kuala Lumpur: Longman Malaysia, 1975. 2 vols. 3 maps.
These two volumes contain illustrations, in colour, of all the species of butterfly confirmed to have been captured in West Malaysia and Singapore. The text gives details of: generic, specific and subspecific names, followed by the name of the author; rarity where applicable; distribution in West Malaysia; forewing length from mid-thorax to apex; descriptive details where necessary; food plant(s) where known; and distribution within the Oriental Region.

72   The birds of the Malay peninsula, Singapore and Penang. An
     account of all the Malayan species, with a note of their occurrence in
     Sumatra, Borneo, and Java and a list of the birds of those islands.
     A. G. Glenister.   Kuala Lumpur: Oxford University Press, 1951.
     First paperback ed., 1971. 291p. map.

This volume divides into two parts. The first is concerned with Malayan birds as
seen in the field, and discusses: the birds of everyday life; some aids to
identification of Malayan birds in the field; the birds and bird families of Malaya.
The second and main part contains a systematic list of all the species recorded
from the Malay peninsula, Singapore, Penang and peninsular Thailand, with a
description of each and a short account of its habits and status. Appendixes
provide a glossary of Malay bird names; a list of the birds of Sumatra, Borneo,
and Java; and a list of Malayan species. There are a large number of colour plates
and black-and-white illustrations.

73   **Mulu. The rain forest.**
     Robin Hanbury-Tenison.   London: Weidenfeld & Nicolson, 1980.
     176p. 2 maps. bibliog.

An account of an expedition to the Mulu area of north-east Sarawak, undertaken
in 1977-78 under the auspices of the Royal Geographical Society and the Sarawak
government. The area had been designated a national park by the Sarawak
authorities, and it was at their invitation that the expedition undertook to draw up
a management plan for the park. A large number of scientists undertook studies
of the ecology of the rain forest, the botanical and zoological resources of the
area, and of the geomorphology of the terrain. Appendixes list the birds and
mammals recorded within the Gunung Mulu National Park.

74   **An introduction to the mammals of Sabah.**
     John Harrison.   Kota Kinabalu, Malaysia: The Sabah Society, 1964
     (reprinted, 1973). 244p. bibliog.

This volume provides a systematic descriptive list of the mammals of Sabah.
There are over sixty black-and-white illustrations.

75   **Orang-utan.**
     Barbara Harrisson. London: Collins, 1962. 224p.

An essentially popular, although serious, account of Barbara and Tom
Harrisson's deep affection for Borneo's most famous inhabitant, and of their great
commitment to halt the alarming decline in his numbers. It recounts their
experiences with particular orang-utan in Sarawak; and considers the conditions
of the orang-utan in the world's zoos. In a postscript, Tom Harrisson asks: has the
orang a future?

76   **Common Malayan wildflowers.**
     M. R. Henderson. London: Longmans, 1961. 69p.

This valuable introductory guide includes only those herbaceous and shrubby
plants that are accessible and abundant in the peninsula. There are a large
number of colour plates.

77 **Malayan wild flowers.**
M. R. Henderson. Kuala Lumpur: Malayan Nature Society.
3 vols.
These three volumes originally appeared as the December 1949, September 1950,
and June 1951 issues of the *Malayan Nature Journal*. They were reprinted by the
Malayan Nature Society in 1955-59. The aim of this work is 'to enable the non-
expert to identify a majority of the smaller plants to be found not only in the
forest, but by the roadsides, on the seashores, and in the waste spaces of Malaya'.

78 **Gardening in the lowlands of Malaya.**
R. E. Holttum. Singapore: Straits Times Press (Malaya), 1953.
323p.
This book seeks to consider briefly all aspects of gardening in the lowlands of the
peninsula (and Singapore). It includes chapters on: garden planning; propagation
and pruning; ornamental shrubs and climbers; trees and palms; lawns; orchids;
vegetables; fruit and fruit trees; and pests and diseases. There are a large number
of line-drawings, and of photographs (both in colour and in black-and-white). The
author was the Director of the Botanic Gardens in Singapore from 1925-49.

79 **Orders and families of Malayan seed plants. Synopsis of orders and
families of Malayan gymnosperms, dicotyledons and
monocotyledons.**
Hsuan Keng. Singapore: Singapore University Press, 1978. rev.
ed. 437p. 4 maps. bibliog.
This volume provides 'a simple and systematic account of all the orders and
families of seed plants, native, naturalized, or commonly cultivated in the Malay
Peninsula and on Singapore Island'.

80 **Mosses of Singapore and Malaysia.**
Anne Johnson. Singapore: Singapore University Press, 1980.
126p. bibliog.
This book includes brief descriptions, frequently accompanied by a pen-line
illustration, of a selection of the estimated 500 species of moss found in Malaysia
and Singapore. For each species included, there is almost invariably a reference to
the localities where it may be found.

81 **Poisonous snakes of Peninsular Malaysia.**
Lim Boo Liat. Kuala Lumpur: Malayan Nature Society, in
association with the Institute for Medical Research [Kuala Lumpur],
1979. 61p. bibliog.
Peninsular Malaysia has some 141 known species of land and sea snakes. Of
these, all the species of sea snake (21) are venomous; but only 16 species of land
snake are poisonous, and of these only 5 species are considered dangerous to
man. This slim volume provides brief descriptions of all species of venomous land
and sea snakes in the peninsula, accompanied wherever possible by colour
photographs. There is also discussion of: the identification of venomous snakes

and recognition of their fang marks; the first aid treatment of snake bites; precautions against snake bites; and the prevention of snakes entering houses.

82   **Kinabalu. Summit of Borneo.**
Edited by Margaret Luping, Chin Wen, E. Richard Dingley.   Kota Kinabalu, Malaysia: The Sabah Society, 1978. 482p. 5 maps. bibliog.

Kinabalu is the mountain which dominates Sabah both physically and indeed spiritually. This volume of sixteen essays, which considers not only the mountain but also the surrounding national park, is divided into three parts. The first considers the mountain itself, and includes a general introduction by Tom Harrisson; an account of expeditions to the mountain over the century from 1851; and discussion of the geomorphology and geology of the area. The second and third parts consider respectively the flora and fauna of the area. Almost all the papers contain extensive bibliographies; and there is a very large number of photographs (approximately half in colour) and numerous line drawings.

83   **Expedition to Borneo. The search for proboscis monkeys and other creatures.**
David Macdonald.   London: J. M. Dent & Sons, 1982. 180p.

This is an account of a 1972 expedition to Borneo, undertaken principally to search for proboscis monkeys. The author warns that this is not a definitive account of the proboscis monkey; rather 'it is the story of encounters with hospitable people, extraordinary animals and intransigent outboard motors, the story of our naïveté and our enchantment, our blisters and disappointments, and, above all, the story of a wonderful place whose charm I want in some small measure to pass on to the reader who has not shared my good fortune in being able to travel there'.

84   **Borneo.**
John MacKinnon.   Amsterdam: Time-Life International (Nederland) B.V., 1975. 184p. map. bibliog.

This coffee-table book consists of relatively brief, but informative, chapters on the plants, insects, mammals (orang-utan), birds, and fish which inhabit the jungles of Borneo. Also includes a large number of superb photographs in colour.

85   **Mammals of Borneo. Field keys and an annotated checklist.**
Lord Medway.   Kuala Lumpur: Malaysian Branch of the Royal Asiatic Society, 1977. rev. ed. 172p. bibliog. (Monograph no. 7).

A detailed and exhaustive annotated checklist of Bornean mammals from the entire island. A substantial introduction discusses: the history of the study of Bornean mammals; their diversity and distribution, and their future in Borneo. There is also a considerable number of black-and-white photographs.

86   **The wild mammals of Malaya (Peninsular Malaysia) and Singapore.**
Lord Medway.   Kuala Lumpur: Oxford University Press, 1978. 2nd
ed. 128p. bibliog.

A comprehensive guide to the native wild mammals of Peninsular Malaysia and
Singapore which seeks 'to give sufficiently detailed descriptions to enable any
mammal to be identified . . . and also to draw attention to such behavioural
aspects and other characteristics as are of general interest or useful aids to
identification'. For each entry, information is provided under the following
headings: distribution, identification, habits, voice, breeding, life history, and
subspecies. Documentary sources of information are fully referenced. There are
15 colour plates and 11 figures.

87   **The birds of the Malay peninsula. A general account of the birds
inhabiting the region from the isthmus of Kra to Singapore with the
adjacent islands. Volume V: Conclusion, and survey of every species.**
Lord Medway, David R. Wells. London: H. F. & G. Witherby;
Kuala Lumpur: Penerbit Universiti Malaya, 1976. 448p. 7 maps.
bibliog.

The first four volumes in this series, under the authorship of H. C. Robinson and
F. N. Chasen, were published by Witherby in London between 1927 and 1939.
This final volume includes three concluding essays. But the major portion consists
of a systematic survey of every species of bird in the Malay peninsula. This is the
standard work on the subject.

88   **Common Malayan butterflies.**
R. Morrell.   London: Longmans, Green, 1960. 64p.

A brief introduction to the butterflies of the Malay peninsula which concentrates
'upon about a hundred species which the collector is most likely to encounter on
his earlier rambles', and gives 'some hint of the treasures which await him when
he ventures farther into the jungle'. There are twenty colour plates.

89   **A handlist of Malaysian mammals. A systematic list of the mammals
of the Malay Peninsula, Sumatra, Borneo and Java, including the
adjacent small islands.**
Frederick Nutter Chasen. Singapore: Government Printing Office,
1940. 209p. map. (Bulletin of the Raffles Museum, Singapore, no.
15).

This handlist, prepared by the then Director of the Raffles Museum, is an
essential work of reference in the field. Note should also be made of: F. N.
Chasen, *A handlist of Malaysian birds*, published in the *Bulletin of the Raffles
Museum, Singapore*, no. 11, December 1935.

90 **The birds of Borneo.**
Bertram E. Smythies, revised by the Earl of Cranbrook [Lord
Medway]. Kota Kinabalu, Malaysia; Kuala Lumpur: The Sabah
Society, with the Malayan Nature Society, 1981. 3rd ed. 473p. map.
bibliog.

This volume provides a systematic descriptive list of Bornean birds, supplemented
by a large number of colour plates. Earlier editions (1960, 1968) also included a
number of important supplementary chapters on such aspects as: birds and men in
Borneo, Iban omen birds, and cave swiftlets.

91 **Common birds of the Malay peninsula.**
M. W. F. Tweedie. Kuala Lumpur: Longman Malaysia, 1970. 2nd
ed. 69p.

This introductory guide provides a brief description of about 150 of the more
common species of birds found in the Malay peninsula, as well as information on
their habits and distribution. Almost all the species included are illustrated in
colour.

92 **Malayan naturalist.**
M. W. F. Tweedie. Singapore: Eastern Universities Press, 1957.
86p. map.

A collection of brief introductory essays by a former curator of the Raffles
Museum in Singapore. The subjects included are: bats; whales; crocodiles and
lizards; frogs and toads; the existence of sea serpents; butterflies; bees and wasps,
corals and allied animals; the giant snail; and grasshoppers, locusts, and crickets.

93 **Poisonous animals of Malaya.**
M. W. F. Tweedie. Singapore: Malaya Publishing House, 1941.
90p.

This volume includes the following chapters: Malayan poisonous snakes;
symptoms and treatment of snake bite; poisonous fish; poisonous insects;
centipedes and millipedes; poisonous invertebrate animals other than arthropods;
and poisonous arachnida (notably, scorpions).

94 **The snakes of Malaya.**
M. W. F. Tweedie. Singapore: Government Printing Office, 1957.
2nd ed. 143p. map. bibliog.

The major part of this volume consists of brief descriptions of the 129 species of
snake found in Peninsular Malaysia, Singapore, and the surrounding seas,
descriptions which will provide adequately for identification. The volume also
includes a systematic list of Malayan snakes with bibliographical references to
complete descriptions of every species; and a note on the distribution of species in
neighbouring territories. There are a large number of line-drawings and 17
photographs.

95 **Malayan animal life.**
M. W. F. Tweedie, J. L. Harrison. London, Kuala Lumpur: Longmans, 1965. 2nd ed. 237p.
This book, by a former Director of the Raffles Museum in Singapore and a former Professor of Zoology at the University of Singapore, seeks to provide 'the young reader, uninstructed in natural history, and visitors from overseas' with a brief introductory outline of the enormous fauna of the peninsula. The volume also includes an alphabetical list of Malay names for the peninsula's fauna, with the English and scientific equivalents.

96 **The Malay archipelago.**
Alfred Russel Wallace. Singapore: Graham Brash, 1983. 515p. 10 maps.
A reprint (unabridged of the 1922 edition) of a classic book of natural history and travel, published originally in London in 1869. From 1854 to 1862, Alfred Russel Wallace (1823-1913) explored the Malay Archipelago (including, of course, the peninsula and the island of Borneo). He observed the numerous different native peoples who inhabited the archipelago; made a detailed description of the abundant animals, birds, and insects that flourished there; and amassed a collection of 125,000 animal and insect specimens, many previously unknown. Wallace argued that the western half of the archipelago is Indian in animal life, whereas the eastern half is Australian. This thesis is now accepted by naturalists, and the line separating the two halves of the archipelago's animal life is called the Wallace line in his honour.

97 **Palms of Malaya.**
T. C. Whitmore. Kuala Lumpur: Oxford University Press, 1973. 132p. 7 maps. bibliog.
The main part of this volume consists of a detailed description of all the genera, and a substantial selection of the species, of wild palms found in Peninsular Malaysia. Brief introductory chapters consider: the construction of the palm; palm cultivation; palms of local interest in Malaya; the palm subfamilies; and keys to Malayan palms and distinctive characters. There are a number of black-and-white photographs, and a very large number of pen drawings.

Into the heart of Borneo. An account of a journey made in 1983 to the mountains of Batu Tiban with James Fenton.
See item no. 67.

The prehistory of Borneo.
See item no. 100.

Rain-forest collectors and traders. A study of resource utilization in modern and ancient Malaya.
See item no. 294.

Orang Asli animal tales.
See item no. 301.

Flora and Fauna

Malay poisons and charm cures.
See item no. 359.

Prehistory and Archaeology

98 **Archaeology in Sarawak.**
Chêng Tê-K'un. Cambridge, England: W. Heffer & Sons,
University of Toronto Press, 1969. 33p. map. bibliog.
This slim volume provides a brief account of the results of archaeological work in
Sarawak in general (as of the late 1960s), and of the excavations at Santubong (on
the delta of the Sarawak River, near Kuching) in particular.

99 **An annotated bibliography of Malayan (West Malaysian)**
archaeology: 1962-1969.
F. L. Dunn, B. A. V. Peacock. *Asian Perspectives*, vol. 14 (1971),
p. 43-48.
This is a comprehensive annotated bibliography, containing some 40 items.

100 **The prehistory of Borneo.**
Tom Harrisson. *Asian Perspectives*, vol. 13 (1970), p. 17-45.
This is an excellent survey and summary of the archaeological work carried out in
Sarawak, and to a lesser extent in Sabah and Brunei, from 1945 through to 1970.
An extensive list of references is attached. The author was government
ethnologist and curator of Sarawak Museum between 1947 and 1966, and was
arguably the most prominent archaeologist, ethnologist, and naturalist at work in
Sarawak in that period. *Journal of the Malaysian Branch of the Royal Asiatic
Society*, vol. 50, part 1 (June 1977) is a memorial issue for him, and contains
assessments of aspects of his work and interests by other scholars in the field. It
includes papers on: the ancient iron industry of the Sarawak river delta; Indian
influence in early Southeast Asia; the Niah caves; and the rhinoceros of Borneo.

101 **The later prehistory of the Malay peninsula.**
B. A. V. Peacock. In: *Early South East Asia. Essays in archaeology, history and historical geography.* Edited by R. B. Smith, W. Watson. New York, Kuala Lumpur: Oxford University Press, 1979. p. 199-214.

Provides an account of the archaeological evidence for the later prehistory of the Malay peninsula, and considers briefly some of the outstanding problems of interpretation. The volume, as a whole, has a most extensive bibliography.

102 **Archaeological researches on ancient Indian colonization in Malaya.**
H. G. Quaritch Wales. *Journal of the Malayan Branch of the Royal Asiatic Society*, vol. 18, part 1, (Feb. 1940), 85p. 15 maps and plans.

A report on archaeological research on Indian cultural expansion, undertaken at sites in Kedah, Perak, and Johor in the late 1930s under the direction of Quaritch Wales. The first part presents 'the body of new facts made available' by the field researches. The second, and more slender part suggests a number of broader conclusions which may be drawn from these findings. There are 89 black-and-white photographs attached to the end of the volume.

103 **The Malay peninsula in Hindu times.**
H. G. Quaritch Wales. London: Bernard Quaritch, 1976. 199p. 8 figs.

This survey by Quaritch Wales of the period of Hindu influence in the Malay peninsula opens with a consideration of textual evidence and early sculptures, before analysing the various Indian settlements, and the religious and commercial influence in the peninsula of Indianized Srivijaya.

104 **Early Malaysia. Some observations on the nature of Indian contacts with pre-British Malaya.**
Kernial Singh Sandhu. Singapore: University Education Press, 1973. 131p. 4 maps. bibliog.

A survey of Indian contacts with the Malay peninsula which covers the period from the earliest times, through the Melaka sultanate, to the Portuguese and Dutch periods. The volume includes a brief comment by Paul Wheatley on the dynamics of the process of Indianization in South East Asia.

105 **Prehistoric Malaya.**
M. W. F. Tweedie. Singapore: Eastern Universities Press, 1965. 3rd rev. ed. 44p. map. bibliog.

This volume appears in a series 'Background to Malaya'. It provides a concise introduction to the archaeological research, and its findings, undertaken in Peninsular Malaya from the end of the 19th century, although primarily from 1917. There are a considerable number of photographs and line-drawings.

106 **Desultory remarks on the ancient history of the Malay peninsula.**
Paul Wheatley. In: *Malayan and Indonesian studies. Essays presented to Sir Richard Winstedt on his eighty-fifth birthday.*
Edited by John Bastin, R. Roolvink. Oxford, England: Clarendon Press, 1964. p. 33-75.
This 'conspectus of the results of some of the [more recent] researches on the ancient history of the Malay peninsula' draws on the material which Wheatley considered at length in *The golden khersonese* (q.v.).

107 **The golden khersonese. Studies in the historical geography of the Malay peninsula before A.D. 1500.**
Paul Wheatley. Kuala Lumpur: University of Malaya Press, 1961. 388p. 53 maps and diags. bibliog.
In this classic study, Wheatley discusses Chinese, Greek, Latin, Indian and Arab sources relating to the historical geography of the peninsula prior to the 16th century. In the final two sections of the work, the author provides a summary of the political geography of the Malay peninsula before AD 1400, and an account of the political geography of Melaka during the 15th century. There are numerous and lengthy quotations in the original from the Chinese, Greek, and Latin sources (followed by translations). Arab and Indian sources are quoted only in translation, but again the quotations are numerous and lengthy. Thus this volume is designed not only as 'an account of the historical geography of the Malay Peninsula but also as a compendium of references'.

108 **Impressions of the Malay peninsula in ancient times.**
Paul Wheatley. Singapore: Donald Moore, for Eastern Universities Press, 1964. 254p. 7 drawings and maps. bibliog.
In this volume Wheatley provides a synthesis of his views on the historical geography of the Malay peninsula prior to the fall of Melaka in 1511, presented at length in *The golden khersonese* (q.v.). This present work is intended for the more general reader.

Rain-forest collectors and traders. A study of resource utilization in modern and ancient Malaya.
See item no. 294.

The peoples of north and west Borneo.
See item no. 315.

History

General

109 Malaysia. Prospect and retrospect. The impact and aftermath of colonial rule.
Richard Allen. London: Oxford University Press, 1968. 335p.
3 maps. bibliog.

This study provides an introductory political history of Malaysia from the Melaka sultanate, although concentrating on the period from the Japanese invasion through to 1967. Particular attention is paid to Malaysia's external relations since independence, notably with Singapore, the Philippines (the dispute over Sabah), and Indonesia (confrontation over the formation of Malaysia in 1963).

110 Malaya. The making of a neo-colony.
Edited by Mohamed Amin, Malcolm Caldwell. Nottingham, England: Spokesman Books, 1977. 265p.

The nine papers in this volume constitute a radical analysis of the history of Malaya from the British intervention in 1874 to independence in 1957, with six of the papers being concerned with the period from 1942. Caldwell himself contributes three papers: the British 'forward movement' between 1874-1914; developments in the period from the First World War through to, and including, the 1930s depression; and the period from the Emergency through to political independence. The remaining chapters include consideration of: the contradictions in pre-war colonialism (1930-41); the rise and fall of Malayan trade unionism between 1945-50; and developments in Singapore between 1945 and 1957.

111 **A history of Malaysia.**
Barbara Watson Andaya, Leonard Y. Andaya.   London;
Basingstoke, England: Macmillan, 1982. 350p. 4 maps. bibliog.
The authors provide a survey of the history of Malaysia from earliest times
through to 1980, giving due attention both to the pre-colonial period and to the
history of the territories of present-day East Malaysia. This is the most
comprehensive and well-balanced introduction to the history of the country which
has appeared to date.

112 **Malaysia. Selected historical readings.**
Compiled by John Bastin, Robin W. Winks.   Nendeln,
Liechtenstein: KTO Press, 1979. 2nd ed. 526p. 2 maps. bibliog.
First published in 1966, this volume consists of substantial extracts from major
writings on the history of Malaysia. The readings, with the assistance of brief
commentaries by Bastin and Winks, form a coherent and consecutive account of
the modern history of the country, with considerable attention being given to the
eastern territories. The first edition covered the period from the early Melaka and
Brunei sultanates to the secession of Singapore in 1965. In this second edition a
number of new readings have been added in an appendix, the majority of which
either supplement the existing material on the early 1960s, or are concerned with
the period 1965-70.

113 **The international personality of the Malay peninsula. A study of the
international law of imperialism.**
Alfred P. Rubin.   Kuala Lumpur: University of Malaya Press,
1974. 327p. bibliog.
This volume is concerned with the theoretical justifications advanced by statesmen
of different societies for their political actions taken in the Malay peninsula from
the time of the Melaka sultanate through to the 1830s. For example, in the
opening chapter there is consideration of 'the concepts of government and
international behaviour existing in the Malay Peninsula before the arrival of
Europeans in politically significant numbers' and of 'the justification felt necessary
by the Europeans for their actions in the Peninsula at the beginning of the
sixteenth century'. Thereafter there is consideration of: the early European
rivalries in the peninsula; the ascendancy of the Dutch; the initial establishment of
British power; the removal of Thai authority in the 1820s; and the subsequent
consolidation of British control.

114 **A critical appraisal of historians of Malaya: the theory of society
implicit in their work.**
Patrick Sullivan. In: *Southeast Asia. Essays in the political economy
of structural change.* Edited by Richard Higgott, Richard
Robison.   London: Routledge & Kegan Paul, 1985. p. 65-92.
This essay 'critically examines the writing of Malay history from the earliest texts
to the present day, uncovers and criticises a common view of society in these
writings, and examines the way this view has been transmitted through
generations of historians'. More specifically it examines three stages of history

writing in Malaya: 'traditional writings and their uses for both traditional and more recent historians; the works of colonial scholar-administrators; and post-colonial works'. Particular attention is paid to 'the construction of Perak history up to the early years of British intervention'.

115 **Papers on Malayan history. Papers submitted to the first International Conference of South-East Asian Historians, Singapore, January 1961.**
Edited by K. G. Tregonning. Singapore: Journal of South-East Asian History, 1962. Published by the Department of History, University of Malaya in Singapore. 273p.

Among the fourteen contributions are papers which consider: the tin industry (Wong Lin Ken); Indian immigration (Kernial Singh Sandhu); British policy in Malayan waters in the nineteenth century (N. Tarling); the British forward movement, 1880-1889 (E. Thio); Kaum Muda-Kaum Tua: innovation and reaction among the Malays, 1900-1941 (W. Roff); and Japanese policy for Malaya under the occupation (Y. Itagaki).

116 **Papers on Malay subjects.**
Edited by R. J. Wilkinson, 1907-16, selected and introduced by P. L. Burns. Kuala Lumpur: Oxford University Press, 1971. 468p.

R. J. Wilkinson (1867-1941) was a senior British official in Malaya and a distinguished scholar of Malay. Between 1907 and 1927 a series of pamphlets 'Papers on Malay Subjects' appeared under his editorship. These were intended essentially to assist British administrative cadets to prepare for the Malay language examination: more generally, they were to introduce British officers to the cultural traditions and history of the Malays. They therefore represent 'the first attempt to write a systematic account of the Malays of the Malay Peninsula, of their society, cultural traditions and history'. This volume reprints a selection of the *Papers*, each concerned with history. It includes: 'A history of the Peninsular Malays with chapters on Perak and Selangor' by Wilkinson himself; the Perak State Council minutes (1877-82); and a number of essays on the history of Negeri Sembilan.

The Malay peninsula prior to British rule (pre-1786)

117 **Perak, the abode of grace. A study of an eighteenth-century Malay state.**
Barbara Watson Andaya. Kuala Lumpur: Oxford University Press, 1979. 444p. 7 maps. bibliog.

In the early 18th century the state of Perak, on the west coast of the Malay peninsula, was prey to periodic attacks from pirates and raiders as well as threatened by Bugis and Minangkabau disputes. But in 1746 Perak signed a treaty with the Dutch East India Company, and from then until the end of the century 'Perak's rulers managed to tread the fine line of diplomacy, maintaining domestic peace and equable relations with their neighbours in a period when invasion and civil war were endemic'. Indeed Perak appears to have enjoyed a prosperity previously unknown. The author is primarily concerned with this period from 1746: and focuses on the Perak sultans' perceptions of the Dutch alliance and the advantage which it brought to their state. The book draws on contemporary Malay sources, as well as European materials.

118   **The kingdom of Johor 1641-1728.**
Leonard Y. Andaya.   Kuala Lumpur: Oxford University Press,
1975. 394p. 7 maps. bibliog.

The author provides an essentially political history of the kingdom of Johor from 1641 when the conquest of Portuguese Melaka by the Dutch and the beginning of a close friendship between Johor and the Dutch enabled the Malay kingdom to enjoy a prolonged period of prosperity and renewed strength; through the murder in 1699 of a wicked and depraved sultan by the Orang Kaya (nobles) of Johor, an event which was followed by pronounced political distintegration; the conquest of Johor by Minangkabau forces in 1718; to the emergence of Bugis political dominance in the kingdom in the 1720s. The book draws predominantly on contemporary Malay sources, as well as European materials.

119   **Kedah 1771-1821. The search for security and independence.**
R. Bonney.   Kuala Lumpur: Oxford University Press, 1971. 215p.
3 maps. bibliog.

Bonney's work provides a diplomatic history of Kedah from 1771, in which year there occurred a serious succession dispute within the state which led to the lease of Kuala Kedah to the English East India Company the following year, to 1821 and the Siamese invasion which brought Kedah within the territory of the kingdom of Siam. Particular attention is paid to the influence of internal political disputes on Kedah's external relations. There is analysis of the circumstances surrounding the lease of Penang to the East India Company in 1786, the persistent Siamese threat to Kedah in the late 18th and early 19th centuries, and the frequent requests from Kedah to the Company for protection against that threat.

120   **Sĕjarah Mĕlayu. Malay Annals.**
A translation of Raffles MS 18, with commentary by C. C.
Brown.   *Journal of the Malayan Branch of the Royal Asiatic
Society*, vol. 25, parts 2 & 3 (Oct. 1952). 276p. 2 maps. bibliog.

The *Sĕjarah Mĕlayu* is a Melaka court text which records the origins, establishment, and rise to pre-eminence of the Melaka empire. This is a translation and commentary upon the earliest extant version of the text, drafted in 1612 and copied at the beginning of the 19th century. The *Sĕjarah Mĕlayu* was not intended to provide a precise account of events. Rather it is regarded as the foremost example of classical Malay prose style, a work of outstanding literary merit as well as a valuable insight into the Malay perception of their past. This study was subsequently reprinted by Oxford University Press (Kuala Lumpur) in 1970, and again in 1983 (with an introduction by R. Roolvink).

121 **Indigenous political systems of western Malaya.**
J. M. Gullick. London: Athlone Press; New York: Humanities Press, 1958. 151p. 2 maps. bibliog.

In this classic study, Gullick describes and analyses the political institutions of the western Malay states (in practice, Perak; Selangor; and Negeri Sembilan) in the period immediately prior to British intervention in 1874. His aim is 'to present indigenous Malay political institutions of the period as a working system of social control and leadership'. There is consideration of the Malay village community as a residential, economic and social unit; the sultanate; the ruling class; the district chief; Malay law as a means of social control; the nature of Malay warfare in this period; the economic aspects of political leadership; and the cohesion of the Malay state.

122 **Malacca fort.**
Graham Irwin. *Journal of Southeast Asian History*, vol. 3, no. 2 (Sept. 1962), p. 19-44.

Irwin provides a primarily architectural history of the stone fort at Melaka from the first construction on that site undertaken by Albuquerque in 1511-12 to the destruction of the fort by the British in 1807.

123 **The population of Kedah in the nineteenth century.**
Zaharah Mahmud. *Journal of Southeast Asian Studies*, vol. 3, no. 2 (Sept. 1972), p. 193-209.

This article provides a detailed examination of the changing size, ethnic composition, spatial distribution, and economic activity of the population of 19th-century Kedah.

124 **The conquest of Malacca.**
Francisco de Sá de Meneses, translated by Edgar C. Knowlton. Kuala Lumpur: University of Malaya Press, 1970. 234p. bibliog.

Malaca conquistada is an epic poem, concerned primarily with the achievements of Afonso de Albuquerque, focusing on the conquest of Melaka by the Portugese in 1511. The first edition of the poem was published in 1634. The poet follows fairly closely the events as recounted by earlier writers, 'but shows an ability to deviate from history when that serves his purpose'.

125 **Kerajaan. Malay political culture on the eve of colonial rule.**
A. C. Milner. Tucson, Arizona: University of Arizona Press, 1982. 178p. 4 maps. bibliog.

Milner's study of Malay political culture on the eve of colonial rule – in essence the Malay perception of their own political order, behaviour, and motivations – focuses primarily on the rise and expansion of the Sumatran state of Deli, and on a civil war which occurred in the peninsular state of Pahang in the late 1850s and early 1860s. The study is based on a searching examination and analysis of classical Malay writings, notably the *Hikayat Deli* and the *Hikayat Pahang*.

126 **The precious gift.** (Tuhfat al-Nafis.)
Raja Ali Haji Ibn Ahmad, an annotated translation by Virginia Matheson, Barbara Watson Andaya. Kuala Lumpur: Oxford University Press, 1982. 476p. 4 maps. bibliog.

The *Tuhfat al-Nafis* was written in the mid-19th century by Raja Ali Haji, a Riau prince of Bugis descent. It provides an extended account of events in the Malay world from the late 17th century. It is therefore one of the most important indigenous manuscript sources for the pre-colonial history of the peninsula. This translation has a brief introduction, and is exhaustively annotated.

127 **Pre-colonial state systems in Southeast Asia. The Malay peninsula, Sumatra, Bali-Lombok, South Celebes.**
Edited by Anthony Reid, Lance Castles. Kuala Lumpur: Malaysian Branch of the Royal Asiatic Society, 1975. 135p. 4 maps. (Monograph no. 6).

This volume of twelve papers, originally presented at a colloqium at the Australian National University in April 1973, contains the following four contributions on the Malay peninsula: 'The structure of power in seventeenth century Johor' (Leonard Andaya); 'Concepts of state in the *Tuhfat al-Nafis*' (Virginia Matheson); 'The nature of the state in eighteenth century Perak' (Barbara Andaya); and 'Kedah – the development of a Malay state' (Dianne Lewis).

128 **The Portuguese administration in Malacca, 1511-1641.**
D. R. SarDesai. *Journal of Southeast Asian History*, vol. 10, no. 3 (Dec. 1969), p. 501-12.

This paper considers the administrative organization of the Portuguese in Melaka, in the context of the Portuguese colonial administration centered in Goa. It is particularly concerned with the methods used by the Portuguese to control the many races and nationalities which inhabited the city-port.

129 **Prince of pirates. The Temenggongs and the development of Johor and Singapore 1784-1885.**
Carl A. Trocki. Singapore: Singapore University Press, 1979. 251p. 5 maps. bibliog.

This is a study of the Temenggong dynasty of Johor – their origins; their position in the old empire of Johor which had disintegrated in the 18th century; and, most importantly, their construction of a new state of Johor during the 19th century. At the beginning of that century the Temenggong's domain extended over the southern tip of the Malay peninsula, Singapore, and the northern part of the Riau archipelago. From the founding of the British settlement at Singapore in 1819, the Temenggongs gradually relinquished their claims to the island and archipelago, and concentrated all their efforts towards building up a government to rule the state which is now called Johor. By 1885 the state had reached its present boundaries. The study draws in part on documents in the Johor archives, and includes analysis of: the related institutions of piracy and slavery in the area; and the close involvement of the Chinese (notably pepper and gambier planters) in the foundation and maintenance of the Temenggong's state in Johor.

130 **Malacca's early kings and the reception of Islam.**
Christopher H. Wake. *Journal of Southeast Asian History*, vol. 5, no. 2 (Sept. 1964), p. 104-28.

Wake examines the major contemporary Malay, Chinese, and Portuguese sources for the history of the Melaka sultanate, in order to reconstruct a list of the Melaka kings for the 15th century and to reconsider the date and circumstances under which the Melaka ruler converted to Islam.

131 **The fall of Śrīvijaya in Malay history.**
O. W. Wolters. Kuala Lumpur: Oxford University Press, 1970. 274p. map. bibliog.

Using mainly the Melaka court text, the *Sĕjarah Mĕlayu*, and Chinese dynastic and travel records, Wolters attempts a reconstruction of the relationship between the collapse of the great Sumatran Malay empire of Śrīvijaya, which arguably occurred in the second half of the 14th century, and the establishment and rise of Melaka. Particular attention is paid to the pre-Melaka career of the founder of Melaka, posthumously known to the Malays as Iskandar Shah. Wolter's interpretation has attracted considerable academic controversy.

The Borneo territories to the end of British rule (pre-1963)

132 **Sabah. The first ten years as a colony 1946-1956.**
M. H. Baker. Singapore: Malaysia Publishing House, for the Department of History, University of Singapore, 1965. 154p.

This account of the opening decade of formal colonial rule in Sabah includes the following chapters: geography and resources; the people; the historical background; constitution and administration; social services and public utilities; trade, labour, and industry; agriculture; and communications. A brief introduction, written in 1964, provides a survey of some of the more prominent changes experienced by Sabah in the years from 1958, the date at which the main text had been completed.

133 **A gambling style of government. The establishment of the Chartered Company's rule in Sabah, 1878-1915.**
Ian Black. Kuala Lumpur: Oxford University Press, 1983. 254p. 3 maps. bibliog.

This volume is concerned with the 'faltering process' by which the British North Borneo Chartered Company secured effective control over the territory of Sabah in the late 19th and early 20th centuries, and the consequences of European occupation for the people of that area. Particular attention is paid to the indigenous reactions to Company rule, including the Mat Salleh revolts in the last years of the 19th century. Black's volume attempts 'to create a history of Sabah under the Company, rather than a history of the Company itself'.

134 **Rajah Charles Brooke. Monarch of all he surveyed.**
Colin N. Crisswell. Kuala Lumpur: Oxford University Press, 1978. 253p. 4 maps. bibliog.

Charles Brooke (1829-1917) was the nephew and successor of Rajah James Brooke. He ruled Sarawak from 1868 until his death. This biography draws mainly on British government records.

135 **The tobacco industry of North Borneo: a distinctive form of plantation agriculture.**
David W. John, James C. Jackson. *Journal of Southeast Asian Studies*, vol. 4, no. 1 (March 1973), p. 88-106.

Provides an account of the tobacco industry of North Borneo from its initial development in the last two decades of the 19th century to its contraction and then virtual demise in the inter-war decades. 'It investigates the role of the industry in the process of economic development in [North Borneo] and also seeks to indicate the particular features of this form of plantation agriculture'.

136 **The towkays of Sabah. Chinese leadership and indigenous challenge in the last phase of British rule.**
Edwin Lee. Singapore: Singapore University Press, 1976. 271p. 5 maps. bibliog.

This study is concerned with the Chinese mercantile and political élite in Sabah in the final years of colonial rule, through the entry of Sabah into Malaysia, to the late 1960s. Particular attention is paid to: Chinese opposition to Malaysia and the community's consequent conflict with indigenous advocates of the Federation; divisions within the Chinese élite during the negotiations and discussions (notably the Cobbold Commission) which eventually led to the creation of Malaysia; the internal political repercussions of the Philippine claim to Sabah, the Indonesian opposition to Malaysia, and the Brunei revolt; the close business interest of the *towkays* in the extraction of Sabah timber and the political implications of timber wealth; and the adjustment of the Sabah *towkays* to the changed circumstances of the state after 1963.

137   **The evolution of urban government in Southeast Asian cities: Kuching under the Brookes.**
Craig A. Lockard.   *Modern Asian Studies*, vol. 12, part 2 (April 1978), p. 245-67.
This article is concerned primarily with the development of local government in Kuching (Sarawak) under the Brooke Raj (1841-1941). In this period Kuching 'had a system of indirect rule through which the Chinese and Malay communities were generally governed separately through their own elites; although a municipal board did exist after 1921, it had fairly limited powers and responsibilities and, most importantly, its membership, too, was based on the principle of communal representation'. Lockard also provides a brief comparative analysis of the historical evolution of urban government in other South East Asian cities, including Kuala Lumpur and Singapore.

138   **Rajahs and rebels. The Ibans of Sarawak under Brooke rule, 1841-1941.**
Robert Pringle.   London: Macmillan, 1970. 410p. 5 maps. bibliog.
This history of the Ibans under the rule of the Brookes places particular emphasis on social change. It is a study 'set far from the main centres of political and commercial life, in the outlying provinces of a thinly populated, overwhelmingly rural state. It is a story of country places, of ten-shop Chinese bazaars, of villages, of longhouses and of individuals'. Pringle's study is intended to complement Benedict Sandin's *The sea dayaks of Borneo before white rajah rule* (q.v.).

139   **The name of Brooke. The end of white rajah rule in Sarawak.**
R. H. W. Reece.   Kuala Lumpur: Oxford University Press, 1982. 331p. 2 maps. bibliog.
Reece's first concern is to explain why Brooke rule in Sarawak came to an end in July 1946 and 'to describe the way in which it [the end] came about'. This involves a consideration of such issues as the nature of Brooke rule in the 1930s; the question of the Brooke succession; the policy of the Colonial Office towards Sarawak between 1934 and 1941; the origins of indigenous political organization in Sarawak between 1930 and 1945; and the impact of the Japanese occupation. In the final two chapters Reece considers the actual cession of Sarawak to the British Crown in 1946, and the subsequent anti-cession movement in the territory in the period 1946-51.

140   **The white rajahs. A history of Sarawak from 1841 to 1946.**
Steven Runciman.   Cambridge, England: Cambridge University Press, 1960. 320p. 3 maps. bibliog.
This book was written at the suggestion of the (British) Government of Sarawak which also financed at least part of the research and allowed access to all the papers and documents in its archives. In addition some surviving members of the Brooke family placed their papers at the disposal of the author. But this is not, Runciman states, an official history. Nevertheless this book offers a distinctly favourable view of Brooke rule. Thus: 'In an age when colonial methods were not always pretty, when the lust for power or for commercial gain too often dictated policy, they showed how a few Europeans could bring peace and contentment to a

fierce and lawless country, with the goodwill and even love of its peoples. Their weapons were human sympathy, selflessness and a high integrity'.

141   A flourish for the bishop. Brooke's friend Grant. Two studies in
      Sarawak history, 1848-1868.
      Max Saint. Braunton, England: Merlin Books, 1985. 284p. map.
      bibliog.
These two complementary and corrobarative studies seek to assess the achievements of two missionaries working in Sarawak in the middle decades of the 19th century, the 'somewhat ebullient' Bishop Frank McDougall and his wife Harrietta. In particular the studies seek 'to restore the Bishop's good name after a century of eclipse and distortion'.

142   Borneo and British intervention in Malaya.
      Nicholas Tarling. *Journal of Southeast Asian Studies*, vol. 5, no. 2
      (Sept. 1974), p. 159-65.
Tarling has two principal concerns in this article: 1] to suggest that British determination to avoid intervention by other major powers along the sea-routes to China in the 19th century was a crucial consideration both in accounting for British intervention in the peninsula in the 1870s and in shaping British official policy towards the Borneo territories from the middle of the century; 2] to examine some of the early [colonial] proposals for bringing the Borneo territories and the peninsular territories into a form of federation or other constitutional association.

143   The burthen, the risk, and the glory. A biography of Sir James
      Brooke.
      Nicholas Tarling.   Kuala Lumpur: Oxford University Press, 1982.
      465p. 2 maps. bibliog.
This is an extremely detailed biography of Sir James Brooke (1803-68), the founding member of the dynasty of 'White rajahs' which ruled Sarawak from 1841 until 1946. This study draws considerably on the unpublished private papers of various members of the Brooke family.

144   Sulu and Sabah. A study of British policy towards the Philippines
      and North Borneo from the late eighteenth century.
      Nicholas Tarling.   Kuala Lumpur: Oxford University Press, 1978.
      385p. 4 maps. bibliog.
The Sulu archipelago forms the southernmost part of the Philippines, situated between Mindanao and Sabah. Tarling's extremely detailed study is concerned primarily with the making of British policy towards the Sulu-Sabah region from the late 18th century through to the end of the 19th century. This is a subject of some contemporary relevance, for it was the earlier authority of the Sultan of Sulu over the north Borneo territory which was to form the basis of the Philippine claim to Sabah in the 1960s.

145   **A history of modern Sabah (North Borneo 1881-1963).**
      K. G. Tregonning.   Kuala Lumpur: University of Malaya Press,
      1965. 2nd ed. 275p. 2 maps. bibliog.
The first edition of this work, published in 1958, was titled, *Under Chartered
Company rule*. This present edition provides a general history of Sabah from the
chartering of the British North Borneo Company in 1881 through to independence
and entry into the Federation of Malaysia in 1963.

146   **The origins of British Borneo.**
      L. R. Wright.   Hong Kong: Hong Kong University Press, 1970.
      237p. 3 maps. bibliog.
This volume is concerned primarily with Britain's progressive involvement in
Borneo from 1860 to 1888, in which latter year British protectorate status was
negotiated for the three territories of Sarawak, Brunei, and North Borneo.
Wright suggests that British interest in the area in this period increasingly derived
from concern over the vulnerability of the trade route to East Asia were another
European power to establish itself on the north-west coast of Borneo.

The Chinese community of Sarawak. A study of communal relations.
See item no. 17.

Life in the forests of the Far East.
See item no. 68.

Colonialism and Iban warfare.
See item no. 329.

Peninsular Malaya under British rule in the period to 1941

Political history (1786-1941)

147   **The Kelantan rising of 1915: some thoughts on the concept of
      resistance in British Malayan history.**
      J. de V. Allen.   *Journal of Southeast Asian History*, vol. 9, no. 2
      (Sept. 1968), p. 241-57.
This article 'does not claim to be an adequate account of the 1915 Kelantan
Rising' but is primarily intended 'to suggest that a fuller study of it would make as
good a starting-point as any for a more general review of the role played by
armed Malay resistance in the history of the British period in Malaya'. A more
detailed analysis of the uprising is provided by: Ibrahim Nik Mahmood, 'The

To'Janggut Rebellion of 1915', in: *Kelantan. Religion, society and politics in a Malay state*, edited by William R. Roff (Kuala Lumpur: Oxford University Press, 1974, p. 62-86).

148   **Malayan Civil Service, 1874-1941: colonial bureaucracy/Malayan élite.**
J. de Vere Allen.   *Comparative Studies in Society and History*, vol. 12, no. 2 (April 1970), p. 149-78.

In the early years of British administration in the Malay States, the European officials were 'a very small and oddly assorted group of men quite separate and different from, and only loosely controlled by, the official colonial establishment in the Straits Settlements'. By the time of the Japanese occupation, there had emerged a highly homogenous and cohesive community of British officers in the Malayan Civil Service. This paper traces this development of a colonial bureaucracy, concentrating upon: the growth in numbers; the emergence of a distinctive *esprit de corps*; 'and the efforts, largely successful, to maintain a certain degree of independence – or at any rate internal self-government – which sometimes led it into disputes or open clashes with Whitehall, with the High Commissioner in Singapore, or with the rest of the European community in Malaya itself'. This paper is followed by some comments by Gayl D. Ness (p. 179-87).

149   **Taming the jungle. The men who made British Malaya.**
Pat Barr.   London: Secker & Warburg, 1977. 172p. map. bibliog.

A popular account of the work and personalities of many of the principal British administrators who served in the Malay States in the last decades of the 19th century, including Birch, Clifford, Low, Maxwell, Swettenham, and Weld.

150   **Our tropical possessions in Malayan India: being a descriptive account of Singapore, Penang, Province Wellesley, and Malacca; their peoples, products, commerce and government.**
John Cameron.   London, 1865. Reprinted, with an introduction by Wang Gungwu; Kuala Lumpur: Oxford University Press, 1965. 408p.

John Cameron was editor of the *Straits Times* in Singapore when this book was written. His description of the peoples, products, commerce and government in the Straits Settlements focuses mainly on Singapore.

151   **The British Foreign Office and the Siamese Malay States, 1890-97.**
Chandran Jeshurun.   *Modern Asian Studies*, vol. 5, part 2 (April 1971), p. 143-59.

This paper is concerned with 'tracing the trend of thought within the Foreign Office [in the 1890s] on the thorny question of the Siamese claim to suzerainty in that part of the Malay Peninsula immediately north of the British-protected states of Perak and Pahang'. It concludes in 1897, when the Colonial Office began to exercise considerable influence over the making of British policy in the Siamese part of the Malay Peninsula; this was also the year which saw the conclusion of the Anglo-Siamese Secret Convention with respect to that area. In 1909 the states in question – Kedah, Perlis, Kelantan and Trengganu – were transferred to British authority.

152 **The reasons for British intervention in Malaya: review and reconsideration.**
E. Chew. *Journal of Southeast Asian History*, vol. 6, no. 1 (March 1965), p. 81-93.

Reviews the evidence concerning the change in Colonial Office policy towards the Malay States in 1873 which led to British intervention in the peninsula at the beginning of the following year. It provides a detailed reconsideration of the work of earlier writers on this subject, including most notably Cowan, MacIntyre, and Parkinson.

153 **Sir Frank Swettenham and the Federation of the Malay States.**
E. Chew. *Modern Asian Studies*, vol. 2, part 1, (Jan. 1968), p. 51-69.

The Federated Malay States (comprising Perak, Selangor, Negeri Sembilan, and Pahang) was formed in 1896, with Swettenham as its first Resident-General. This article considers Swettenham's view of the causes of federation, 'and then discusses the origins of the concept of a Malay federation and [Swettenham's] role in the formation of the FMS'.

154 **Nineteenth-century Malaya. The origins of British political control.**
C. D. Cowan. London: Oxford University Press, 1961. 286p. 4 maps. bibliog.

The principal concern of this study is to analyse the way in which Britain came to intervene in the affairs of the western Malay states in the 1870s. It suggests that the critical influence on British policy was the fear of foreign (German) intervention in the peninsula should Britain fail to take action, and the awareness that the presence of another European power in the peninsula would threaten the eastern approaches to India and the sea-route to China. Cowan also considers the actual introduction of British Residents in Perak, Selangor, and Sungai Ujong in 1874; the early Malay reaction to this British presence (notably the murder of the Perak Resident, J. W. Birch, in 1875); the evolution of the Resident system after 1876; and, briefly, the extension of British authority to the remainder of the peninsula south of Siam by 1914.

155 **Malaysia. A study in direct and indirect rule.**
Rupert Emerson, with an introduction by John Bastin. Kuala Lumpur: University of Malaya Press, 1964. 536p. 2 maps.

Emerson, who was Professor of Government at Harvard in the 1930s, published this study in 1937. It is concerned with both British Malaya and the Netherlands East Indies, although the emphasis is on the former territory. It first provides an account of the advance of British administration in the peninsula, and thus includes discussion of early Western contact with the area; the British forward movement towards the end of the 19th century; and the consolidation and character of colonial administration into the 20th century. Second, and more valuably, Emerson analyses the confused political structure of the Federated Malay States, Unfederated Malay States, and the Straits Settlements in the inter-war decades, and in particular considers the 'decentralization' debate which dominated the colonial administration in the early part of that period. When it first appeared, this study was vigorously attacked by former members of the Malayan Civil Service as being harshly biased against British rule, although present-day readers may regard Emerson's judgements on British colonialism as being relatively mild. The study is now widely regarded as a classic work in the field – probably the most insightful account of British administration in Malaya between the world wars.

156 **British Malaya. A bibliographical and biographical compendium.**
Robert Heussler. New York, London: Garland Publishing, 1981. 193p.

This work divides into two parts. The first is a lightly annotated, selective bibliography of British Malaya, focusing mainly on the period 1867-1942. There are 499 entries divided into: bibliographies and directories; history and social science; British policy and administration; biography and autobiography; Malay studies; immigrant peoples – Chinese and Indian; war, insurrection and terrorism; miscellaneous. There is both a subject and an author index. The second part of the book provides brief biographical sketches for each of the administrative officials who served in British Malaya.

157 **British rule in Malaya. The Malayan Civil Service and its predecessors, 1867-1942.**
Robert Heussler. Oxford, England: Clio Press, 1981. 356p. map. bibliog.

This study is concerned with the British officials who administered Malaya from 1867 (when responsibility for the Straits Settlements passed from the India Office to the Colonial Office) to 1942. It focuses on their backgrounds and education, on their work in Malaya, and on the moral and professional precepts which developed within the service over that period. There is consideration, for example, of the founding of the Residency system and of the early work of the Residents in the later 19th century; the Chinese Protectorate; the Labour Department; administration on the east coast; the making of policy and the exercise of power; and the life and work of the Residents and District Officers in the Federated Malay States in the inter-war years. As well as working from official primary sources, Heussler has utilized a substantial body of private papers and written reminiscences by retired members of the Malayan Civil Service. He has also drawn on correspondence with many retired officials as well as transcripts of interviews with them.

158 **Completing a stewardship. The Malayan Civil Service, 1942-1957.**
Robert Heussler.   Westport, Connecticut; London: Greenwood
Press, 1983. 240p. 6 maps. bibliog.

This is the sequel to Heussler's *British rule in Malaya: The Malayan Civil Service and its predecessors, 1867-1942*. The focus of the study is 'on the spirit, the values and the working posture of the MCS (The Malayan Civil Service) in the closing days of its life . . . the views and daily work of men who were at the center of affairs', through the outbreak of war in December 1941 and the occupation; the re-establishment of British administration after 1945; the Emergency; and the end of colonial rule in 1957.

159 **The emergence of the modern Malay administrative elite.**
Khasnor Johan.   Singapore: Oxford University Press, 1984. 230p.
bibliog.

This study examines the emergence of a new class of English-educated modern Malay administrators within the administrative service of the FMS from the early 20th century. It is concerned 'more with the social implications of the emergence of [this] Malay official class than with its administrative experience'. In particular it focuses on the various acculturation processes experienced by this class, as the British administration sought to mould them into 'suitable' administrative officers; and on the consequences of that experience for the relations of the class with the British official community, the traditional Malay élite, and the *rakyat*; and for their own perceptions of themselves as a social group.

160 **The origin of British administration in Malaya.**
Khoo Kay Kim.   *Journal of the Malaysian Branch of the Royal Asiatic Society*, vol. 39, part 1 (July 1966), p. 52-91.

This article provides a detailed examination of the motives 'for the Colonial Office's decision to assume responsibilities for the administration of some of the Malay States in 1873'. Khoo suggests that the intervention policy of 1873 'was actuated very much by economic motives', most notably by concern that the prevailing anarchy in the Malay states 'was injurious to the development of Straits commercial enterprise in the Peninsula'. British intervention was prompted primarily by concern for the development of British trade and commerce in the Straits area: with respect to Cowan's argument that the Colonial Office was primarily concerned at the possibility of German intervention, Khoo suggests that 'there are innumerable reasons to suspect that [the genuineness of Kimberley's fear of intervention by another power] was false and none to indicate that it was true'.

161 **The western Malay states 1850-1873. The effects of commercial development on Malay politics.**
Khoo Kay Kim.   Kuala Lumpur: Oxford University Press, 1972.
244p. 4 maps. bibliog.

Khoo's principal concern is with the commercial links between the Straits Settlements and the western Malay states in the two decades prior to British intervention in early 1874, and the impact of those commercial interests on the politics of the peninsular states. There is consideration of the growth of Straits commercial and mining activities in the peninsula; political disorder in the western states arising from acute dissension within the Malay polity and conflicts between the various Chinese secret societies; and the involvement of Straits merchants in the mounting disorder in the western Malay states through to the early 1870s.

162 **The Kuomintang-Communist united front in Malaya during the National Salvation period, 1937-1941.**
Stephen Leong. *Journal of Southeast Asian Studies*, vol. 8, no. 1 (March 1977), p. 31-47.

Leong considers the extent to which the united front between the Kuomintang in China and the Chinese Communist Party, formed during the Sino-Japanese War from 1937, was reflected by the Kuomintang in Malaya and the Malayan Communist Party. His conclusion challenges previous interpretations by suggesting that the degree of collaboration between the two parties in Malaya was in fact substantially limited: the united front in Malaya lasted a mere ten months in 1937-38.

163 **The Malayan overseas Chinese and the Sino-Japanese war, 1937-1941.**
Stephen Leong. *Journal of Southeast Asian Studies*, vol. 10, no. 2 (Sept. 1979), p. 293-320.

Leong examines the response of the Malayan overseas Chinese to the Sino-Japanese war, from the outbreak of hostilities in July 1937 to the Japanese invasion of Malaya in December 1941. Particular attention is paid to the fund-raising activities of the Chinese community in Malaya, (Leong suggests that from 1939 'monetary contributions from the Malayan Chinese helped to prevent the Chinese Government from becoming bankrupt'), and their boycott of Japanese goods. He notes the tolerant and sympathetic attitude of the colonial administration in Malaya towards the patriotic activities of the Chinese in this period.

164 **Britain's intervention in Malaya: the origin of Lord Kimberley's instructions to Sir Andrew Clarke in 1873.**
D. MacIntyre. *Journal of Southeast Asian History*, vol. 2, no. 3 (Oct. 1961), p. 47-69.

MacIntyre provides a detailed consideration of the background and origin of the instructions given to Sir Andrew Clarke, the incoming Governor of the Straits Settlements, by Lord Kimberley, the Colonial Secretary, on 20 September 1873. These instructions may be said to have indicated the abandonment of the established British policy of non-intervention in the peninsula, and to have led to the initial establishment of British administration in Perak, Selangor, and Sungai Ujong early in 1874.

165 **Perak and the Malays.**
J. F. McNair. Kuala Lumpur: Oxford University Press, 1972.
454p. 2 maps.

Major McNair, a long-time resident of the Straits Settlements, visited Perak immediately prior to the disturbances which led to the murder of the first British Resident, J. W. W. Birch, in 1875; he was also with the British military force subsequently sent to that state. This volume, which was first published in 1878, provides an extremely detailed and comprehensive description of the state of Perak and its inhabitants at that time. There is also an account of the British intervention in 1874, the events leading to the murder of Birch, and the subsequent British suppression of the Malay uprising.

166 **British intervention in Malaya 1867-1877.**
C. Northcote Parkinson. Singapore: University of Malaya Press, 1960. 384p. 10 maps.

This study of British intervention in the western Malay states in the 1870s covers the period from the transfer of the Straits Settlements from the authority of the India Office to that of the Colonial Office in 1867, through the actual interventions in Perak, Selangor, and Sungai Ujong in 1874, to the initial, violent, Malay response (the Perak uprising) and its suppression. Parkinson argues that critical elements in the British decision to intervene in 1874 were: the petition in March 1873 from Chinese Straits merchants to the Colonial Office calling for British action to restore order in the Malay states; and the contemporaneous change of administration in England, with Disraeli eventually replacing Gladstone in early 1874.

167 **The Kuomintang in Malaya, 1912-1941.**
Png Poh Seng. *Journal of Southeast Asian History*, vol. 2, no. 1 (March 1961), p. 1-32.

Png provides an account of the activities of the Kuomintang in Malaya up to the Japanese invasion, and a consideration of the essentially sympathetic attitudes and policies of the British colonial administration towards those activities. He suggests that the KMT performed three functions in Malaya: 1) 'it nurtured and strengthened the patriotic and nationalist spirit of a substantial portion of the Chinese-educated'; 2) it was mainly responsible for developments in Chinese education in Malaya; 3) 'it served as an important co-ordinating and propaganda agent which roused the Chinese in Malaya to make substantial and sustained contributions to China in its time of peril'.

168 **The origins of Malay nationalism.**
William R. Roff. Kuala Lumpur: University of Malaya Press; New Haven, Connecticut: Yale University Press, 1967. 297p. bibliog.

This volume is concerned with the development of communal and nationalist aspirations among the peninsular Malays over the period from the later 19th century to the fall of Malaya to the Japanese in 1941, and with the Malay voluntary associations 'of a potentially nationalist nature' which emerged in this period. Roff identifies three new Malay élites in these decades: an urban bourgeoisie in the Straits Settlements who were usually of Arab or South Indian origin; a Malay intelligentsia with rural origins and vernacular education; and the English-educated sons of the established Malay aristocracy. He considers in particular the social origins and educational background of each élite group – and this involves an examination of the varying influences of the Arab world – as well as the relationship of each group with the traditional Malay élite and with the mass of the Malay peasant population. There is also discussion of the relationships between British educationalists and administrators and the English-educated Malay élite, many of whom held positions in the Malay Administrative Service and the legislative councils.

169   **The Protected Malay States 1874-1895.**
Emily Sadka.   Kuala Lumpur: University of Malaya Press, 1968.
464p. map. bibliog.

Sadka is primarily concerned with the formation of British policy and the development of the structure of government in particular in Perak and Selangor, but also Negeri Sembilan and Pahang, over the first two decades of British formal rule in the peninsula. Particular attention is paid to the observation that although British Residents appointed to those states were nominally appointed simply to advise the Malay sultans, in practice they came to exercise almost complete executive authority. Sadka considers the manner in which the Residential system thus evolved and the part consequently played by Malay sultans and chiefs in the government of their own states. There is also analysis of the policies introduced in the states in this period to promote economic development and social change.

170   **British trade and expansion in Southeast Asia 1830-1914.**
D. R. SarDesai.   New Delhi: Allied Publishers, 1977. 302p.
bibliog.

Two chapters in this study are directly concerned with the expansion of British interests in the Malay peninsula during the 19th century. Chapter 2 considers the 'country trade' in the Straits and the establishment and development of the free port of Singapore. Chapter 5 is primarily concerned with British intervention in the west coast states of the peninsula in the 1870s. SarDesai rejects C. D. Cowan's view that intervention was occasioned primarily by British fear of foreign (German) intrusion into the affairs of the states. Rather he lays particular emphasis on: increasing willingness on the part of the metropolitan authorities to protect existing and potential British trading interests by intervention – a willingness born largely from the increasingly competitive nature of international trade in the later 19th century; the long-standing relationship between Straits merchants and the Malay chiefs in the peninsula; and the ambitious, independent, nature of the new Governor of the Straits Settlements, Sir Andrew Clarke.

171   **The political structure of the state of Kedah, 1879-1905.**
Sharom Ahmat.   *Journal of Southeast Asian Studies*, vol. 1, no. 2
(Sept. 1970), p. 115-28.

Sharom Ahmat provides a detailed account of the structure and organization of the Kedah political system in the three decades immediately preceding the introduction of British administration. In so doing, he demonstrates why political conditions in that state had been, from the middle of the 19th century, extremely stable; and why, on the eve of the British intrusion, Kedah continued to display 'all the signs of successful and intelligent administration'.

172 **Administration in the Federated Malay States 1896-1920.**
Jagjit Singh Sidhu. Kuala Lumpur: Oxford University Press, 1980. 227p. map. bibliog.

Sidhu provides a detailed study of British administrative methods in Malaya from the formation of the Federation in 1896 until 1920. He is particularly concerned with the impact of changes in colonial administration on the Malay aristocracy and, more importantly, on the Malay masses in the states of the Federation. He concludes that by 1920 the sultans in the FMS (Federated Malay States) had been reduced to the position of political nonentities; that there were very few political opportunities for the remainder of the Malay aristocracy; and that the Malay peasantry 'was in danger of being completely submerged by the hard-working and materialistic Chinese and Indian immigrants'.

173 **Malay nationalism, 1896-1941.**
Radin Soenarno. *Journal of Southeast Asian History*, vol. 1, no. 1 (March 1960), p. 1-28.

This account of the 'peaceful and evolutionary' growth of Malay nationalism in the four decades prior to the Japanese occupation gives particular emphasis to the Malay political organizations and associations which emerged in that period. The article also contains a valuable comparison between the development of Malay and Indonesian nationalisms in the period prior to the war.

174 **The historiography of Malaysia: recent writings in English on the history of the area since 1874.**
A. J. Stockwell. *Journal of Imperial and Commonwealth History*, vol. 5, no. 1 (Oct. 1976), p. 82-110.

This article consists of 'a list of the principal books and articles on [the history of] Malaysia published in English since and including 1960', preceded by a brief discussion of the recent historiography of Malaysia.

175 **Piracy and politics in the Malay world. A study of British imperialism in nineteenth-century South-East Asia.**
Nicholas Tarling. Melbourne: F. W. Cheshire, 1963. 273p. 2 maps.

Tarling is concerned with the part played by the 'suppression of piracy' in British policy in the Malay archipelago from the early 19th century through to the 1870s. The analysis considers piracy and politics with reference to Johor, Brunei, Sulu and Mindanao, and Aceh.

176 **Britain's search for security in north Malaya, 1886-1897.**
Eunice Thio. *Journal of Southeast Asian History*, vol. 10, no. 2
(Sept. 1969), p. 279-303.

In the last two decades of the 19th century there was strong pressure from officials
in the Straits Settlements and the Malay States for the extension of the system of
Residents into the northern portion of the peninsula, then under nominal Siamese
authority. This pressure was neutralized by the British Foreign Office, which
sought alternative means of protecting British interests in that area. Thio
examines the various arrangements which were considered (at a time when the
intervention of another European power in that portion of the peninsula appeared
possible), culminating in a secret convention between Britain and Siam signed in
1897.

177 **The Straits Settlements 1826-67. Indian Presidency to Crown
Colony.**
C. M. Turnbull. London: Athlone Press, 1972. 428p. 6 maps.
bibliog.

This study of the Straits Settlements (Singapore, Melaka, Penang) from 1826 to
1867, covers the period from when they were brought together to form a
Presidency of British India, to the time they were removed from Indian
administration and became a Crown Colony. It is concerned primarily with the
British administration of the Settlements and with the development of Straits
society as a whole. There is discussion of, for example: the immigrant character of
Straits society; the structure of government; government and society; the
economy; social conditions (health, poverty, and education); external defence;
piracy; relations between the Straits Settlements and the Malay States; and the
actual transfer of the Settlements from the India Office to the Colonial Office in
the 1860s.

178 **Traditional leadership in a new nation: the Chinese in Malaya and
Singapore.**
Wang Gungwu. In: *Leadership and authority. A symposium.*
Edited by Gehan Wijeyewardene. Singapore: University of
Malaya Press, for the Centre for Southeast Asian Studies in the
Social Sciences, University of Singapore, 1968. p. 208-22; and, in:
Community and nation. Essays on Southeast Asia and the Chinese.
Wang Gungwu. Singapore: Heinemann Educational Books
(Asia), for the Asian Studies Association of Australia, 1981.
p. 159-72.

Wang analyses the changing structure of leadership in the Chinese community in
Malaya and Singapore since the early 20th century, using the traditional Chinese
hierarchy of scholar-official, merchant/shopkeeper, artisan and peasant.

179 **Start from Alif: count from one. An autobiographical mémoire.**
Sir Richard Winstedt. Kuala Lumpur: Oxford University Press,
1969. 186p.

Sir Richard Winstedt was an official in the Malayan Civil Service from 1902-35.
On his retirement from the service he joined the staff of the School of Oriental
and African Studies in London. Throughout his adult life he was a prolific writer
on Malay language, customs, and history. This autobiographical fragment,
published after his death in 1966 at the age of 87, covers his life from his Oxford
days to 1916, when in Malaya he was appointed Assistant Director of Education
in charge of the Malay vernacular schools of the FMS and Straits Settlements.

180 **Islam and Islamic institutions in British Malaya, 1874-1941. Policies
and implementation.**
Moshe Yegar. Jerusalem: Magnes Press, The Hebrew University,
Jerusalem, 1979. 302p. map. bibliog.

The officially declared policy of the British administration in Malaya was to
refrain from interfering in matters affecting Malay religion and custom. Yegar's
study is concerned with the partial erosion of that policy in the face of the
practical requirements of governing. He concentrates on the administrative and
legal features of British policy in matters of Islamic religion and Malay custom,
with analysis of, for example: the religious elements in the constitutions of the
individual states; the principles of the legal system; the religious courts; the
administration of religious affairs, including the codification of Islamic law, and
the regularization of the *haj* – (pilgrimage to Mecca) – because of the possible
social and health hazards which the pilgrimage might have presented; and
religious education.

181 **Overseas Chinese nationalism in Singapore and Malaya 1877-1912.**
Yen Ching-Hwang. *Modern Asian Studies*, vol. 16, part 3 (July
1982), p. 397-425.

Yen seeks to explain, using Singapore and Malaya as case studies, how and why
overseas Chinese nationalism arose in the late 19th and early 20th centuries. He
argues that two types of nationalism, cultural and political, co-existed in the
Chinese communities in Singapore and Malaya in this period. The former was
'mainly intended to restore Confucian cultural values in the local communities',
while the latter encompassing pro-Ch'ing nationalism, reformist nationalism, and
revolutionary nationalism was 'chiefly motivated by the change of politics in
China'. Yen concludes that 'overseas Chinese nationalism was an offshoot of
modern Chinese nationalism, and not a component part of indigenous nationalism
in Southeast Asia'.

182 **The grooming of an elite: Malay administrators in the Federated
Malay States, 1903-1941.**
Yeo Kim Wah. *Journal of Southeast Asian Studies*, vol. 11, no. 2
(Sept. 1980), p. 287-319.

Yeo provides a detailed account of the training, recruitment, and development of
Malay administrators in the FMS from 1903, when Sultan Idris of Perak first

requested the employment of Malays in administrative posts, to 1941. It should be noted that the Westernized Malay bureaucrats who emerged by this process of training and recruitment during the inter-war decades, were the only new Malay élite group in that period who could provide an alternative leadership to the traditional Malay ruling class: and indeed after 1945 they, along with the élite of the Unfederated Malay States, led the struggle for complete Malayanization of the administration and for national independence.

183   **The politics of decentralization. Colonial controversy in Malaya 1920-1929.**
Yeo Kim Wah.   Kuala Lumpur: Oxford University Press, 1982.
395p. map. bibliog.

The decentralization controversy in Malaya in the 1920s involved proposals to devolve administrative powers and functions within the Federated Malay States (FMS) from the federal authorities (notably the Chief Secretary) to the individual states. The main objectives of the proposal were: to provide opportunities for the Malays to bear a larger measure of administrative responsibility; to overcome the administrative restlessness of the British Residents in each state; and to create a decentralized administration, in order to attract the Unfederated Malay States into a peninsula-wide federation. This detailed study includes consideration of: the formulation of decentralization proposals by George Maxwell, Chief Secretary of the FMS, in 1920; the proposal in 1925 by Laurence Guillemard, the High Commissioner, to abolish the office of Chief Secretary; and the subsequent abandonment of decentralization as a result, in large part, of opposition from European commercial interests in Malaya and, in particular, from within the Malayan Civil Service itself. See also a review article by Yeo Kim Wah (of K. K. Ghosh, not included here) in *Journal of Southeast Asian Studies*, vol. 12, no. 2 (Sept. 1981), p. 487-511.

184   **The Selangor succession dispute, 1933-38.**
Yeo Kim Wah.   *Journal of Southeast Asian Studies*, vol. 2, no. 2
(Sept. 1971), p. 169-84.

Under British rule, although the succession to a Malay throne was a matter of Malay custom, it had come to be controlled and regulated by the colonial administration. In the 1930s, the old sultan of Selangor openly resisted an attempt by the colonial government to impose on the state an heir apparent who was unacceptable to him and to a section of his family. The result was 'a deplorable [and unusual] failure in British Malay diplomacy'. Yeo discusses the origins and course of the dispute, which 'raged for five years in Malaya and London' and considers its repercussions on British policy towards the Malay States.

185   **The Kuomintang movement in Malaya and Singapore, 1912-1925.**
C. F. Yong, R. B. McKenna.   *Journal of Southeast Asian Studies*,
vol. 12, no. 1 (March 1981), p. 118-32.

The article considers the history of the KMT (Kuomintang) in Malaya from the registration of the first branch in Singapore in 1912 to the imposition of a ban on KMT branches by the British administration in 1925. In particular, there is an examination of KMT organization, leadership, and ideology in Malaya during this period; and a consideration of the causes and rationale for the 1925 ban. The article draws largely on the Colonial Office and Foreign Office records.

186   **The Kuomintang movement in Malaya and Singapore, 1925-30.**
       C. F. Yong, R. B. McKenna.   *Journal of Southeast Asian Studies*,
       vol. 15, no. 1 (March 1984), p. 91-107.
This paper considers KMT organizations and membership in Malaya and Singapore, and examines the nature and composition of KMT leadership and ideology, between 1925 when a ban was imposed on local KMT branches and 1930 when the British authorities in Malaya began to enforce that ban more severely. During those five years, 'the KMT managed to remain a viable and formidable political force among the Chinese in Malaya and Singapore' despite harrassment and repression by the colonial authorities. The paper does not, however, elaborate on British policy towards the KMT in Malaya during this period.

Economic and social history (1786-1941)

187   **The myth of the lazy native. A study of the image of the Malays,
       Filipinos and Javanese from the 16th to the 20th century and its
       function in the ideology of colonial capitalism.**
       Syed Hussein Alatas.   London: Frank Cass, 1977. 267p. bibliog.
This study considers the origins of the myth of the lazy native – the alleged indolence of the native Malay, Filipino and Javanese – as the myth evolved from the 16th to the 20th century; and the function of that myth as a significant element in colonial ideology. There is consideration of, for example: the British image of the Malays in the late 19th and 20th century; colonial capitalism and its attitude towards labour; the Malay concept of industry and indolence; Mahathir's analysis of Malay economic backwardness in *The Malay dilemma*; and the distortion of the Malay character. The author is Professor of Malay Studies at the National University of Singapore.

188   **Tales from the South China Seas. Images of the British in South-
       East Asia in the twentieth century.**
       Charles Allen, in association with Michael Mason.   London:
       André Deutsch & the British Broadcasting Corporation, 1983.
       240p. map.
This volume derives from a series of oral history documentaries, originally broadcast on BBC radio. It is assembled from the taped recollections of European men and women who had spent a major part of their lives in the former British colonial territories which surround the South China Sea, principally Malaya; and attempts to show 'what life was really like in the Malayan archipelago for the seafarers, traders, planters, tin-miners and government servants, and for their wives and children'. The recollections concentrate on the period between the wars.

189 **Western enterprise in Indonesia and Malaya. A study in economic development.**
G. C. Allen, Audrey G. Donnithorne. London: Allen & Unwin, 1954. 321p. map. bibliog.

This is a study of the part played by Western individuals, firms and governments in the economic development of Indonesia and Malaya from the early nineteenth century to the mid-1950s, with particular emphasis on the period from 1945. With respect to Malaya, there is consideration of: the instruments of Western enterprise; rubber, palm oil, and cocoa production; mining; banking; shipping; public utilities; commerce; and manufacturing industries. The authors argue that 'along with good government and freedom to trade and migrate, the Westerners furnished an endowment of capital, scientific knowledge, experience and resource without which development [in Indonesia and Malaya] could not have begun'.

190 **The rubber industry. A study in competition and monopoly.**
P. T. Bauer. London: Longmans, Green & Company, 1948. 404p.

A classic study of the world crude rubber producing industry. Inevitably it is concerned in large part with the Malayan industry. Bauer considers not only the cultivation of rubber in plantations and smallholdings, but also international rubber regulation; the rise of the synthetic rubber industry, chiefly in the United States; and, from the perspective of the later 1940s, the principal aspects of future competition between natural and synthetic rubber. The study is divided into the following parts: the rubber industry, 1929-33; the establishment of international regulation; rubber regulation in peace and war; plantation labour and developments in technique; the threat to the monopoly of natural rubber from synthetic production; and the present (late 1940s) position and prospects of the industry, with particular reference to the Malayan rubber industry.

191 **The impact of Chinese secret societies in Malaya. A historical study.**
Wilfred Blythe. London: Oxford University Press, 1969. 566p. 8 maps. bibliog.

Blythe was Secretary for Chinese Affairs in the Federation of Malaya in the immediate post-war period, and later Colonial Secretary in Singapore. This volume, written after his retirement, is based on police and government records as well as interviews with secret society leaders and members. It is concerned with the history, organization, functioning and impact of the societies in Malaya, and considers in very great detail such aspects as: their repeated threats to public order in the 1850s and 1860s; attempts by the authorities to control and then suppress them from the middle of the 19th century; the relations of the secret societies with the Malayan Communist Party before and during the Emergency; and their activities in both Malaya and Singapore in the post-war period and upto the middle 1960s.

192 **Memsahibs in colonial Malaya: a study of European wives in a British colony and protectorate 1900-1940.**
Janice N. Brownfoot. In: *The incorporated wife*. Edited by Hilary Callan, Shirley Ardener. London: Croom Helm, 1984, p. 186-210.

This paper, which draws primarily on 'extensive oral interviews and question-naires with a range of former Malayan residents, male as well as female', considers the lives and experiences of European wives in colonial Malaya, and examines the influence which they – as individuals and as a group – had on the character of racial and cultural interchange in the Malaya of that period.

193 **The British in Malaya 1880-1941. The social history of a European community in colonial South-East Asia.**
John G. Butcher. Kuala Lumpur: Oxford University Press, 1979. 293p. 4 maps. bibliog.

This study has two principal foci: it is concerned 'with the way in which Europeans adapted to life in Malaya, the occupational and social structure of the European community, and the role of women within the community'; it also considers 'the general position of the Europeans in Malayan society, social relations between Europeans and Asians, the tensions which at times character-ized relations between the two groups, and relations between European men and Asian women'. Butcher argues that the concept of a European standard of living is important for an understanding of 'aspects of both . . . these broad sets of issues'. There are some 25 excellent photographs.

194 **The demise of the revenue farm system in the Federated Malay States.**
John G. Butcher. *Modern Asian Studies*, vol. 17, part 3 (July 1983), p. 387-412.

Butcher is concerned with the abolition of the major revenue farms in the FMS, involving opium, spirits, pawnshops, and public gambling, completed in the space of a few years around 1910. He argues that the demise of the revenue farm system arose from 'the rapid increase in the power of Western mines and plantations that took place after 1900 and a change in the relationship between the government and the Chinese businessmen who operated the major farms'. Up to the 1890s the leading Chinese of the FMS 'had been the key to the economic prosperity of the Malay States, and the farms had been used as a way of encouraging their activities. By the early 1900s Western capital had become dominant, and the farmers were at best revenue collectors, but even in this respect they were found wanting, and the government moved to terminate the farm system'.

195 **Towards the history of Malayan society: Kuala Lumpur District, 1885-1912.**
John G. Butcher. *Journal of Southeast Asian Studies*, vol. 10, no. 1 (March 1979), p. 104-18.

The author seeks to argue that the history of Malayan society should be approached less through a concentration on particular ethnic groups – for this 'tends to obscure the relationships, however tenuous, which have existed *between* these groups, and the fact that these relationships have undergone important changes' – than through an examination of Malayan society as a whole. To illustrate his argument he provides a brief account of society in the town and district of Kuala Lumpur between the death of Yap Ah Loy (1885) and 1912.

196   The development of British Malaya 1896-1909.
Chai Hon-Chan.   Kuala Lumpur: Oxford University Press, 1967.
2nd ed. 366p. 5 maps. bibliog.

Chai provides a comprehensive account of developments in the Federated Malay States (Perak, Selangor, Pahang, and Negeri Sembilan) between 1896, when the Federation came into being, until 1909 when the Federal Council was created. There is consideration of: the structure and administrative practices of the Federation; currency reform; immigration and labour; economic development (agriculture and tin-mining); railways; health and medical research; and education.

197   Colonialism and communalism in Malaysia.
B. N. Cham.   *Journal of Contemporary Asia*, vol. 7, no. 2 (1977),
p. 178-99.

Cham seeks to emphasize class rather than race in analysing the history of Malaysia and the structures of contemporary Malaysia. Specifically he considers the impact of colonial rule on the main Malayan communities, to argue that 'communal contradictions in Malaysia are . . . a product of the semi-feudal and semi-capitalist environment created and shaped by British rule and perpetuated in the post-independence era by the upper class élites of both the Malay and the non-Malay communities seeking to build their support base in their respective community purely along communal lines'.

198   The traders. A story of Britain's South-East Asian commercial adventure.
Sjovald Cunyngham-Brown.   London: Newman Neame, for
Guthrie & Company (U.K.), 1971. 352p. bibliog.

This study is essentially a history of Guthrie and Company in Malaya and Singapore from the 1820s to the 1960s. The company was perhaps the foremost British merchant firm/agency house in the region during the colonial period. This history is more concerned with individuals than economics.

199   Investment in the rubber industry in Malaya c.1900-1922.
J. H. Drabble.   *Journal of Southeast Asian Studies*, vol. 3, no. 2
(Sept. 1972), p. 247-61.

Drabble provides a detailed analysis of investment in the Malayan rubber industry from the time the crop was first widely planted for commercial purposes to the imposition of the first restriction scheme at the beginning of the 1920s. He is concerned principally with the investment activities of European rubber growers. Drabble draws on material which was to appear in his *Rubber in Malaya, 1876-1922: the genesis of the industry* (Kuala Lumpur: Oxford University Press, 1973).

200 **Peasant smallholders in the Malayan economy: an historical study with special reference to the rubber industry.**
J. H. Drabble. In: *Issues in Malaysian development*. Edited by James C. Jackson, Martin Rudner. Singapore: Heinemann Educational Books (Asia), for the Asian Studies Association of Australia, 1979. p. 69-99.

The aim of this study is 'to trace the changing situation of the rubber smallholder' throughout the history of the rubber industry in Malaya – from the 'pioneer' period of rapid growth up to 1920, through the decades of depression and restriction between the wars, to the post-1945 period 'in which the dominant concern has been the rejuvenation of the industry's productive powers'.

201 **Rubber in Malaya 1876-1922. The genesis of the industry.**
J. H. Drabble. Kuala Lumpur: Oxford University Press, 1973. 256p. map. bibliog.

This is a strictly chronological study of the natural rubber industry in Malaya from the first plantings in the 1870s through to late 1922, on the eve of the introduction of the Stevenson rubber restriction scheme. The analysis illustrates the continuous interaction of capital, labour, entrepreneurial activity, government policy, and technical research which secured the rapid expansion of the industry in this period. Drabble draws in large measure on commercial records (including those of Guthries; the Rubber Growers' Association; Boustead; and Harrisons and Crosfield). The main focus of the study is consequently on the plantation rather than the smallholding sector of the industry.

202 **Some thoughts on the economic development of Malaya under British administration.**
J. H. Drabble. *Journal of Southeast Asian Studies*, vol. 5, no. 2 (Sept. 1974), p.199-208.

From this brief survey of the main features of economic change in Malaya under British rule, Drabble concludes that 'the advent of colonial administration in Malaya was not by itself sufficient to determine the pattern of economic development which emerged subsequently'. The open-ness of the Malayan economy (i.e. the high dependence of the Malayan economy on the level of economic activity in the industrialized countries which purchased rubber and tin), 'was an influence at least as strong, if not more so, as the colonial administration in affecting the pace and direction of economic development'.

203 **The British agency houses in Malaysia: survival in a changing world.**
J. H. Drabble, P. J. Drake. *Journal of Southeast Asian Studies*, vol. 12, no. 2 (Sept. 1981), p. 297-328.

This article provides a brief history of the agency houses in Malaysia, from their origins as merchant firms in the early 19th century; through their transformation into primarily managing agencies, notably for the rubber plantations, at the beginning of the 20th century; to their further restructuring, in response to the problems of economic reconstruction and economic diversification and to the issues raised by growing national aspirations and policies, in the period since 1945. Drabble and Drake do not present a history of the individual firms, but rather examine their development as a general class of business, emphasizing the ways in which they have adapted their structures to changing local and world conditions over a period of nearly 160 years.

204 **The economic development of British Malaya to 1914: an essay in historiography with some questions for historians.**
P. J. Drake. *Journal of Southeast Asian Studies*, vol. 10, no. 2 (Sept. 1979), p. 262-90.
In this important paper, Drake seeks 'to identify the main forces of Malayan economic growth, and the interactions between them, in the half-century before 1914'. In essence he argues that 'nineteenth-century improvements in technology, transport, and communications fostered the rapid growth of the international economy and caused Europe and America to search the world for raw materials for their industries and markets for their products. These developments led in Malaya to the implantation of foreign forces – government, labour, capital, and enterprise – which supplied the driving power for economic development'. The final four pages of the article outline possible areas for future research. The article is followed, p. 291-92, by a highly critical comment from Lim Chong Yah.

205 **The growth of a plural society in Malaya.**
Maurice Freedman. *Pacific Affairs*, vol. 33, no. 2 (June 1960), p. 158-68.
Freedman provides a broad analysis of the historical growth of the plural society in Malaya through the colonial period to independence. In a concluding passage he argues that 'through most of its modern history Malaya has shown important cultural and "racial" divisions, but these divisions had not created cleavages running the length and breadth of the society . . . [but with the attainment of independence] Malays, Chinese, and Indians are forced to confront one another and [are] pushed into speaking for their own ethnic communities on a national scale . . . of course the ethnic alignment is not complete; there are other cleavages in the society (some within ethnic groups, to weaken them; others marking divisions across ethnic groups)'.

206 **The story of Kuala Lumpur (1857-1939).**
J. M. Gullick. Singapore: Eastern Universities Press, 1983. 178p. bibliog.
A popular account of the history of Malaysia's capital city, from its earliest days as a small tin mining community in the late 1850s to the eve of the Japanese occupation, when it was by far the dominant urban concentration in the peninsula, and the administrative centre of the Malay States.

207 **The chersonese with the gilding off.**
Emily Innes, with an introduction by Khoo Kay Kim. Kuala
Lumpur: Oxford University Press, 1974. 2 vols.

Emily Innes was the wife of a minor government official who was stationed in the
Malay States from 1876 to his resignation in 1882, a resignation, he alleged, which
had been 'forced upon him because he [had] refused to condone the wrong
perpetrated by his superiors'. When he left the government administration he
tried to secure compensation from the Colonial Office for his six years' service in
Malaya: the subsequent failure of this petition led his wife to write the present
volume, which was first published in 1885. It is a record of life in certain parts of
the Malay States at that time – the pettiness of colonial society and, more
extensively, the life of the *kampong* – written by a woman who retained few fond
memories of her years in Malaya. It seeks to present a very different view of the
Malay States from that offered in Isabella Bird's, *The golden chersonese* (q.v.),
which had been published two years earlier.

208 **Planters and speculators. Chinese and European agricultural
enterprise in Malaya, 1786-1921.**
James C. Jackson. Kuala Lumpur: University of Malaya Press,
1968. 312p. 31 maps. bibliog.

This study is divided into three parts. The first considers shifting commercial
agriculture, and discusses, for example: Chinese planters in Singapore and Johor;
gambier and pepper planters in western Malaya; and the Chinese tapioca
industry. The second part is concerned with sedentary plantation agriculture, and
analyses: the early plantations in the Straits Settlements; sugar planting from the
1820s; and the European coffee estates. The final part considers the rubber
plantation industry from the early plantings of the 1870s through to the restriction
scheme introduced at the beginning of the 1920s.

209 **Malay society, 1874-1920s.**
Khoo Kay Kim. *Journal of Southeast Asian Studies*, vol. 5, no. 2
(Sept. 1974), p. 179-98.

This broad survey of the more important changes which took place in Malay
society in the half century from the establishment of British administration, pays
particular attention to the provision and content of Malay and religious education
during this period. Khoo suggests that 'throughout the greater part of the
twentieth century, the dynamic elements in the Malay society were to be found
not so much among the English-educated intelligentsia but among the products of
the religious schools, Malay private schools and even Government Malay
schools'.

210 **Recent Malaysian historiography.**
Khoo Kay Kim. *Journal of Southeast Asian Studies*, vol. 10, no. 2
(Sept. 1979), p. 247-61.

Khoo is particularly concerned with the recent growth in historical research into
various aspects of Malay society and economy, undertaken in the main by
undergraduates at the principal Malaysian universities as graduation exercises.
This research has provided 'a broad perspective of Malay society as a whole',

whilst at the same time giving 'a useful insight into community life in particular settlements, making fine distinction, sometimes, between sub-ethnic groups'.

211 **Sino-Malaya relations in Peninsular Malaysia before 1942.**
Khoo Kay Kim. *Journal of Southeast Asian Studies*, vol. 12, no. 1 (March 1981), p. 93-107.
This work is concerned with the Malay perceptions of, and response to, the increasing Chinese presence in the peninsula from the mid-19th century – but notably from the beginning of the 20th century. Khoo suggests that the attitude of the Malays towards the Chinese in the later period developed 'from a feeling of neglect and despair', as political power had been transferred to the British, whilst economic power appeared to be largely in the hands of the Chinese. But he notes that despite the frequent verbal antagonism between prominent Chinese and Malays in the period up to 1942, there was no serious outbreak of communal violence. The opening two words of the title should surely read: 'Sino-Malay'.

212 **The chettiar and the yeoman. British cultural categories and rural indebtedness in Malaya.**
Paul H. Kratoska. Singapore: Institute of Southeast Asian Studies, 1975. 28p. (Occasional Paper no. 32).
This paper considers some of the cultural conceptions held by the British in Malaya during the colonial period, and how they influenced British attitudes and responses to the question of rural indebtedness in the Malay States [mainly the Krian District in Perak], and the role of chettiar money-lenders in the creation of that indebtedness.

213 **'Ends that we cannot foresee': Malay reservations in British Malaya.**
Paul H. Kratoska. *Journal of Southeast Asian Studies*, vol. 14, no. 1 (March 1983), p. 149-68.
The author is concerned with rural land policy in Malaya from the 1890s to the 1930s, and in particular with the impact of that policy on Malay economic development. He argues that British officials 'attempted to use the Malay Reservations Enactment to serve two different and incompatible objectives: the preservation of a village-based Malay subsistence economy, and the creation of a protected arena for Malay economic development'.

214 **Rice cultivation and the ethnic division of labor in British Malaya.**
Paul H. Kratoska. *Comparative Studies in Society and History*, vol. 24, no. 2 (April 1982), p. 280-314.
Kratoska challenges the view that British colonial administration 'created and perpetuated an ethnic division of labour in Malaya in order to serve the needs of British capital and to maximize government revenue'. In detail, this is the argument that 'immigrant labor . . . was denied the opportunity to build an economic base in Malaya in order to keep wages low, while the indigenous Malay population was discouraged from growing export produce (particularly rubber) in order to stimulate rice cultivation, thereby creating a cheap supply of food'. The

author suggests that the above analysis is in error on two important points. 'The first is the claim that the British administration did not permit non-Malays to plant rice or become peasant cultivators; except for the 1930s this contention is untrue. The second is the suggestion that Malays were expected to produce rice for the non-Malays employed as estate and mine workers; in fact, until 1930, the government as a matter of policy made no attempt to substitute locally produced rice for imported grain'. Cf. Lim Teck Ghee, *Kajian Malaysia* (Dec. 1984).

215 **British Malaya. An economic analysis.**
Li Dun Jen.   Kuala Lumpur: Institute for Social Analysis, 1982. 2nd ed. 200p. bibliog.

First published in 1955, this volume aims to provide an analysis of British 'imperialism at work', covering the period 1895-1938. There are chapters on: finances; trade; tin; rubber; population and labour. In this reprinting, the important notes and tables omitted in 1955 are now included.

216 **Economic development of modern Malaya.**
Lim Chong-Yah.   Kuala Lumpur: Oxford University Press, 1967. 388p. 5 maps. bibliog.

This volume is divided into three parts. The first considers various aspects of economic change in Malaya from 1947-60, notably the nature and causes of economic growth. The second part examines the principal products of the economy – tin, rubber, palm oil, and rice. The final part considers population, currency and banking, taxation, and the infrastructure of the Malayan economy. The second and third parts are historical in approach, covering the period, in essence, from British intervention in the peninsula in 1874 through to the Malaysia agreement in 1963. There is a lengthy statistical appendix.

217 **British colonial administration and the 'ethnic division of labour' in Malaya.**
Lim Teck Ghee.   *Kajian Malaysia* (Journal of Malaysian Studies), vol. 2, no. 2 (Dec. 1984), p. 28-66.

In a period when the Malaysian government is strenuously seeking to diminish, if not eliminate, the identification of race with occupation in Malaysian society, it is not surprising that an increasing interest has emerged in academic circles, and in the community at large, in the origins of that ethnic differentiation: whether it can be explained by the 'inherent' characteristics of each ethnic group, or whether other factors were at work. Lim argues that 'notwithstanding the complexity of factors that go to explain any social phenomenon, the colonial government must be regarded as playing the decisive role in the development of ethnic occupational differentiation'. He suggests that 'British policy towards the Malays, Chinese and Indians in land, labour, education and economy clearly reveals the racial stereotypes that underpinned British thinking'; and that 'the result of [colonial] policy was to structure or enhance the stagnation of Malays in the padi fields and Indians in the plantations'. Cf. Paul H. Kratoska, *Comparative studies in society and history* (April 1982).

218 **Origins of a colonial economy. Land and agriculture in Perak 1874-1897.**
Lim Teck Ghee.   Penang: Federal Publications, on behalf of
Universiti Sains Malaysia, 1976. 230p. map. bibliog.

This work was, in effect, a preliminary study for the author's *Peasants and their agricultural economy in colonial Malaya, 1874-1941* (q.v.). It was in fact Lim's MA thesis (for the University of Malaya), whilst the later, more substantial work was his PhD dissertation (for the Australian National University). The present work considers: colonial land policy in Perak 1874-97; the peasant padi economy; the plantation economy; the British colonial administration's pursuit of a dual policy (i.e. native and plantation) for agriculture in Perak; the political and economic effects of colonial land policy on development in the state.

219 **Peasants and their agricultural economy in colonial Malaya 1874-1941.**
Lim Teck Ghee.   Kuala Lumpur: Oxford University Press, 1977.
291p. map. bibliog.

This study is principally concerned with the changes in Malayan peasant society and agricultural economy in the Federated Malay States over the period 1874-1941, and the influence of the British colonial administration in effecting those changes. For example he considers: government policy towards the alienation of land (notably the Malay Reservations Enactment of 1913); the provision of agricultural credit; and the restriction of agricultural over-production (notably the Stevenson Rubber Restriction Scheme of 1922-28). Particular attention is paid to the vigorous response of the Malay peasantry towards opportunities to cultivate rubber for the world market from the 1900s; and in contrast, the determination of government that the peasantry should concentrate instead on the cultivation of rice. Lim concludes: 'It would not be an exaggeration to say that the colonial government's activities favouring the plantation sector were often tantamount to an anti-peasant agriculture policy and stunted peasant development during a period when conditions were conducive for growth.' There is a substantial statistical appendix.

220 **Leadership and power within the Chinese community of Sarawak: a historical survey.**
Craig A. Lockard.   *Journal of Southeast Asian Studies*, vol. 2, no.
2 (Sept. 1971), p. 195-217.

The purpose of this essay is 'to examine the nature of the changes manifested within the Chinese elite [in Sarawak], and to analyse the ways in which the criteria for the selection of leaders and the exercise of power have changed from the establishment of Chinese settlement in the 1830s to the contemporary situation as part of the Malaysian Federation'. Lockard argues that in recent decades, the sources of political power within the Chinese community have diversified: 'wealth, speech group and kinship are declining [as sources of political power] although they are still important. Education and political party activity have attained importance that transcends to some extent particularism and business interests.'

221 **The Malay States 1877-1895. Political change and social policy.**
Philip Loh Fook Seng.   Kuala Lumpur: Oxford University Press,
1969. 233p. 6 maps. bibliog.

This study considers 'some of the attitudes and motives which had a part in
determining both the political formation and the social framework of the
Federated Malay States established in 1895'. The work is divided into two parts.
The first considers the political setting, specifically the political adjustment which
took place after the Perak War in 1875-76, and the extension of British control in
the peninsula from the appointment of Weld as Governor of the Straits
Settlements in 1880 through to the creation of the Federation. The second part,
'The Social Framework', considers land, labour and education policy in the states
under British control in the period 1877-95.

222 **Colonialism, dualistic growth and the distribution of economic
benefits in Malaysia.**
Ozay Mehmet.   *Southeast Asian Journal of Social Science*, vol. 5,
no. 1-2 (1977), p. 1-21.

This paper examines 'the experience of colonial Malaya and independent
Malaysia with respect to economic growth and the impact of that growth on the
general economic wellbeing of the Malaysian population'. It is divided into two
main parts. The first analyses economic change during the colonial period, 'to
show that the dual economy was the result of colonial policies and [that] it
drained resources from Malaya to Britain'. The second part examines income
distribution since independence 'to show that the principal beneficiaries of rapid
growth during the 1960s have been the urban Malay elite controlling the
bureaucracy and the rural non-Malays'. Among the conclusions are that with
independence, political power was transferred by the British to the Malay ruling
class. However, economic planning and policy has continued to be conducted on
traditional, colonial lines. Also the present official policy of seeing 'the inter-racial
disparities as the major, or the sole cause of income and wealth maldistribution in
Malaysia is not only misleading, but also potentially highly risky. It is bound to
make non-Malays feel insecure and less than fully enthusiastic supporters of
government policies'.

223 **Colonial labor policy and administration: a history of labor in the
rubber plantation industry in Malaya, c.1910-1941.**
J. Norman Parmer.   Locust Valley, New York: J. J. Augustin
Incorporated Publisher, 1960. 294p. 2 maps. bibliog. (Monograph
of the Association for Asian Studies, no. 9).

This study of labour in the rubber plantation industry in Malaya seeks 'to set out
and evaluate official labor policy and to find the sources of policy'; and 'to
examine and appraise the conduct of labor administration, to study the relations
between government officials and employers and briefly to indicate some of the
effects of British labor policy and administration in Malaya'. Specifically,
consideration is given to the formation of the estate labour force, from Indians,
Chinese, and Javanese; labour legislation and administration; wage policy, and
unemployment policy.

224 **The wandering thoughts of a dying man. The life and times of Haji Abdul Majid bin Zainuddin.**
Edited with an introduction and notes by William R. Roff. Kuala Lumpur: Oxford University Press, 1978. 169p. bibliog. (of Abdul Majid's published writings).

Abdul Majid (1887-1943), one of the most prominent Malays of his generation, was an educationalist and teacher (he was the first Malay Assistant Inspector of Schools, and later, the first Malay to be a college principal), and then the first Malayan Pilgrimage Officer (1924-40), travelling to Jeddah with the first ship every year and returning seven months later with the last. This autobiographical sketch, published here for the first time from a manuscript deposited with the National Archives of Malaysia, covers his life upto his first pilgrimage to Mecca in 1923; and gives the reader 'a vivid picture of, and a good deal of insight into, many central aspects of Malay life' during the first quarter of the 20th century.

225 **Agricultural policy and peasant social transformation in late colonial Malaya.**
Martin Rudner. In: *Issues in Malaysian development*. Edited by James C. Jackson, Martin Rudner. Singapore: Heinemann Educational Books (Asia), for the Asian Studies Association of Australia, 1979. p. 7-67.

Rudner examines 'the acute policy tensions of late colonial [post-1945] agriculture between the long-standing objective of preserving intact the subsistence agrarian framework of a traditional Malay cultural and social order, and the post-war thrust towards greater self-sufficiency in rice production'.

226 **The legacy of Malaysian Chinese social structure.**
Laurence K. L. Siaw. *Journal of Southeast Asian Studies*, vol. 12, no. 2 (Sept. 1981), p. 395-402.

This brief but valuable article, which draws upon Weber's 'ideas about the nature of a community in relation to ethnicity', argues principally that the Malaysian Chinese community was inherently divisive. Immigrant Chinese displayed not so much 'the universally acknowledged characteristics of Chineseness . . . as their own variety of social, cultural, religious, and linguistic traditions which only members of their own group could understand and appreciate fully'. Siaw's analysis also argues in this context that the Malayan social structure created under British rule encouraged 'social class and status along ethnic or racial lines'.

227 **Class, race and colonialism in West Malaysia. The Indian case.**
Michael Stenson. St. Lucia, Australia: University of Queensland Press, 1980. 234p. bibliog.

Almost all the writings on the political and economic changes which have occurred in Peninsular Malaysia in the colonial and post-colonial periods have interpreted those changes in communal terms. Stenson offers a vigorous challenge to this approach. He argues that an understanding of the historical evolution of Malaysian society and economy 'is to be found not so much in the cultural dynamics of the Malay, Chinese or Indian communities as in the evolution of the world capitalist economy and the class structure of Malaysian society'. Class and colonialism/capitalism, rather than race, are the critical elements in the historical development of the political economy of Malaysia. Specifically Stenson uses the case of the Indians in Malaya 'to illustrate the structure and functioning of the colonial and neo-colonial order'. He considers, for example: Indians in the colonial economy 1907-41; the emergence of Indian/communal nationalism from the 1930s; the mobilization of Indian labour, 1938-41; the class and non-communal affiliations of the Indians prior to the war; communalism and class during the Japanese occupation; the working-class alliance and the Malayan Indian Congress, 1945-48; insurgency and counter-insurgency, 1948-57; and government by the Alliance, 1957-69, which 'expressed the common interests of the Malay élite and Chinese *towkays* in sustaining and expanding the capitalist economy'. There is a very brief discussion of 1969 and its aftermath. Stenson concludes that the major part of the great volume of surplus value produced by Indian labour from the colonial period 'went to the metropolitan capital, or in more recent years, to the local bourgeoisie'. And then 'the emancipation of the Indian proletariat in Malaysia lies in class rather than communal politics'. One of the main themes of this study is the 'incapacity of communal organizations to assist the Indian proletariat as a whole within the structure of neo-colonial capitalism'.

228 **Cinemas and censorship in colonial Malaya.**
Rex Stevenson. *Journal of Southeast Asian Studies*, vol. 5, no. 2 (Sept. 1974), p. 209-24.

Stevenson examines 'the British reaction to the growth of the cinema as a social force in the Straits Settlements and the FMS during the 1920s and 1930s'. He is concerned with 'the attempts of officialdom to come to terms with a new and powerful social phenomenon rather than with providing a detailed account of the cinema itself'. In the inter-war decades, concern was frequently expressed by sections of the European community in Malaya that films which portrayed white men and women in an unflattering light or undignified manner (and in the nature of things, this would include the majority of films produced in that period), seriously undermined the prestige of European rule in the East.

229 **The white man's burden and brown humanity: colonialism and ethnicity in British Malaya.**
A. J. Stockwell. *Southeast Asian Journal of Social Science*, vol. 10, no. 1 (1982), p. 44-68.

The first part of this paper considers the socio-cultural experience of Europeans in colonial Malaya, 'including the alienation of the individual, the growth of white tribalism and the emergence of a colonial ideology which was partly common to the empire as a whole and partly peculiar to Malaya'. It then examines 'European perceptions of non-Europeans (especially Malays) and the way ethnic attitudes affected colonial administration'. The paper concludes by briefly considering 'the British influence upon the Malays' image of themselves'.

230 **Social relations of dependence in a Malay state: nineteenth century Perak.**
Patrick Sullivan. Kuala Lumpur: The Malaysian Branch of the Royal Asiatic Society, 1982. 88p. 7 maps. bibliog. (Monograph no. 10).

The primary aim of this study is 'to describe "dependent" social relations (slavery and debt-bondage) in Perak . . . in the period just prior to their abolition by British fiat in 1883'. The three main chapters provide 'a history of the cultural influences that contributed to the structure' of the state of Perak; an economic and political description of Perak in the 19th century; and an account and analysis of slavery and debt-slavery in 19th-century Perak. This work is intended as a contribution not only to the history of Malaya itself but also to the comparative study of societies, in particular their servile systems.

231 **After its own image. The Trengganu experience, 1881-1941.**
Shaharil Talib. Singapore: Oxford University Press, 1984. 302p. 6 maps. bibliog.

Shaharil Talib seeks to examine: 1] the response of the ruling class in the east coast state of Trengganu to the accelerated inflow of outside capital and entrepreneurship which occurred in the late 19th century, and to the imposition of colonial rule which soon followed in 1909; and 2] the increasing social differentiation which took place within Trengganu society as it came under these external pressures. The result is a highly detailed study of the political, economic and social changes experienced by a major Malay state during a crucial period of transition: a study, in the words of the author, 'on the dissolution and reconstitution of the Malay social order by capitalist penetration backed by the coercive apparatus of the colonial state to serve the needs of the global expansion of capital'.

232 **Voices from the Kelantan desa 1900-1940.**
Shaharil Talib. *Modern Asian Studies*, vol. 17, part 2 (April 1983), p.177-95.

This article is concerned with 'the attitudes and other subjective feelings of the peasantry in Kelantan as they experienced the crushing of the natural economy, the pre-colonial economy of the peasants which combined food-gathering, hunting, agriculture and craft work, by 20th-century capitalist penetration backed by a pervasive colonial administration'. It draws on petition letters from the peasantry to the colonial authorities, written from the early 20th century. These documents are examined under three broad categories: the peasants and the colonial state; the experience of the peasants in their relationship with local officials; and conflicts between peasants and the plantations.

233 **Malay reservations and Malay land ownership in Semenjih and Ulu Semenjih *mukims* Selangor.**
Voon Phin Keong. *Modern Asian Studies*, vol. 10, part 4 (Oct. 1976), p. 509-23.

This study is based on an examination of land titles in the Malay Reservations in two *mukim* (the lowest administrative unit in Malaysia) in the state of Selangor for the period from the 1890s to 1968. Its main purpose is to 'outline the background to the creation of these Malay Reservations and to assess the role played by the Reservations in terms of Malay land ownership in the rural areas in the two *mukims*'. Voon concludes that 'whatever the disadvantages associated with these Reservations, especially with reference to the proper development of the land, the primary objective of guaranteeing Malay interests in land was achieved'.

234 **Western rubber planting enterprise in Southeast Asia 1876-1921.**
Voon Phin Keong. Kuala Lumpur: Penerbit Universiti Malaya, 1976. 210p. approx. 40 maps. bibliog.

This study of the growth of the Western-owned sector of the rubber industry in South East Asia from the introduction of rubber to the region in the 1870s to the eve of the first rubber restriction scheme of the inter-war decades, gives appropriate consideration to the very major developments in the Malay peninsula. Voon examines, *inter alia*, the role of the agency house system and the prevalence of interlocking directorships among plantation companies in securing the dominance of Western interests in the rubber industry of South East Asia during that period.

235 **The economic history of Malaysia: a bibliographic essay.**
Wong Lin Ken. *Journal of Economic History*, vol. 25, no. 2 (June 1965), p. 244-62.

Confining himself principally to the period of British rule, and solely to works in the English language, Wong provides a primarily descriptive survey of the literature in this field (as at the mid-1960s) and suggests briefly further areas for research (again, as at the mid-1960s).

236 **The Malayan tin industry to 1914. With special reference to the states of Perak, Selangor, Negri Sembilan and Pahang.**
Wong Lin Ken. Tucson, Arizona: University of Arizona Press, 1965. 302p. bibliog.

Wong's study of the tin industry in Malaya from the early part of the 19th century through to 1914 is concerned primarily with the circumstances which led to the rapid expansion of the industry after British intervention in the peninsula in 1874, and with the principal features of that expansion. Particular attention is paid to the contrasting features of Chinese and European mining practices and organization, in an attempt to explain the increasing prominence of Western enterprise in the industry towards the end of the period. There is also a consideration of such aspects as: the relationship between the revenue farms and Chinese mining activity; the supply of mining labour; and colonial policy towards

European mining companies. There is a lengthy statistical appendix, as well as nine, mainly contemporary, photographs of mining operations.

237 **Twentieth-century Malayan economic history: a select bibliographic survey.**
Wong Lin Ken. *Journal of Southeast Asian Studies*, vol. 10, no. 1 (March 1979), p. 1-24.
This article brings up to the late 1970s, the survey of the literature in English on the modern economic history of Malaya (defined here as Peninsular Malaysia and Singapore), which Wong had provided for the *Journal of Economic History* in 1965. Here he covers approximately the period of the 20th century to 1965. This article is more analytical than the earlier piece – more an essay in historiography – and is thus an excellent introduction to the major issues in this field, at least as seen at the end of the 1970s.

238 **Western enterprise and the development of the Malayan tin industry to 1914.**
Wong Lin Ken. In: *The economic development of South-East Asia. Studies in economic history and political economy*. Edited by C. D. Cowan. London: George Allen & Unwin, 1964. p.127-53.
This paper considers the growth in the demand for tin in the industrial economies through the second half of the 19th century, and the expansion of Western mining enterprise in Malaya through to 1914. Wong's particular concern is to explain how Western enterprise came to challenge, and eventually overthrow, the Chinese dominance of the Malayan tin industry. His explanation concentrates on such considerations as: the effectiveness of particular forms of mining technique and business organization in relation to the physical nature of the tin deposits; capital resources; and the policy of the colonial administration towards Chinese economic and social authority in the Malay states from the end of the 19th century.

239 **The development of the tin mining industry of Malaya.**
Yip Yat Hoong. Kuala Lumpur, Singapore: University of Malaya Press, 1969. 446p. 2 maps. bibliog.
A standard work on the history of the tin mining industry in Malaya. The opening and concluding chapters consider the industry in the late 1960s and, from the perspective of that time, the industry's 'present trends and future prospects'. The intervening chapters provide an exhaustively detailed account and analysis of tin mining in Malaya, essentially from the imposition of British administration in the 1870s through to the 1960s.

240 **The Japanese community in Malaya before the Pacific War: its genesis and growth.**
Yuen Choy Leng. *Journal of Southeast Asian Studies*, vol. 9, no. 2 (Sept. 1978), p. 163-79.
This study is concerned with the growth and changing character of the Japanese community in Malaya from the early 20th century, when it consisted primarily of prostitutes, to the late 1930s, when the Japanese were 'a socially cohesive [and

self-contained] community [in Malaya] with important stakes in the country's
economy'.

241 **Japanese rubber and iron investments in Malaya, 1900-1941.**
Yuen Choy Leng. *Journal of Southeast Asian Studies*, vol. 5, no.
1 (March 1974), p. 18-36.
Yuen traces the development of Japanese investment in rubber planting and,
more important, in iron mining in Malaya, 'and shows how these ventures
contributed to the expansionist impulse which, among other factors, eventually
led to the military invasion of Malaya in December 1941'. The article contains
detailed information on the Japanese individuals and organizations involved in
these two fields of investment; and a consideration of the varied response of the
British administration to the Japanese commercial advance.

**Waiting for China. The Anglo-Chinese College at Malacca, 1818-1843,
and early nineteenth-century missions.**
See item no. 353.

**The London Missionary Society: a written record of missionaries and
printing presses in the Straits Settlements, 1815-1847.**
See item no. 354.

The impact of railroads on the Malayan economy, 1874-1941.
See item no. 626.

The Japanese Occupation, the
Emergency and the Independence
Campaign (1942-57)

242 **Japanese policy towards the Malayan Chinese 1941-1945.**
Yoji Akashi. *Journal of Southeast Asian Studies*, vol. 1, no. 2
(Sept. 1970), p. 61-89.
Akashi examines the fluctuating and ambivalent policy of the Japanese towards
the Chinese community in Malaya during the occupation, a policy which moved
between moderation and a search for cooperation, and brutal repression. The
article draws heavily on Japanese sources, and on interviews with former
members of the Japanese occupation administration.

243 **The Malayan Union.**
James de V. Allen. New Haven, Connecticut: Yale University,
Southeast Asia Studies, 1967. 181p. (Monograph Series, no. 10).
The Malayan Union was a major constitutional reform for peninsular Malaya,
officially promulgated in April 1946 but rapidly abandoned in the face of fierce

opposition from Malay interests. This study, which draws considerably on the
author's interviews with many of those who were involved in the Malayan Union
scheme, considers primarily the reasons why this constitutional reform was
attempted, and why it failed so quickly. Approximately one-third of the volume is
given over to appendixes which reproduce some of the major documents
concerned with the formulation and introduction of the Malayan Union, and,
more importantly, with the vigorous opposition to it. See also M. R. Stenson,
Journal of Southeast Asian History (Sept. 1969).

244 **The Indian minority and political change in Malaya 1945-1957.**
Rajeswary Ampalavanar. Kuala Lumpur: Oxford University
Press, 1981. 260p. map. bibliog.
This volume is concerned principally with political developments within the
minority Indian community of Malaya as the country moved from occupation in
1945 towards independence in 1957. In particular it considers the evolution of the
community from one politically orientated primarily towards India, to one which
increasingly owed allegiance to an independent Malaya. Particular attention is
paid to the influence of Indian nationalism on the Malayan Indians; the political
aspirations and activities of Indian labour; political factionalism within the Indian
community; and the movement of the Malayan Indian Congress towards alliance
with the United Malays National Organization and the Malayan Chinese
Association, which was finally achieved in 1955.

245 **Indian society of Malaysia and its leaders: trends in leadership and
ideology among Malaysian Indians, 1945-60.**
S. Arasaratnam. *Journal of Southeast Asian Studies*, vol. 13,
no. 2 (Sept. 1982), p. 236-51.
This work is concerned with the variegated ethnic segments within the Indian
community of Malaysia, 'the kinds of leadership' the segments produced, and 'the
interactions of that leadership among each other', for the period 1945-60. He
considers leadership among Indian labour (the trade unions); the political and
national leadership of the Malaysian Indians; and Indian social, religious, and
cultural leadership in that period.

246 **The war of the running dogs. How Malaya defeated the communist
guerrillas, 1948-60.**
Noel Barber. London: Collins, 1971. 284p. map. bibliog.
This is a dramatic account of the communist insurrection and its defeat. It draws
considerably on information supplied to the author by Special Branch officers who
served in Malaya during the Emergency. A notable feature of the work is the
attention given to the activities and personalities of the principal communists
involved in the insurrection.

247 **The jungle is neutral.**
F. Spencer Chapman. London: Chatto & Windus, 1949. 436p. 5
maps.
This is a most vivid account of the author's punishing experiences in enemy-
occupied Malaya, harassing the Japanese forces and laying preparations for an

History. The Japanese Occupation, the Emergency and the
Independence Campaign (1942-57)

anticipated British military re-occupation. It is a work of very considerable
courage and endurance, both physical and mental.

248   **The masked comrades. A study of the Communist united front in
      Malaya, 1945-48.**
      Cheah Boon Kheng.   Singapore: Times Books International,
      1979. 172p.

Cheah's concern is with the Malayan Communist Party and some of its principal
front organizations (notably the Malayan Democratic Union), in the period 1945-
48. He considers in particular the people involved, 'how they worked, why they
worked with the communists, what their personal backgrounds and the areas of
inter-organizational conflicts and cooperation were, as well as . . . the various
conflicts of ideas and personalities'.

249   **Red star over Malaya. Resistance and social conflict during and
      after the Japanese occupation of Malaya, 1941-1946.**
      Cheah Boon Kheng.   Singapore: Singapore University Press,
      1983. 366p. 3 maps. bibliog.

This study focuses primarily on race relations (mainly involving Malays and
Chinese) and political change in Malaya during the Japanese occupation and, in
particular, in the immediate post-war period of the British Military Administration (BMA). It therefore considers such themes as: the social impact of the
occupation; the Malayan Communist Party (MCP) and the anti-Japanese
movement; the communal violence, the Malay-MCP-Chinese conflict after the
Japanese surrender; and the conflict between the communists and the BMA in the
same period. Cheah points out in an introduction that the communal violence
which occurred in the post-Japanese interregnum was on a far more serious scale
than that which occurred in May 1969; moreover, he suggests that only by
understanding the events of that brief post-surrender period is it possible to
comprehend the subsequent developments in Malayan/Malaysian politics and
society.

250   **Sino-Malay conflicts in Malaya, 1945-1946: communist vendetta and
      Islamic resistance.**
      Cheah Boon Kheng.   *Journal of Southeast Asian Studies*, vol. 12,
      no. 1 (March 1981), p. 108-17.

A detailed description and analysis of the armed conflicts between Chinese and
Malays in the immediate aftermath of the war. Whilst the Chinese community had
been very harshly treated by the Japanese during the occupation, many prominent
Malays had collaborated with the occupation forces. Then after the Japanese
surrender, increasing militancy from the predominantly Chinese-led MCP and
MPAJA provoked Malay resistance which was led by Islamic religious leaders,
determined to defend their race and religion from the dangers of communism.
Cheah concludes that 'the absence of widespread Malay support in the communist
struggles today [1980s] could well have its roots in the racial clashes' of the
immediate post-war months, when the Malays saw Chinese as communists, and
communists as Chinese.

251 **Some aspects of the interregnum in Malaya (14 August-3 September 1945).**
Cheah Boon Kheng. *Journal of Southeast Asian Studies*, vol. 8, no. 1 (March 1977), p. 48-74.

This article provides an analysis of the political and social situation in Malaya in the three weeks between the collapse of Japanese administration and the return of British military forces. Cheah then seeks to explain why the Malayan Communist Party did not use the political and social tensions and confusion of that period to attempt to seize power, and thus present the returning colonial forces with a *fait accompli*.

252 **Malaya upside down.**
Chin Kee Onn. Kuala Lumpur: Federal Publications, 1976. 3rd ed. 205p. map.

First published in Singapore in January 1946, this book provides a most vivid, but balanced, first-hand account of Malaya under the Japanese occupation.

253 **Templer. Tiger of Malaya. The life of Field Marshal Sir Gerald Templer.**
John Cloake. London: Harrap, 1985. 508p. 10 maps. bibliog.

Sir Gerald Templer (1898-1979), appointed High Commissioner to Malaya in February 1952, is widely recognized as the man primarily responsible for the political-military initiatives which led to the defeat of the communist insurrection. Cloake provides a very detailed account of Templer's life, paying full attention to his Malayan years and achievements.

254 **Riot and revolution in Singapore and Malaya 1945-1963.**
Richard Clutterbuck. London: Faber & Faber, 1973. 321p. 26 maps and diags. bibliog.

Clutterbuck served in the army in Malaya and Singapore between 1956-58, and from 1966-68. He retired from service in 1972 with the rank of Major-General. This volume is concerned with the urban and rural insurgency carried out in Singapore and Malaya by the Malayan Communist Party (MCP) in the post-war decades, and focuses in particular on the 'points of contact' between the insurgents and the people in those two theatres. With regard to Singapore, Clutterbuck is particularly concerned to examine the clandestine organization of the communists among the Chinese students and trade unions, their attempt to gain control of the political party in power, and their eventual defeat by the authorities. In Malaya he considers in particular the clandestine, hierarchical organization of the Malayan Communist Party, from the leaders, down through the cadres to the villagers, and the intelligence techniques employed by the Special Branch to break those lines of communication. See also, *Conflict and violence in Singapore and Malaysia 1945-1983*. Richard Clutterbuck. (Singapore: Graham Brash, 1985. revised, updated and enlarged ed. 412p. 37 maps and diags. bibliog.). This volume consists, in effect, of a reprinting of the 1973 study, with the addition of a substantial discussion of the 1964 and 1969 riots in Singapore and Malaysia respectively.

255 SOE in the Far East.

Charles Cruickshank. Oxford, England: Oxford University Press, 1983. 285p. 6 maps. bibliog.

The Special Operations Executive (SOE) was created by the British Government in mid-1940 to undertake or assist sabotage, subversive activities and black propaganda in enemy, enemy-controlled, and neutral countries. This is the official history of the operations of SOE in Asia, and it thus draws on the unreleased archives of the department itself. One full chapter is devoted to the Malayan operations: and there are numerous scattered references to Malaya elsewhere in the book.

256 The communist struggle in Malaya.

Gene Z. Hanrahan. Kuala Lumpur: University of Malaya Press, 1971. 237p. bibliog.

Hanrahan's work was first published in 1954. It provides an analysis of the strategy and tactics of the communist movement in Malaya, tracing the origins and early development of the movement in the 1920s; the creation of the Malayan Communist Party at the beginning of the 1930s; communist activities during the Japanese occupation (including the activities of the Malayan Peoples' Anti-Japanese Army); and the move to armed revolt in the post-war years. Particular attention is paid to the doctrines and practices of the Malayan Communist Party – armed insurrection; revolutionary techniques; labour activities; guerrilla warfare. Hanrahan concludes (in 1954) that neither the communists nor the government was capable of victory. This reprint contains a brief postscript by Sir Robert Thompson (a Secretary for Defence in Kuala Lumpur at the end of the 1950s) which reviews Hanrahan's analysis in the light of later developments. A lengthy appendix reproduces important Malayan Communist Party documents.

257 The social and ideological origins of the Malayan Chinese Association.

Heng Pek Koon. *Journal of Southeast Asian Studies*, vol. 14, no. 2 (Sept. 1983), p. 290-311.

Heng examines the role of the MCA (The Malayan Chinese Association) 'in the evolution of organization modes developed by the Chinese community in Malaya to regulate its social, economic, and political affairs'. She argues: 1) that the MCA 'was the vehicle that bridged the divide between traditional and modern modes of community regulation'; and 2) that it 'linked the political concerns of the Chinese community, which hitherto had been largely China-orientated, with the mainstream development of Malayan nationalism and the emerging Malayan nation state during the years 1949-57'.

258 Dato Onn and Malay nationalism 1946-1951.

Ishak bin Tadin. *Journal of Southeast Asian History*, vol. 1, no. 1 (March 1960), p. 56-88.

Dato Onn bin Ja'afar was the first President of the United Malays National Organization, founded in May 1946. In June 1951 he resigned from the UMNO having failed to open membership of the party to non-Malays, and founded the Independence of Malaya Party which was open to all races in Malaya. Ishak bin

History. The Japanese Occupation, the Emergency and the Independence Campaign (1942-57)

Tadin provides a detailed account of these years; and, in conclusion suggests that Dato Onn 'must be remembered as the indispensable pioneer of the Malay national movement'.

259 **Japanese-trained armies in Southeast Asia. Independence and volunteer forces in World War II.**
Joyce C. Lebra. Hong Kong: Heinemann Educational Books (Asia), 1977. 226p. bibliog.
This study of Japan's sponsorship and training of local military forces in Japanese-occupied South East Asia pays appropriate attention to events in Malaya. In the peninsula the Japanese organized and trained important Malay volunteer corps, but perhaps their major initiative involved the recruitment of Indians into the Indian National Army.

260 **Jungle war in Malaya. The campaign against communism 1948-60.**
Harry Miller. London: Arthur Barker, 1972. 220p. 2 maps.
Miller was a journalist who covered the Emergency for the *Straits Times*. His account of the campaign, which draws on personal recollections and records, is 'purely a newspaperman's report of the course of the war and its dramatic highlights and depressing failures – from both sides'. A concluding chapter examines the resurgence of communist activity in Malaysia in the late 1960s and early 1970s.

261 **Malaya: a political and economic appraisal.**
Lennox A. Mills. Minneapolis, Minnesota: University of Minnesota Press, 1958. 234p.
Writing immediately after the country's independence, Mills provides an economic and political assessment of peninsula Malaya over the period 1945-57. There is consideration of: post-war change and reconstruction; the communist rebellion; communalism and self-government; *merdeka*; Malaya and Commonwealth defence; natural and synthetic rubber; rubber and taxes. There is also a chapter on contemporaneous developments in Singapore.

262 **Malaya: the communist insurgent war, 1948-60.**
Edgar O'Ballance. London: Faber & Faber, 1966. 188p. map. bibliog.
This is an outline account of the Emergency, drawn from published sources. The opening chapters describe the rise of communism in Malaya in the 1930s; the war-time resistance to the Japanese; and the political confusion of the post-war years. There follows a chronological account of the insurrection through to its suppression. A final chapter considers the main causes of the communist failure – aggressive anti-guerrilla tactics by the authorities; resettlement of sections of the population by the government; and the existence of support for the authorities amongst the mass of the Malayan population. Two appendixes provide information on: the numbers of people killed or wounded during the insurrection; and the British, Commonwealth and Gurkha units that served in Malaya during the Emergency.

History. The Japanese Occupation, the Emergency and the Independence Campaign (1942-57)

263 The British and Malayan nationalism, 1946-1957.
James P. Ongkili. *Journal of Southeast Asian Studies*, vol. 5, no. 2 (Sept. 1974), p. 255-77.

Ongkili provides an account of political change in Malaya from the Malayan Union in 1946 to independence in 1957. His article divides into the following sections: political developments until 1955; the 1955 elections and nationalism; and the road to *merdeka*. He argues that although British rule 'had [left] its inevitable stamp on the political outlooks and perceptions of Malayan leaders . . . the political and economic "bargain" between the Malays and the non-Malays, the development of Malayan citizenship and nationality, the distinctive ideological underpinnings of party politics, and, above all, the inter-communal approach to national problems [each characteristic of the period 1946-57] were clearly the products of Malayan minds that had comprehended the meaning of freedom and independence'.

264 Nation-building in Malaysia, 1946-1974.
James P. Ongkili. Singapore: Oxford University Press, 1985. 275p. bibliog.

Ongkili provides 'a broad historical view of the efforts made by the Malayan/Malaysian leadership [in the period 1946-1974] to weld together' Malaya/Malaysia's disparate communities 'into a cohesive whole, and their attempts to develop a general sense of national consciousness'. He seeks to view Malaysia's peculiar communal problems 'from the perspective of those who have been entrusted with the practical responsibility of running the government of the country'. Specific chapters consider: the unification of the Malay peninsula, 1946-48; in quest of racial unity (covering the Emergency to the 1955 elections); independence and the independence settlement; the creation of Malaysia; the challenges to the Malaysian concept; and the [communal] 'bargain' and the New Economic Policy. A former civil servant and academic, James Ongkili is now a cabinet minister in the Malaysian Government.

265 The Malayan Chinese Association, 1948-65.
Margaret Roff. *Journal of Southeast Asian History*, vol. 6, no. 2 (Sept. 1965), p. 40-53.

The author provides a brief survey of the history of the Malayan Chinese Association from its formation in 1948 [1949] until the mid-1960s. She draws attention to the 'cautious, right-wing, middle-class and capitalist image' of the MCA in those years; and throws doubt on the party's claim in that period that it spoke for the majority of the Chinese in Malaya.

266 The organization of the British Military Administration in Malaya, 1946-48.
Martin Rudner. *Journal of Southeast Asian History*, vol. 9, no. 1 (March 1968), p. 95-106.

The British Military Administration was established on 15 August 1945, immediately following the Japanese surrender, as the effective government of Malaya and Singapore pending the restoration of a civilian administration. It was brought to an end by the creation of the Malayan Union and Colony of Singapore

on 1 April 1946. Rudner is concerned with the governmental structures, rather
than the policy and politics, of the BMA.

267 The communist insurrection in Malaya 1948-1960.
Anthony Short. London: Frederick Muller, 1975. 547p. map.
bibliog.

This study had its origins in an agreement, made in the early 1960s, between the
University of Malaya, in which Anthony Short was then a lecturer, and the
Government of Malaya under which the author was granted full access to the
administration's confidential and secret papers relating to the communist
insurrection. These sources have remained closed to all other scholars.
Consequently this volume must be considered the most comprehensive and
authoritative study of the insurrection to appear thus far. The origins and
outbreak of the revolt in June 1948; the military campaigns; the counter-
insurgency programmes; and the circumstances of the insurrection's disintegration,
are each considered in great detail. Particular attention is paid to the resettlement
of the Chinese squatters into the New Villages, and to the importance of
intelligence information from Chinese sources for the counter-insurgency
campaign; for Short argues that it was mainly through intelligence that the
authorities were able to cut off the insurgents from their support, recruits and
supplies, to the point where the organization of the Malayan Communist Party
simply crumbled.

268 Malayan federalism 1945-1963. A study of federal problems in a plural society.
B. Simandjuntak. Kuala Lumpur: Oxford University Press, 1969.
347p. bibliog.

This work falls into two parts. The first 'is concerned with the reasons for the
introduction of the federal solution into Malaya and Malaysia [and] the working
of the federal experiment up to 1963', and thereby includes examination of: the
Malayan Union experiment; the Federation of Malaya inaugurated in 1948; the
Merdeka Federation; and the Malaysia Federation introduced in 1963. The second
part considers 'the problems posed by the plurality of Malaya's and Malaysia's
society in the implementation of the federal idea', and thereby includes
examination of: citizenship; language and education; federal finance; economic
integration; defence; and federalism and parliamentary government.

269 Counter-insurgency operations: 1. Malaya and Borneo.
E. D. Smith. London: Ian Allan, 1985. 112p. 10 maps. bibliog.

This book provides a vivid account of the counter-insurgency tactics and methods
employed by the United Kingdom and Commonwealth forces during the Malayan
Emergency and the Borneo Confrontation. Brigadier E. D. Smith served in both
campaigns. There are a very large number of black-and-white photographs.

270   **Tan Cheng Lock. His leadership of the Malayan Chinese.**
Soh Eng Lim.   *Journal of Southeast Asian History*, vol. 1, no. 1
(March 1960), p. 29-55.

Tan Cheng Lock was the most prominent political figure in the Chinese
community in Malaya in the period following the Japanese occupation to
independence in 1957. This article provides an account of his political leadership
principally during this period; and concludes that his leadership was an
'intellectual and indirect' one, for as a direct practical politician, Tan Cheng Lock
'was a failure'. See also: 'The social and political ideas of Tun Datuk Sir Tan
Cheng Lock', by Tjoa Hock Guan, in: *Melaka. The transformation of a Malay
capital c1400-1980*, edited by Kernial Singh Sandhu and Paul Wheatley (Kuala
Lumpur: Oxford University Press, 1983. vol. 2, p. 299-323).

271   **From Malayan Union to Singapore separation. Political unification
in the Malaysia region 1945-1965.**
Mohamed Noordin Sopiee.   Kuala Lumpur: University of Malaya
Press, 1974. 353p. bibliog.

Considers the numerous and varying attempts which were made at political
unification involving Peninsular Malaya, Singapore, Sabah, Sarawak, and Brunei
in the period 1945-65. Particular attention is paid to: the British attempt in 1946
to establish the Malayan Union and the subsequent surrender to Malay
opposition; the formation of the Federation of Malaya in 1948 and the later,
unsuccessful, secessionist movements 'mounted by Penang nationalist and pro-
colonial elements, Johore royalists, and Kelantan parochialists'; the struggle from
1946-60 to achieve the merger of Singapore and Malaya; the formation of
Malaysia in 1963 (including Brunei's decision not to join the federation); the
events leading to Singapore's separation from Malaysia in 1965, and the expulsion
itself. There is a lengthy pictorial appendix, consisting mainly of newspaper and
official photographs capturing the principal political events of the period.

272   **The ethnic and urban bases of communist revolt in Malaya.**
Michael Stenson. In: *Peasant rebellion and communist revolution in
Asia*. Edited by John Wilson Lewis.   Stanford, California:
Stanford University Press, 1974. p. 125-50.

Provides an essentially chronological survey of the origins of the communist
insurrection in Malaya. Stenson considers, for example: the early sources of
communism in Malaya; the creation of a mass base, 1937-42; the Japanese
occupation – a national liberation campaign foregone; the post-war united front
strategy; and the transition to revolutionary politics. In conclusion Stenson argues
that 'the resort to armed revolt came . . . not at the peak of popular frustration
and political mobilization, but as the result of the specific frustrations of a radical
minority . . . international events, notably the atmosphere of militant Cold War
confrontation and the successes of the CCP (Chinese Communist Party),
convinced an inexperienced, provincial leadership that what was in reality an act
of desperation was both necessary and timely . . . Begun in disarray and isolation
from the Party's bases of mass Chinese urban support, the revolt exposed the
MCP as the leader of a minority group of radical Chinese within a plural society
where politically awakened Malays regarded Communism as a specifically Chinese
disease'. The MCP was doomed to stage 'a festering revolt which, in the absence

of fundamental social and political transformations, could never develop into a true revolution'. See also: *Repression and revolt: the origins of the 1948 communist insurrection in Malaya and Singapore.* by Michael R. Stenson (Athens, Ohio: Ohio University, Center for International Studies, Southeast Asia Program, 1969. 31p.).

273 **Industrial conflict in Malaya. Prelude to the communist revolt of 1948.**
M. R. Stenson. London: Oxford University Press, 1970. 271p. bibliog.

Stenson is concerned with the development from the 1930s of the immigrant Chinese and Indian labourers in Malaya into a politically conscious labour movement 'which demanded fundamental social, economic and political reforms leading to independence from colonial rule'. He examines the government and employer early reaction – hesitant proposals for limited reform – and then the greatly increased divergence between the aspirations of the trade unions, and the repression of the government and employers in the years immediately following the end of the Japanese occupation. The major part of the volume is concerned with the growing conflict between organized labour and government in the period 1945-48, leading to the passage of restrictive trade union legislation, the outbreak of the communist revolt, and the declaration of the Emergency in the middle months of 1948. A postscript surveys the experience of the trade union movement in Malaysia and Singapore in the 1950s and 1960s.

274 **The Malayan Union and the historians.**
M. R. Stenson. *Journal of Southeast Asian History*, vol. 10, no. 2 (Sept. 1969), p. 344-54.

This is an extended review of J. de V. Allen's *The Malayan Union* (q.v.). Stenson argues that Allen fails 'to throw any more light upon the basic problems of British policy making, to present an entirely satisfactory explanation of official decisions, to adequately explore the attitudes of the Chinese and Indians, or to demonstrate the real significance of the events to subsequent Malayan history'. He is particularly critical of Allen's failure to consider effectively the insensitivity and the ignorance of Chinese and Indian attitudes and ambitions, displayed by British planners in the conception, introduction and abandonment of the Malayan Union.

275 **British imperial policy and decolonization in Malaya, 1942-52.**
A. J. Stockwell. *Journal of Imperial and Commonwealth History*, vol. 13, no. 1 (Oct. 1984), p. 68-87.

Stockwell argues that British policy towards Malaya in the post-war years is usually seen to have passed through three phases: 1) 1945-48, which saw the supposedly aberrant and abortive Malayan Union experiment; 2) 1948-51, a period of apparent drift; and 3) 1951- , which saw a new determination and clear direction in the conduct of Malayan affairs. Working from recently released papers at the Public Record Office, Stockwell modifies the account summarized above in significant respects. He suggests that there was 'a clear appreciation in the highest circles of the significance of Malaya in the post-war period for Britain's influence in Asia and her recovery at home'. In particular he suggests 'an essential continuity in British strategy stretching from the so-called "deviant"

History. The Japanese Occupation, the Emergency and the Independence Campaign (1942-57)

Malayan Union through the years of apparent "drift" to the supposedly "new course" of 1952-57'.

276 British policy and Malay politics during the Malayan Union experiment, 1942-1948.

A. J. Stockwell. Kuala Lumpur: The Malaysian Branch of the Royal Asiatic Society, 1979. 206p. bibliog. (Monograph no. 8).

This detailed study of the war-time formulation and post-war implementation of a major constitutional reform for Malaya and the Malay response to that constitutional experiment, considers: the effect of the Japanese occupation on Malay political developments and on British policy towards Malaya; Anglo-Malay relations in the immediate post-war period, and in particular the Malay response to the Malayan Union; the Anglo-Malay constitutional negotiations in the period 1946-48; and, again in the period 1946-48, the position of the UMNO (the United Malays National Organization) within the Malay community, Malay radicalism and the Indonesian influences on Malay politics, and the struggle for political support from the *kampong*. An appendix contains short, but valuable biographical notes on the main persons involved in these events.

277 The formation and first years of the United Malays National Organization (UMNO) 1946-1948.

A. J. Stockwell. *Modern Asian Studies*, vol. 11, part 4 (Oct. 1977), p. 481-513.

Stockwell provides an analysis of the UMNO from its foundation in May 1946 to the declaration of the Emergency in June 1948. In an introduction he notes 'in its early years the party's leaders were more concerned to safeguard Malay rights *vis à vis* the other races of Malaya, and were more inclined to collaborate with the British authorities in opposition to radicalism within their own community, than to struggle for self-government . . . [Nevertheless] for the first time a mass and pan-peninsula Malay movement [had] emerged to attack British policy . . . UMNO amounted to an unprecedented Malay response to colonial rule'.

278 The United Malays National Organization, the Malayan Chinese Association, and the early years of the Malayan Emergency, 1948-1955.

Richard Stubbs. *Journal of Southeast Asian Studies*, vol. 10, no. 1 (March 1979), p. 77-88.

Stubbs is concerned with some of the links between the development of political parties in Malaya prior to 1955, notably the UMNO and the MCA, and the course of the Emergency. For example he argues that the development of those parties was assisted by the restrictions imposed by the government on left-wing political organizations in the late 1940s; and that the work of the UMNO and the MCA in recruiting the electoral support of the rural population was of considerable importance in undermining the strength of the communists in the 1950s.

279 **Tan Cheng Lock: a Malayan nationalist.**
K. G. Tregonning. *Journal of Southeast Asian Studies*, vol. 10,
no. 1 (March 1979), p. 25-76.

This is a lengthy, sympathetic, account of the life and political career of Tan
Cheng Lock, based on the subject's private papers which are now deposited in the
National Archives of Malaysia. Tregonning gives very considerable attention to
Tan Cheng Lock's activities in the pre-war and occupation periods as well, of
course, to the period after 1945 when he was the dominant political figure in the
Chinese community, and was closely involved in the political events which took
Malaya to independence in 1957.

280 **Operations most secret. SOE: the Malayan theatre.**
Ian Trenowden. London: William Kimber, 1978. 231p. 15 maps
and diags. bibliog.

A vivid account of the operations of Force 136 of the Special Operations
Executive (SOE) against the Japanese in the Malayan theatre. Trenowden draws
considerably on the accounts of these operations provided by surviving
participants; and therefore his book places as much emphasis on the "human
incidents" as on the "tactical achievements" of Force 136 in that area. Also
published under the title *Malayan operations most secret – Force 136* (Singapore:
Heinemann Educational Books [Asia], 1983).

281 **British planning for post-war Malaya.**
C. M. Turnbull. *Journal of Southeast Asian Studies*, vol. 5, no. 2
(Sept. 1974), p. 239-54.

Turnbull examines some of the principal influences behind the war-time
formulation and post-war implementation of the Malayan Union.

282 **The anti-federation movement in Malaya, 1946-48.**
Yeo Kim Wah. *Journal of Southeast Asian Studies*, vol. 4, no. 1
(March 1973), p. 31-51.

When the Malayan Union encountered strong Malay opposition in 1946, the
British authorities began to advance alternative constitutional proposals – the
Federation Proposals. This, in turn, was resisted by the Chinese and Indian
communities who, together with left-wing Malays, organized an anti-federation
movement, consisting of the Pan-Malayan Council of Joint Action (PMCJA) and
the Pusat Tenaga Ra'ayat (PUTERA). This paper examines 'the origin,
leadership and organization of the PMCJA-PUTERA as well as its agitation
against the Federation scheme during the years 1946-1948'.

**Prince and premier. A biography of Tunku Abdul Rahman Putra Al-
Haj. First Prime Minister of the Federation of Malaya.**
See item no. 401.

Population and Demography

283 **Demographic impact on socio-economic development. The Malaysian experience.**
Cheong Kee Cheok, Lim Lin Lean. Canberra: The Australian National University, 1982. 129p. bibliog. (Development Studies Centre, Monograph no. 29).

This study examines the impact of population changes in contemporary West Malaysia on the rate of economic growth, on structural change in the economy, and on the provision of social welfare and basic needs. A final chapter evaluates the extent to which population factors have been integrated into Malaysian development plans and considers the implications of future population trends.

284 **The population of Borneo. A study of the peoples of Sarawak, Sabah and Brunei.**
L. W. Jones. London: Athlone Press, 1966. 213p. map. bibliog.

A study which is primarily concerned with the growth and characteristics (notably sex ratio, marital status, distribution and internal migration, literacy and education, and religion) of the populations of Sarawak, Sabah, and Brunei, particularly for the period after 1945, to a lesser degree for the pre-war period. There is also consideration of the sources of demographic information; a demographic analysis of economic activity; and an assessment of future (from the mid-1960s) demographic prospects in the territories of northern Borneo.

285 **Population and settlement in Sarawak.**
Lee Yong Leng. Singapore: Donald Moore for Asia Pacific Press, 1970. 257p. 45 maps and diags. bibliog.

A consideration of the population and settlement features of Sarawak which is divided into three parts. The first provides an introduction to the physical environment and human settlement of the territory. The second considers the historical growth, distribution, and composition of the Sarawak population (with reference to the three ethnic groups – Malays, Dayaks, Chinese). The final part discusses the impact of population on the Sarawak landscape, with analysis of, for example: land use; agricultural patterns; planned villages; and urban settlements. There are twenty-six photographs.

286 **Population and development: theory and empirical evidence. The Malaysian case.**
Lim Lin Lean. Petaling Jaya: International Book Service, 1983. 318p. map. bibliog.

This book provides both a theoretical and empirical (in terms of a peninsular Malaysia case study) examination of the relationships between demographic change and economic/social development. Lim adopts two approaches. The first involves a discussion of the impact of economic and social development on demographic patterns (mortality; fertility; marriage patterns; migration). The second approach involves, conversely, a consideration of the consequences of demographic change for economic and social development. A final chapter 'discusses population policies and the integration of population considerations in Malaysia's various five-year plans'. Attached to each chapter is both a general and Malaysia-specific bibliography.

287 **Malaysia: patterns of population movement to 1970; Malaysia: a demographic analysis of internal migrants; Malaysia: migration and development: a regional synthesis; Malaysia: population distribution and development strategies.**
Robin J. Pryor. In: *Migration and development in South-East Asia. A demographic perspective.* Edited by Robin J. Pryor. Kuala Lumpur: Oxford University Press, 1979. p. 79-136. 10 maps. bibliog.

These four papers offer, respectively: a description of the major patterns of population movement in Malaysia up to 1970; an analysis of the main demographic characteristics of internal migrants; a description of the inter-relationships between migration and the level of economic development and modernization; and an examination of the implications of the Third Malaysia Plan (1976-80) and other regional development studies for population distribution. The analysis is concerned primarily with West Malaysia.

288 **A bibliography of the demography of Malaysia and Brunei.**
Saw Swee-Hock, Cheng Siok-Hwa. Singapore: University Education Press, 1975. 103p.

The scope of this bibliography is 'restricted to published works in the English language in the form of books, booklets, reports, articles and ordinances'. There are 644 titles, classified into 18 sections according to subject matter. There is an author index.

Population and Demography

289 **Population dynamics in a plural society: Peninsular Malaysia.**
Manjit S. Sidhu, Gavin W. Jones. Kuala Lumpur: University of
Malaya Co-operative Bookshop, 1981. 282p. 39 maps and figs.
This is a collection of twelve papers on various aspects of population change in
Peninsular Malaysia. There is a consideration of: population distribution and
growth; urbanization; population mobility; and the characteristics of the
population of Peninsular Malaysia (namely: sex composition, 1921-70; ethnic and
regional differences in marital status; trends in marriage and divorce; literacy and
educational attainment; and religious composition). In general the data is taken
up to 1970, although there is some material up to the mid-1970s. An appendix
outlines the sources of population data in Peninsular Malaysia. See also: 'Recent
and prospective population trends in Malaysia', by Gavin W. Jones and P. C. Tan
Journal of Southeast Asian Studies, vol. 16, no. 2 (Sept. 1985), p. 262-80.

290 **Immigration and permanent settlement of Chinese and Indians in
Malaya: and the future growth of the Malay and Chinese
communities.**
T. E. Smith. In: *The economic development of South-East Asia.
Studies in economic history and political economy.* Edited by C. D.
Cowan. London: George Allen & Unwin, 1964. p. 174-85.
The first part of this paper traces 'the settlement of the population of [non-Malay]
origin and argues that the increase of permanent Chinese settlement was in fact
quite rapid some time before official policy was shaped to an acceptance of
Malaya as a country with a permanently settled multi-racial population'. The
second part briefly considers the future (from the perspective of the early 1960s)
growth of the Malay and Chinese communities.

291 **Population growth in Malaya. An analysis of recent trends.**
T. E. Smith. London, New York: Royal Institute of International
Affairs, 1952. 126p. 2 maps.
This detailed study of demographic change in the peninsula, completed towards
the end of the colonial period, draws not only on the extensive official statistical
data but also on the author's intimate knowledge of Malaya and its peoples, as a
senior member of the Malayan Civil Service. The demographic pattern of each of
the three main ethnic communities – Malays, Chinese, Indians – is analysed in
three separate chapters. Two concluding chapters consider: the principal
economic activities of the Malayan peoples and the possible future development
of the economy; and the long-term relation between economic and social changes
and population growth in Malaya.

The population of Kedah in the nineteenth century.
See item no. 123.

Indigenous Minority Peoples

West Malaysia

292 **Orang Asli. The aboriginal tribes of Peninsular Malaysia.**
Iskandar Carey.   Kuala Lumpur: Oxford University Press, 1976.
376p. map. bibliog.

Carey provides 'a general sociological survey' of the Orang Asli, or aborigines, of Peninsular Malaysia. The first three parts of the book consider the three main categories of Orang Asli tribes – the Negritos, the Senoi, and the Proto-Malays. Attention is directed towards such aspects as: social organization; economic activities; agriculture; and magic and religion. The final part of the book considers the Orang Asli in the modern world: there is a description of the Malaysian government's administration of the aborigines, and a consideration of the effects that recent social and economic changes (including those associated with the Emergency) have had on those peoples. Carey was in the Department for Orang Asli Affairs until his retirement in 1969, latterly as Commissioner. There are a large number of plates and illustrations.

293 **The Semai. A nonviolent people of Malaya.**
Robert Knox Dentan.   New York: Holt, Rinehart & Winston,
1968. 110p. map. bibliog.

This is a short general introduction to the Semai, an aboriginal people who live in or near the hills and mountains of central Peninsular Malaysia. It considers, for example: their subsistence agricultural practices; kinship system; housing arrangements; and socioeconomic obligations. But particular attention is paid to the most distinctive feature of the Semai – their non-violent orientation. Dentan describes not only 'how interpersonal and marital relationships, sex, and aggression are influenced by the nonviolent image the Semai hold of themselves', but also how the Semai 'conceive of life, death, pain, and the diagnosis and treatment of disease'.

85

294 **Rain-forest collectors and traders. A study of resource utilization in modern and ancient Malaya.**
F. L. Dunn. Kuala Lumpur: Malaysian Branch of the Royal Asiatic Society, 1975. 151p. 10 maps. bibliog. (Monograph no. 5).

Dunn seeks to apply some of the data and techniques of anthropology, history (and archaeology), and ecology in a detailed study of the collection of, and the trade in, forest products in the southern Malay peninsula. The final three chapters examine forest product collecting and trade in prehistoric times; between the 5th and 19th centuries; and in modern Malaya. Earlier chapters consider: geographical heterogeneity and diversity in the southern Malay peninsula; present-day biotic and non-biotic resources in the forests of the Malayan interior; protohistoric and prehistoric resources in the forests of the southern Malay peninsula.

295 **Batek negrito religion. The world-view and rituals of a hunting and gathering people of Peninsular Malaysia.**
Kirk Endicott. Oxford, England: Clarendon Press, 1979. 234p. 2 maps. bibliog.

This study of the world-view and religious rites of the Batek Negrito considers such aspects as: Batek cosmology; Batek views of their forest environment; their views of human beings and superhuman beings; and their deities. It is based on extensive fieldwork among the Batek of Kelantan in the early and mid-1970s.

296 **The impact of economic modernization on the Orang Asli (aborigines) of northern Peninsular Malaysia.**
Kirk Endicott. In: *Issues in Malaysian development.* Edited by James C. Jackson, Martin Rudner. Singapore: Heinemann Educational Books (Asia), for the Asian Studies Association of Australia, 1979. p. 167-204.

Endicott examines those processes of economic modernization occurring in rural Malaysia 'that are likely to impinge on the Negritos and Temiar [who are among the most isolated of the Orang Asli] and attempts to determine what effect [those modernization processes] will have on their ways of life'.

297 **Chewong myths and legends.**
Signe Howell. Kuala Lumpur: The Malaysian Branch of the Royal Asiatic Society, 1982. 137p. map. bibliog. (Monograph no. 11).

Howell presents 71 Chewong myths and legends in full, with the purpose of making 'available the oral traditions of an aboriginal people of the Malay Peninsula'. There is no attempt to make a detailed analysis of the material, although a brief introduction provides a context essential for an understanding of the myths which follow.

298 **Society and cosmos. Chewong of Peninsular Malaysia.**
Signe Howell. Singapore: Oxford University Press, 1984. 294p.
2 maps. bibliog.
The Chewong are a small group (numbering about 260 individuals) of aboriginal
people who live in central Pahang. Howell's study is concerned with 'the
principles which govern the way the Chewong act, based on their understanding
of themselves, each other, their environment, and the supernatural'. Fieldwork
was undertaken mainly in the late 1970s.

299 **The Orang Asli: an outline of their progress in modern Malaya.**
Alun Jones. *Journal of Southeast Asian History*, vol. 9, no. 2
(Sept. 1968), p. 286-305.
This paper considers the changes which have taken place in the Orang Asli's
relationships and contacts with the Malays and Chinese, and with the various
governments in the peninsula, from the establishment of British administration to
the post-Emergency period – although particularly from the Japanese occupation.

300 **Ethnic groups of mainland Southeast Asia.**
Frank M. LeBar, Gerald C. Hickey, John K. Musgrave. New
Haven, Connecticut: Human Relations Area Files Press, 1964.
288p. map. bibliog.
This descriptive survey of the peoples and cultures of mainland Southeast Asia
includes a brief section on the Malays (p. 255-62) which contains an account of,
for example: their location; linguistic affiliation; demography; settlement pattern
and housing; economy; kin groups; marriage and family; sociopolitical organization; and religion. There are also sections on the Jakun [aboriginal Malays of
Johor] (p. 262-63); and the Moken, the Sea Gypsies of the coastal waters of
western Malaya (p. 263-66).

301 **Orang Asli animal tales.**
Lim Boo Liat. Singapore, Kuala Lumpur: Eastern Universities
Press, 1981. 58p.
Lim presents fourteen stories related to him by the Orang Asli (aboriginal tribes)
in Selangor, each story being concerned with a different common small mammal.
For each animal there is also a brief description of their appearance; distribution;
habits; and economic and medical importance; and a photograph. The book is of
interest (for varying reasons), to folklore specialists, children, and naturalists.

302 **Pagan races of the Malay peninsula.**
Walter William Skeat, Charles Otto Blagden. London:
Macmillan & Company, 1906. 2 vols. 7 maps. bibliog.
This very substantial work provides a detailed ethnographical description of the
minority races of the Malay peninsula. Its main divisions are titled: manners and
customs; religion; and language. There are a very large number of excellent
black-and-white photographs. By far the greater part of the study was written by
Skeat, a member of the FMS civil service, who had spent a considerable number
of years in districts of the peninsula partly occupied by aboriginal peoples.

303 **Jah-hĕt of Malaysia, art and culture.**
Roland Werner. Kuala Lumpur: Penerbit Universiti Malaya, 1975.
626p. 2 maps. bibliog.
The Jah-hĕt are a numerically small Senoi people found in central Pahang,
perhaps most frequently noted for their wood-carvings which embody their belief
in spirits. The opening two sections of this immensely detailed work provides a
general background to the Jah-hĕt and a brief consideration of their mythology
and ceremonies. But the major part of the book – running to well over 500 pages
and with towards 700 photographic illustrations – is concerned with their wood-
carvings and the spirit beliefs which they embody. In practice this section consists
largely of an illustrated and annotated catalogue of Jah-hĕt wood carvings.

East Malaysia

304 **Studies in Borneo societies: social process and anthropological
explanation.**
Edited by G. N. Appell. DeKalb, Illinois: Northern Illinois
University, Center for Southeast Asian Studies, 1976. 156p.
3 maps. bibliog. (Special Report no. 12). Exclusive distribution by
The Cellar Book Shop, Detroit, Michigan.
The seven papers in this collection 'deal primarily with problems of social
process'. They are said 'to illustrate how an adequate understanding of Bornean
societies requires the perspectives of various social sciences and interpretation
from a variety of theoretical approaches'. They include: a review of social science
research in Sarawak; interethnic relations and culture change in Sabah under
colonial rule; ritual process in a Bornean rice harvest (among the Lun Dayeh);
the role of the *shaman* in Iban society; the afterlife beliefs and rituals of the
Berawan peoples; an analysis of the rituals of headhunting in Borneo.

305 **Ulu. The world's end.**
Jørgen Bisch, translated from the Danish by Reginald
Spink. London: George Allen & Unwin, 1961. 142p.
A popular account of an expedition to the interior of Borneo in the late 1950s,
and of meetings with the Iban, Punan, and Kalabit. The author is a professional
writer-traveller. There are a large number of colour photographs, the vast
majority of bare-breasted tribal women.

306 **Longhouse in Sarawak.**
Mora Dickson. London: Victor Gollancz, 1971. 239p. 2 maps.
This is a popular account of community development work carried out among the
Dayaks in Budu [Sarawak] from the early 1950s, carried out principally by John
Wilson who had first come to the colony in 1949 as a government teacher.
Wilson's work in Sarawak was important in shaping the Voluntary Service

Overseas programme which began in 1958; indeed a considerable number of the early VSO volunteers went to Budu.

307 The religion of the Tempasuk Dusuns of North Borneo.
I. H. N. Evans.   Cambridge, England: Cambridge University Press, 1953. 579p. map.

This extremely detailed study of the religion of the Dusun peoples inhabiting the Tempasuk (Kota Belud) district of Sabah, north along the coast from Kota Kinabalu in the shadow of Mt. Kinabalu, is divided into three main sections: general beliefs, ceremonies, and folk stories.

308 The family system of the Iban of Borneo.
J. D. Freeman. In: *The developmental cycle in domestic groups.* Edited by Jack Goody.   Cambridge, England: Cambridge University Press, 1958. p. 15-52.

The author presents a description of the Iban family structure, which includes consideration of: the Iban long-house; the *bilek* family – the family group which owns and occupies one apartment of a long-house, and thus the basic unit of Iban social and economic organization; marriage; inheritance; death customs; and the division of the *bilek* family estate. Among Freeman's conclusions: 'a child is always a member of either its father's or its mother's natal *bilek*, depending on whether its parents practice virilocal or uxorilocal marriage'. The author's fieldwork was undertaken in 1949-51.

309 The Iban of Western Borneo.
J. D. Freeman. In: *Social structure in Southeast Asia.* Edited by George Peter Murdock.   Chicago: Quadrangle Books; London: Tavistock Publications, 1960. (Viking Fund Publications in Anthropology). Reprinted in 1971 by Johnson Reprint Corporation, New York and London, p. 65-87.

Freeman is particularly concerned in this paper with 'the wider cognatic social, structure of the Iban and their system of kinship and affinity'. This study should be read in conjunction with his 1958 paper which provides 'a more detailed account of the Iban family and the kinds of residence and descent associated with it'.

310 Report on the Iban.
Derek Freeman.   London: Athlone Press; New York: Humanities Press, 1970. new ed. 317p. 3 maps.

This study is primarily 'an account of Iban methods of shifting dry rice cultivation in pioneer areas' of Sarawak. There is consideration of: Iban social organization (including analysis of the *bilek*-family and the long-house community); land tenure; agricultural practices; the economics of agriculture; and Iban methods of land usage. Freeman carried out his research between 1949 and 1951, and a first edition of this study appeared in 1955. This 'new' edition is in fact essentially a republication of the first printing, with the text substantially unchanged.

311 **The home-life of Borneo head-hunters. Its festivals and folk-lore.**
William Henry Furness. New York: AMS Press, 1979. Reprint of
a book first published in 1902 by J. B. Lippincott, Philadelphia.
197p.

This work is mainly concerned with the Kayans and Kenyahs of the Baram district
of Sarawak. It considers such aspects of their lives as: the early training of a head-
hunter; a war expedition; personal embellishment; and some Bornean forms of
taboo. There are a very large number of contemporary [early 20th century]
photographs.

312 **Nine Dayak nights.**
W. R. Geddes. London: Oxford University Press, 1957.
Reprinted, Singapore: Oxford University Press, 1985. 144p.
2 maps.

The final, lengthy, section of this book consists of the tale of a Dayak folk-hero,
Kipachi, as told by a village *shaman*, in the presence of Geddes, during nine
consecutive and festive evenings in November 1950. The tale is preceded by a
substantial description (spread over eight chapters) of the Dayak way of life – its
varieties of work and entertainment; courtship and family life; ritual and belief.
This serious study succeeds also in being highly entertaining.

313 **Common efforts in the development of rural Sarawak, Malaysia.**
B. G. Grijpstra. Assen/Amsterdam: Van Gorcum, 1976. 231p.
3 maps. bibliog.

It is frequently argued that traditional communities, where people share their
resources and production, and are willing to make sacrifices for the welfare of the
community as a whole, provide an ideal basis for co-operative development
projects. From research among the Bidayuh, a dialect group of the Land Dayak
in south-west Sarawak, Grijpstra challenges that view. He examines, for example,
the Bidayuh residential pattern; household, marriage and kinship system;
religion; land tenure; labour; agriculture and other economic activities; village
organization; and the socio-economic structure of Bidayuh villages. And
concludes that Bidayuh villages quickly disintegrate 'when they are incorporated
in the market economy and political system of Sarawak; . . in Bidayuh villages a
traditionally integrated pattern of behaviour is not a strong basis for new co-
operative activities'.

314 **Head-hunters. Black, white, and brown.**
Alfred C. Haddon. London: Methuen, 1901. Reprinted, New
York: AMS Press, 1978. 426p. 6 maps.

This is a general account of an expedition to British New Guinea and Sarawak
undertaken by a party drawn mainly from the University of Cambridge (Haddon
was a university lecturer in ethnology) in 1898-99. With respect to the Sarawak
part of the expedition, there are the following chapters: journey from Kuching to
Baram; the war-path of the Kayans; the country and people of Borneo; a trip into
the interior of Borneo; notes on the omen animals of Sarawak; the cult of skulls
in Sarawak; and peace-making at Baram.

315 **The peoples of north and west Borneo.**
Tom Harrisson. In: *Malaysia: a survey*. Edited by Wang Gungwu.
Singapore: Donald Moore Books, 1964. p. 163–78.
A very brief anthropological and archaeological introduction to the peoples who
inhabit north and west Borneo, written in the early 1960s.

316 **The Iban and their religion.**
Erik Jensen. Oxford, England: Clarendon Press, 1974. 242p.
3 maps. bibliog.
This volume provides an ethnographical account of the behaviour of the Iban
people, or Sea Dyaks, of Sarawak: specifically 'the religious beliefs which are the
basis for their way of life, the framework within which these exist, and the ends to
which they are directed'. There are chapters on, for example: social organization;
property and labour; religious sources; myths and legends; world-view; men and
the spirits; and Iban attitudes to rice.

317 **Essays on Borneo societies.**
Edited by Victor T. King. Oxford, England: Oxford University
Press, for the University of Hull, 1978. 256p. map. bibliog.
(Monographs on South-East Asia, no. 7).
A collection of essays which focuses on the main elements of social organization
of nine peoples of Borneo – Coastal Melanau; Selako Dayak; Kayan (Sarawak);
Lun Dayeh; Rungus Dusun; Bajau Laut (Sabah); Maloh; Ma'anyan of Paju Epat
(Kalimantan); and the Kenyah (Kalimantan and Sarawak). A lengthy introduc-
tory essay by King offers some 'general, and in some cases tentative remarks on
Bornean social organization or social systems'.

318 **Ethnicity in Borneo: an anthropological problem.**
Victor T. King. *Southeast Asian Journal of Social Science,*
vol. 10, no. 1 (1982), p. 23-43.
King is concerned with the numerous difficulties which anthropologists (and
others) working on Borneo 'face in formulating comprehensive and static
classifications of neatly delineated ethnic groupings, and the problems which
various classifications have generated'. In illustrating 'the problems of studying
ethnic identity and of attempting to formulate ethnic classifications', King draws
mainly on his field research in the Upper Kapuas region of West Kalimantan,
concentrating primarily on the Maloh people.

319 **Ethnic groups of insular Southeast Asia.**
Edited and compiled by Frank M. LeBar. New Haven,
Connecticut: Human Relations Area Files Press, 1972. 2 vols.
17 maps. bibliog.
The first volume of this descriptive survey of the peoples and cultures of insular
Southeast Asia contains a section on the ethnic groups of Borneo (p. 147-97),
including the Dusun, Murut, and the Iban. For each ethnic group there is an
account of, for example: location; linguistic affiliation; demography; settlement

91

pattern and housing; economy; kinship; marriage and family; sociopolitical organization; and religion.

320 **Borneo people.**
Malcolm MacDonald. London: Jonathan Cape, 1956. 376p.

Malcolm MacDonald, (son of Ramsay MacDonald), was Governor-General of Malaya and British Borneo in 1946; and Commissioner-General, Southeast Asia between 1948 and 1955. He was a frequent and fascinated visitor to the Borneo territories. This volume provides an informed, personal account of the Land Dayaks; the Ibans; the Kayans and the Kenyahs; and the Melanaus, Malays, and Chinese. There are forty-four photographs, and a drawing by the author.

321 **A Borneo journey into death. Berawan eschatology from its rituals.**
Peter Metcalf. Philadelphia: University of Pennsylvania Press, 1982. 275p. 5 maps. bibliog.

This is a detailed study of the death rituals of the Berawan people of central northern Borneo. For the most part the study follows a chronological sequence, 'dealing with the rituals as they unfold from death to final disposal perhaps years later'. This book draws on the author's extensive fieldwork among the Berawan.

322 **Modernization among the Iban of Sarawak.**
Peter Mulok Kedit. Kuala Lumpur: Dewan Bahasa dan Pustaka, Kementerian Palajaran Malaysia, 1980. 238p. 5 maps. bibliog.

This study is based on a three months' survey research among 684 Iban from three distinctive geographical areas in Sarawak. Two early chapters consider the Iban cultural heritage; and provide a brief survey of Sarawak's history, placing particular emphasis on the period of rule by the Brookes. The remaining chapters describe the survey; and present the ethnographic and data analysis. Kedit draws out the different attitudes toward modernization as displayed by the different groups of Iban in each selected geographical area: and concludes that Iban generally 'could readapt themselves to the needs of urbanism without losing their cultural identity'.

323 **Migration and its alternatives among the Iban of Sarawak.**
Christine Padoch. The Hague: Martinus Nijhoff, for Koninklijk Instituut voor Taal-, Land- en Volkenkunde, Leiden; no. 98, 1982. 126p. 3 maps. bibliog.

Padoch is concerned with 'some of the technological, demographic and other adjustments made by groups of shifting cultivators – communities of Iban in Sarawak – in response to changing environmental conditions, in particular, to variations in resource availability'. She seeks to determine 'whether and what significant changes appear in Iban patterns of land use as the length of settlement of an area increases, the supply of unexploited land dwindles, and as the frontier recedes'. An early chapter considers the history of Iban migrations. Later chapters discuss: land use and land tenure; agricultural methods, labour and yields; human fertility and population growth; and trade and sources of income for the Iban.

324 The natives of Sarawak and British North Borneo.
Henry Ling Roth. London: Truslove & Hanson, 1896. 2 vols.
map. bibliog.

This work is based chiefly on a collection of very incomplete manuscripts by 'an eccentric young gentleman named Hugh Brooke Low' (1849-87), the son of Sir Hugh Low, secretary to the governor of Labuan and later Resident in Perak. It provides the most detailed account of the Borneo natives under British authority: including their physique; marriage; religion; feasts, festivals and dancing; daily life, fire, food and narcotics; agriculture, land tenure, and domestic animals; head-hunting; human sacrifices and cannibalism; music; and languages. A lengthy appendix in volume two reproduces a large number of vocabularies from the relevant languages. There are a very large number of illustrations.

325 The pagans of North Borneo.
Owen Rutter. London: Hutchinson & Company, 1929. 288p. 2 maps. bibliog.

Rutter is almost wholly concerned with the Dusun and Murut peoples. He discusses such aspects as: personal characteristics; social organization; agriculture; jungle and river craft; arts and manufactures; trade and barter; pagan law; headhunting and war; beliefs and ceremonies; and folklore. There are a large number of black-and-white illustrations.

326 Iban adat and augury.
Benedict Sandin. Penang: Penerbit Universiti Sains Malaysia, for the School of Comparative Social Sciences, Penang, 1980. 151p. bibliog.

This study divides into two parts. The first concerns Iban *adat* law and custom, and thus includes an examination of Iban religious festivals; the order of life in the long-house; and weaving, traditional pastimes, dance and music. The second part considers Iban augury: 'as traditionally practiced by the Iban, augury is based on a belief that the gods reveal their favour, or issue warnings to mankind through the behaviour of a class of augural birds, seven in number, that act as message-bearers on their behalf'. The author is himself an Iban. He was a senior figure at the Sarawak Museum from 1952-73. This book also has a lengthy introduction to Iban *adat* and augury, written by Clifford Sather.

327 The Sea Dayaks of Borneo before white rajah rule.
Benedict Sandin. London: Macmillan, 1967. 134p. 7 maps.

Benedict Sandin, an Iban, provides a history (as opposed to ritual, legend, or story), of his people from the time of their initial migrations into Sarawak territory from approximately the late 16th century, but primarily from the end of pioneer settlement in the early 18th century to the arrival of Brooke rule in the mid-19th century. The study is based almost entirely on oral materials known to the author. See also: Robert Pringle, *Rajahs and rebels. The Ibans of Sarawak under Brooke rule, 1841-1941* (London, 1970).

328 **Contributions to the ethnology of central northeast Borneo (parts of Kalimantan, Sarawak and Sabah).**
W. F. Schneeberger.   Berne: University of Berne, Institute of Ethnology, 1979. 143p. 3 maps. bibliog.

The data for this ethnological report were collected by the author during travels throughout northeastern Kalimantan, southern Sarawak and southwestern Sabah in 1939. The report is primarily concerned with the Murut and Kelabit peoples, and considers such aspects as: house types; linguistic characteristics; burial customs; ceremonies whilst receiving guests; agricultural techniques; salt-making; and megalithic monuments.

329 **Colonialism and Iban warfare.**
Ulla Wagner.   Stockholm: OBE-Tryck Sthlm, 1972. 211p. 2 maps. bibliog.

Wagner argues that the 'pacification' of the Sarawak territory by the Brookes from the mid-19th century in reality meant an increase of warfare and opportunities for head-hunting on the part of the Iban: but that paradoxically, the Brookes ended head-hunting. Brooke policy 'stimulated head-taking and was also responsible for its ending'. In order to resolve this apparent paradox, Wagner first provides an analysis of the art and manner of Brooke policy and administration, and an examination of the basic meaning of head-hunting and warfare for Iban society, before considering the 'suppression' of Iban head-hunting.

330 **The Dusun. A North Borneo society.**
Thomas Rhys Williams.   New York: Holt, Rinehart & Winston, 1965. 100p. map. bibliog.

This is a case study in cultural anthropology of the Dusun people of Sabah. The principal chapters consider: conceptions of the natural world; religious belief and behaviour; omens, luck, and chance; sickness and death; social relations; property, order, and authority; subsistence and economy; life experience and world view.

Life in the forests of the Far East.
See item no. 68.

The Malay archipelago.
See item no. 96.

The Malay peoples of Malaysia and their languages.
See item no. 332.

Languages

General

331 **Language and society in Malaysia.**
Asmah Haji Omar. Kuala Lumpur: Dewan Bahasa dan Pustaka, Kementerian Pelajaran Malaysia, 1982. 203p. bibliog.

This volume aims at giving 'a broad picture of the linguistic situation in Malaysia and the issues and problems arising from the use of language in society, and in particular those that are related to the use of Malay'. Included in the ten papers are: language and national ideology; implications of the use of the Malaysian national language in a multi-lingual society; and ethnic diversity and the integration of the Malaysian Chinese and Indians through language medium.

332 **The Malay peoples of Malaysia and their languages.**
Asmah Haji Omar. Kuala Lumpur: Dewan Bahasa dan Pustaka, Kementerian Pelajaran Malaysia, 1983. 682p. map. bibliog.

This work provides a descriptive analysis of twenty-three Malaysian languages: Bahasa Malaysia [Malay proper]; twelve languages found spoken in Sabah; and ten languages from Sarawak. For each ethnic community whose language(s) are examined, there is also a substantial ethnographical description, involving a consideration of the community's history of settlement; subsistence economy; religious system and beliefs; art and craft; and social organization. An introductory chapter considers the characteristics of the Austronesian languages of Malaysia.

Dictionaries and grammars (Malay)

333 Kamus Dwibahasa: Bahasa Inggeris – Bahasa Malaysia.
Kuala Lumpur: Dewan Bahasa dan Pustaka, Kementerian
Pelajaran Malaysia, 1981. 1,457p. bibliog.

This is arguably the most comprehensive and precise contemporary English-Malay
dictionary. Reference should also be made to: *Kamus pembaca; Inggeris-Melayu:
Reader's dictionary; English-Malay*, by A. S. Hornby, E. C. Parnwell, Daud
Baharum, and Asraf (Kuala Lumpur: Oxford University Press, 1972. 416p.).

334 A Dictionary and grammar of the Malayan language.
William Marsden. Singapore: Oxford University Press, 1984.
2 vols.

This is a finely-produced reprint of two volumes which originally appeared in
1812. The dictionary, which constitutes the first volume, provides both Malay-
English ['the essential portion of the work'] and English-Malay. The Malay entries
are given both in transliteration and *jawi* [Arabic letters]. Marsden's *Dictionary*
was pre-eminent in at least the British-influenced areas of the Malay world until
the appearance of R. J. Wilkinson's dictionary in 1901, and remains a work of
very considerable lexicographical interest. This reprint includes an introduction
(with references) to both the dictionary and the grammar by Russell Jones.

335 An unabridged Malay-English dictionary.
R. O. Winstedt. Singapore: Marican & Sons, 1957. 2nd ed. 370p.

The standard concise Malay-English dictionary of the mid-20th century which has
passed through a number of subsequent revisions and editions. Reference should
also be made to: *A Malay-English dictionary (Romanised)*, by R. J. Wilkinson
(Mytilene, Greece: Salavopoulos & Kinderlis, 1932. 2 vols.); also: *An unabridged
English-Malay dictionary*, by Sir Richard Winstedt (Kuala Lumpur: Marican &
Sons, 1965. 4th ed. 437p.)

Religion

General

336 **Contemporary issues on Malaysian religions.**
Tunku Abdul Rahman Putra, Tan Sri Dr. Tan Chee Khoon, Dr.
Chandra Muzaffar, Lim Kit Siang. Petaling Jaya: Pelanduk
Publications, 1984. 212p.

This volume consists of the proceedings of a seminar, 'Common religious values
for nation building', organized by the Consultative Council of Buddhism,
Christianity, Hinduism, and Sikhism, and held in Kuala Lumpur in April 1984.
The contributions aim to encourage a dialogue between Muslim, Buddhist, Hindu,
Christian and Sikh Malaysians in order to establish common religious values for
nation-building. The sections thus include: constitutional provisions for religious
freedom in Malaysia; common religious values for nation building; problem areas
that hinder inter-religious harmony; and towards national unity through inter-
religious understanding. Thus the focus of the volume is on the political
implications of religious diversity, rather than on religious beliefs and practices as
such.

Islam

337 **Islamic revivalism and the political process in Malaysia.**
Mohamed Abu Bakar. *Asian Survey*, vol. 21, no. 10 (Oct. 1981),
p. 1040-59.
A consideration of the origins of the current Islamic resurgence in Malaysia; the
policy of the Malaysian government toward the resurgence; and the impact on party
politics (notably the UMNO and Parti Islam) of Islamic revivalism. In his
concluding comments, Mohamed Abu Bakar, whilst acknowledging the more
pervasive influence of Islam in contemporary Malaysia, notes that the 'new' Islam
may in time raise a powerful challenge to itself, even from among the Malay
population. For example, 'the core of the Malay populace, still imbued with the
old conception of religion, is likely to remain opposed to the current revivalism',
whilst the UMNO 'will continue to contain the forces of Islam'.

338 **Some aspects of Ṣūfism as understood and practiced among the
Malays.**
Syed Naguib al-Attas. Singapore: Malaysian Sociological
Research Institute, 1963. 106p. bibliog.
This study divides into three main sections: an introduction to the origin, spread,
development and culmination of Ṣūfism in Islam; an examination of Ṣūfism as
understood among the Malays, an examination drawn in large part from a reading
of prose and poetry written by Malay mystics of the 16th and 17th centuries; and
an analysis of the practical and ritual aspects of Ṣūfism among the Malays.

339 **Adat and Islam in Malaya.**
M. B. Hooker. *Bijdragen tot de Taal-, Land- en Volkenkunde*,
vol. 130, part 1 (1974), p. 69-90.
This article has two objectives. First, 'to describe the relationship between the
system of law (*adat*) and a religious system which is also a legal system (Islam) as
these co-exist in contemporary Malaya'. Hooker points out that the relationship is
an important one 'because although both systems apply to the same persons – the
Malay peasants – their respective rules in such important matters as marriage and
inheritance are dissimilar and indeed conflict in certain important respects'.
Second, to attempt a better understanding between academic lawyers and
anthropologists in their study of *adat*, Islam, and the relationships between them.
Data is drawn primarily from Negeri Sembilan.

340 **Islam in South-East Asia.**
Edited by M. B. Hooker. Leiden, The Netherlands: Brill, 1983.
262p. bibliog.
A collection of seven essays which seeks 'to provide a concise and introductory
discussion of some fundamental aspects of Islam in South-East Asia'. Those
essays which consider, to some degree, Malaysia are: the translation of Islam into
South-East Asia; Islam and the Muslim state; social theory, ethnography and the
understanding of practical Islam in South-East Asia; Islamic philosophy in South-

East Asia; Muhammadan law and Islamic law; and the contemporary political dimension of Islam.

341 Malaysia: Islamic revivalism and political disaffection in a divided society.
Clive S. Kessler. *Southeast Asia Chronicle*, no. 75 (Oct. 1980), p. 3-11.

Kessler provides a brief account of the *dakwah* movement (a politically informed religious resurgence), which has become a central feature of contemporary Malaysian society. Primarily, he places *dakwah* in its historical, political and economic context. Kessler argues that what is on the one hand 'a genuinely religious movement also constitutes, on the other, a critique of the bureaucratic state, its economic policies and its deracinating cultural effects'. With the emergence of *dakwah*, Islam has come to serve as 'the ideology and mechanism of a popular moral repudiation of the post-colonial state, for excluding rather than embodying popular interests'.

342 Public policy toward religion in Malaysia.
Gordon P. Means. *Pacific Affairs*, vol. 51, no. 3 (fall 1978), p. 384-405.

Means observes in an introductory passage that 'because the legal definition of a Malay is tied to adherence to Islam, and because of state support and promotion of Islam as the official religion, government policies of giving preferential aid to the Malays have become entwined with public policies toward religion'. His article considers how public policies toward religion in contemporary Malaysia 'are related to the economic and social goals enunciated by the Malaysian Government'. In addition some attention is given to 'religious and social trends and to the longer-term consequences of the government's religious policies, especially in matters of ethnic identities and inter-ethnic relations'. Specifically there is consideration of, for example: independence and the constitutional status of Islam; legal privileges associated with Islam; the changing role of Islam in contemporary Malaysia; religion in Malaysian politics; and an evaluation of religious policy.

343 The role of Islam in the political development of Malaysia.
Gordon P. Means. *Comparative Politics*, vol. 1, no. 2 (Jan. 1969), p. 264-84.

This article examines 'the changing role of Islam in Malaysia' and evaluates 'its impact upon the modernization of the political system'. It considers: Islam in traditional Malay society; the role of religion in pre-colonial Malay society; the colonial impact on the role of religion; Islamic law and administration under colonial rule; Islam in the post-war era; the changing role of government in religious affairs; and the effects of religious policies upon modernization. Means concludes that 'it is extremely difficult to determine with precision or clarity whether religion has impeded or promoted political and economic development'. It should be noted that this article was written before the major resurgence of Islam in Malaysia, although clearly it is mainly concerned with the historical role of Islam in the country.

344 **The new fundamentalism: Islam in contemporary Malaysia.**
Judith Nagata. *Asian Thought and Society: An International Review*, vol. 5, no. 14 (Sept. 1980), p. 128-41.

Nagata notes that 'the contemporary Islamic or *dakwah* movement in Malaysia in its organized form is principally urban-based, with its strongest appeal to the younger and more highly educated, middle class sector of the Malay community'. Her article is mainly concerned with the beliefs, organization and influence of the three distinctive *dakwah* groups which form the core of the fundamentalist revival in Malaysia: Darul Arqam; Jema'ah Tabligh; and the Islamic Youth Movement (ABIM). In a conclusion she suggests that 'even though at one level, the Islamic revival has the effect of dividing the Muslim-Malay community, at another level it also operates as a powerful symbol of ethnic unity, and provides for the Malays a renewed sense of identity'.

345 **The reflowering of Malaysian Islam. Modern religious radicals and their roots.**
Judith Nagata. Vancouver, British Columbia: University of British Columbia Press, 1984. 282p. bibliog.

The author is concerned with the rise and flowering of the *dakwah* movement in Malaysia during the 1970s and 1980s, *dakwah* being 'a parochial form of a more widespread . . . revitalization process in the broader Islamic world'. In detail, she considers: the Islamic foundations of Malay culture and consciousness; rural *ulama* (religious scholar/teacher) and the basis of their authority; the urban religious revival – development of *dakwah*; modes of transmission of *dakwah* in Malay-Muslim society; responses to the *dakwah* movement; *dakwah* and the search for ethnic Malay identity; and the roots of the new Malay radical – class and religious ideology.

346 **Religious ideology and social change: the Islamic revival in Malaysia.**
Judith Nagata. *Pacific Affairs*, vol. 53, no. 3 (fall 1980), p. 405-39.

This work provides 'a preliminary review of how the Islamic revival has impressed itself on the Muslim population of Malaysia and become an integral part of the political, economic, ethnic, linguistic and cultural scene'. The main sections of the article provide an analysis of: the social and political background to the Islamic revival in Malaysia; the religious revival in Malaysia – the meaning of *dakwah*; the national-level *dakwah* organizations; the political response to *dakwah*; *dakwah* and the legitimacy of authority; and *dakwah* and 'class interest'. In conclusion, Nagata argues: 'Since 1969, the most salient conflicts in Malaysian society have centered on the issues of language, education, youth, rural-urban imbalances and Malay identity and rights. Higher education . . . and western contacts have led many Malay youth to question the validity of western values, creating cultural and personal conflicts. Ultimately all these conflicts have converged and found a common expression in the religious revival, which mirrors many lines of communication and cleavage already existing in the Malay community'.

The Malays. A cultural history.
See item no. 39.

Malacca's early kings and the reception of Islam.
See item no. 130.

Islam and politics in a Malay state. Kelantan 1838-1969.
See item no. 440.

Islam, society and political behaviour: some comparative implications of the Malay case.
See item no. 441.

Muslim identity and political behaviour in Kelantan.
See item no. 442.

Kelantan. Religion, society and politics in a Malay state.
See item no. 445.

The Islamic Party of Malaysia. Its formative stages and ideology.
See item no. 447.

Malay religion, society and politics in Kelantan.
See item no. 448.

The social organization of Islam in Kelantan.
See item no. 449.

The Malay Islamic Hikāyat.
See item no. 676.

Chinese religious practices

347 **Chinese ancestor worship in Malaya.**
Leon Comber. Singapore: Donald Moore, 1954. 41p. bibiog.
This is a brief, popular, account of Chinese ancestor worship in Malaya, based in large part on Comber's own observations during government service in the country in the late 1940s and early 1950s. The book includes twenty black-and-white photographs, mainly concerned with Chinese funeral practices.

348 **The study of Chinese society. Essays by Maurice Freedman.**
Selected and introduced by G. William Skinner. Stanford, California: Stanford University Press, 1979. 491p. bibiog.
Maurice Freedman was one of the most distinguished anthropologists and sinologists of the post-war decades, with a particular interest in Chinese family and marriage, lineage and ancestor worship, and religion. A major part of his research was conducted in Singapore. This volume brings together twenty-four of

his essays. Of particular interest in the present context are eight papers concerned with kinship and religion in China: and one (written with Marjorie Topley) 'Religion and social realignment among the Chinese in Singapore' [Reprinted from: *Journal of Asian Studies*, vol. 21, no. 1 (1961), p. 2–23]. Topley has also published extensively in this field in her own right: a list of references to her work in this area is included in the bibliography of this volume.

349 **Buddhism in Malaya.**
     Colin McDougall.   Singapore: Donald Moore, 1956. 61p. bibliog.
The first half of this slim book provides a brief introduction to Buddhism – the life of Buddha; the growth of Buddhism; and Buddhist doctrine. Only one (if more substantial), chapter is given over to a consideration of Buddhism in Malaya and Singapore. There is also included a list of some of the Buddhist associations, temples and societies in Singapore and Malaya (as of the mid-1950s); a note on Buddhist relics in Malaya; and a series of black-and-white photographs, mainly of Buddhist temples.

350 **Some aspects of Chinese religious practices and customs in Singapore and Malaysia.**
     Tadao Sakai.   *Journal of Southeast Asian Studies*, vol. 12, no. 1 (March 1981), p. 133-41.
This article is concerned with 'the Taoist creed and common Chinese religious beliefs, in particular the religious customs of *poeh* (the practice of seeking divination) and the worship of the local god of the soil'. In a broader sense it is concerned with the relationship, frequently conflict, between the Chinese culture of China itself and that of Southeast Asia, particularly that of the Singapore-Malaysia region.

Hinduism

351 **Indian festivals in Malaya.**
     S. Arasaratnam. Kuala Lumpur: Department of Indian Studies, University of Malaya, 1966. 51p. bibliog.
This slim volume provides a simple and precise account of all the religious festivals celebrated by the Indian community in Malaysia. There are some nine black-and-white plates. Wherever possible the author points out the differences between the ways in which Indian festivals are celebrated in Malaysia and the ways in which they are celebrated in India itself.

352 **Sai Baba, salvation and syncretism: religious change in a Hindu movement in urban Malaysia.**
Raymond L. M. Lee. *Contributions to Indian Sociology (NS),*
vol. 16, no. 1 (Jan.-June 1982), p. 125-40.
This brief paper is primarily concerned with the organization and dynamics of the Sai Baba movement in urban Malaysia. In a more general sense, it examines the relationship between contemporary Hinduism and sociocultural developments in the Malaysian Indian community. Sri Sathya Sai Baba is an Indian religious figure who rose to prominence in the 1960s. See also: *Patterns of Hindu religious beliefs and practices among the people of Tamil origin in West Malaysia,* by R. Rajoo (Kuala Lumpur: MA diss., Department of Indian Studies, University of Malaya, 1970. 317p. bibliog.). Further references may be found in: *Indians in Peninsular Malaysia. A study and bibliography,* by Rajakrishnan Ramasamy and J. Rabindra Daniel (Kuala Lumpur: University of Malaya Library, 1984. 62p.).

Christianity

353 **Waiting for China. The Anglo-Chinese College at Malacca, 1818-1843, and early nineteenth century missions.**
Brian Harrison. Hong Kong: Hong Kong University Press, 1979.
212p. bibliog.
Harrison is primarily concerned with the creation and development of the Anglo-Chinese College at Malacca, founded by Robert Morrison (the first Protestant missionary to China), and sponsored by the London Missionary Society. His focus is on the educational ideas and achievements of the college and its founder rather than on their religious work as such. See also: 'The Anglo-Chinese College at Malacca, 1818-1843', by Brian Harrison, in: *Southeast Asian history and historiography: essays presented to D. G. E. Hall,* edited by C. D. Cowan and O. W. Wolters (Ithaca, New York; London: Cornell University Press, 1976. p. 246-61); and 'The Anglo-Chinese College and early modern education', by Brian Harrison, in: *Melaka. The transformation of a Malay capital c1400-1980,* edited by Kernial Singh Sandhu and Paul Wheatley (Kuala Lumpur: Oxford University Press, 1983. vol. 1, p. 297-310).

354 **The London Missionary Society: a written record of missionaries and printing presses in the Straits Settlements 1815-1847.**
Leona O'Sullivan. *Journal of the Malaysian Branch of the Royal Asiatic Society,* vol. 57, part 2 (Dec. 1984), p. 61-104.
This is primarily a very detailed, illustrated, account of the evangelical printing work carried out by the Straits Settlements missions of the London Missionary Society in the first half of the nineteenth century. It draws principally on the LMS archives, now deposited in the School of Oriental and African Studies, London.

355 **Khabar gembira (the good news). A history of the Catholic Church in East Malaysia and Brunei (1880-1976).**
John Rooney. London; Kota Kinabalu, Malaysia: Burns & Oates, with Mill Hill Missionaries, 1981. 292p. 6 maps. bibliog.
This is a detailed, academic, study of the history of the Catholic Church in Sabah, Sarawak, and Brunei. It seeks to examine not only the growth of the church's activities in those states but also her contribution to the social and cultural aspirations of Borneo and her relations with local political authority. The work is based on an extensive use of ecclesiastical primary sources. Rev. Fr. Rooney worked as a missionary (the Mill Hill Mission), in Sabah during the 1960s.

356 **The Portuguese missions in Malacca and Singapore (1511-1958).**
Manuel Teixeira. Lisbon: Agência Geral do Ultramar, 1961, 1963. 3 vols. maps. bibliog.
An exhaustively detailed, uncritical, account of the apostolic work of the Portuguese missions in Malacca and Singapore over a period of four centuries.

Life in the forests of the Far East.
See item no. 68.

A flourish for the bishop. Brooke's friend Grant. Two studies in Sarawak history 1848-1868.
See item no. 141.

Animistic beliefs

357 **An analysis of Malay magic.**
Kirk Michael Endicott. Kuala Lumpur: Oxford University Press, 1970. 188p. bibliog.
Endicott is concerned with the magical beliefs and practices (the folk religion), of the Malays of the Malay peninsula. He describes the basic magical beliefs and their inter-relationships, and analyses the logic behind the various 'magical' practices of the Malays. The study draws on the existing published literature, most notably Walter William Skeat's *Malay magic* (q.v.).

358 **Faith and scepticism in Kelantan village magic.**
Raymond Firth. In: *Kelantan. Religion, society and politics in a Malay state*. Edited by William R. Roff. Kuala Lumpur: Oxford University Press, 1974. p. 190-224.
This paper has two aims: 'ethnographically, to give data on Kelantan Malay magic in the coastal area near Bachok, mainly from 1939-40, before modern education reached the people; and more theoretically, to explore the problem of local beliefs in magic, and to challenge mono-lithic views of Malay magic as a unitary self-sufficient system of general credence'. It is argued that 'even a generation ago, in a part of Malaya which has been recognized as a stronghold of magical

practices, Malays have been more pragmatic, shown more variation in their beliefs, been more experimental in their attitudes, than could be inferred from the [existing] literature'.

359 Malay poisons and charm cures.

John D. Gimlette. Kuala Lumpur: Oxford University Press, 1971. 301p. bibliog. (following each chapter).

The first edition of this book was published in 1915. This is a re-printing of a 3rd edition, originally published in 1929. Dr. Gimlette spent eighteen years, from 1896, working in the Malay States (mainly in Kelantan), and his study provides a valuable scientific account of medicine as practised by the Malay *bomor*, (Malay medicine-man), or *pawang* in the early 20th century. The study is divided into two parts. The first includes consideration of: methods of poisoning and Malay charms in general; the work of the *bomor* in relation to clinical medicine; charms and amulets; black art in Malay medicine; and spells and soothsaying. The second part examines the poisons obtained by Malays from fish; animals; the jungle plants; and from inorganic sources.

360 The bomoh and the hantu.

Haji Mohtar bin H. Mohammed Dom. Kuala Lumpur: Federal Publications, 1979. 71p. (Federal Cultural Series).

A *bomoh* is a Malay medicine-man; a *hantu* is the Malay devil. This brief volume, written primarily for the general reader, examines the supernatural forces in Malay beliefs – their origins, the different forms they take and, above all, the influence which they still strongly exert amongst the rural Malay.

361 Malay superstitions and beliefs.

Haji Mohtar bin H. Mohammed Dom. Kuala Lumpur: Federal Publications, 1979. 62p. (Federal Cultural Series).

Written mainly for the general reader, this brief volume discusses those Malay superstitions and beliefs associated with the main stages of life; those which arise in games and the arts; and those which appear in folk-tales. There is also a discussion of Malay taboos, and *padah*, or omens.

362 Traditions and taboos.

Haji Mohtar bin H. Mohammed Dom. Kuala Lumpur: Federal Publications, 1979. 71p. (Federal Cultural Series).

This brief volume is intended for the general reader. It examines traditional Malay beliefs and taboos; Malay traditions and taboos associated with birth and confinement, with building a new house, and with funerals; the customs concerning children; and some Kadazan customs.

363 **Malay magic. Being an introduction to the folklore and popular religion of the Malay peninsula.**
Walter William Skeat. London: Macmillan, 1900. 685p. bibliog. Reprinted with an introduction by Hood Salleh: Singapore: Oxford University Press, 1984.

A classic study of Malay folklore and animistic beliefs, which was written by a British colonial administrator. The major part of the work examines Malay magic rites connected with the various aspects of nature; and Malay magic rites as affect the life of man [for example, birth-spirits; marriage; funerals; medicine; war and weapons]. Preliminary, brief chapters consider: man and his place in the universe; relations with the super-natural world; and the Malay pantheon.

364 **The Malay magician, being Shaman, Saiva and Sufi.**
Richard Winstedt. London: Routledge & Kegan Paul, 1961. Revised and enlarged ed., 180p. bibliog. Reprinted, Kuala Lumpur: Oxford University Press, 1982.

This is a study of Malay magical beliefs and their practical application. There is analysis of, for example: animism; primitive gods, spirits and ghosts; Hindu influence; the ritual of the rice-field; the séance; sacrifice; the magician and Sufi; Muslim magic; and magic in daily life. Sir Richard Winstedt was probably the most distinguished scholar-official in Malaya during the colonial period.

Batek negrito religion. The world-view and rituals of a hunting and gathering people of Peninsular Malaysia.
See item no. 295.

Jah-hët of Malaysia, art and culture.
See item no. 303.

The religion of the Tempasuk Dusuns of North Borneo.
See item no. 307.

The Iban and their religion.
See item no. 316.

Iban adat and augury.
See item no. 326.

The Dusun. A North Borneo society.
See item no 330.

Social Conditions, Health and Welfare

365 **The role of the private sector in housing the urban poor in Peninsular Malaysia.**
D. W. Drakakis-Smith. In: *Issues in Malaysian development.*
Edited by James C. Jackson, Martin Rudner. Singapore:
Heinemann Educational Books (Asia), for the Asian Studies
Association of Australia, 1979. p. 305-37.

The author emphasizes the importance of the smaller and less formal building
'firms', including illegal squatter builders, in the provision of low-cost housing in
Malaysia, whilst acknowledging that as yet little is known 'either of the extent or
the organization of [such] small scale [building] activity, whether legal or illegal'.
A considerable part of the paper consists of an examination of the scope for
reducing the general production costs of housing – the costs of land purchase and
preparation, building materials, labour; and the revision of building and planning
regulations.

366 **Women in Malaysia.**
Edited by Hing Ai Yun, Nik Safiah Karim, Rokiah Talib. Petaling
Jaya: Pelanduk Publications, 1984. 312p. bibliog.

A collection of thirteen papers concerned with the various problems encountered
by women in contemporary Malaysia. Contributions include: women and work in
West Malaysia; developing the rural women; impact of industrialization on the
social role of rural Malay women; women and divorce among the urban Malays;
Indian women in urban Malaysia; traces of Confucianist influence on Malaysian
Chinese women and its implications; the legal status of women in a multi-racial
Malaysian society; and women's organizations in Malaysia. There is an excellent
bibliography.

Social Conditions, Health and Welfare

367 **Malaysian women. Problems and issues.**
Edited by Evelyn Hong. Penang: Consumers' Association of Penang, 1983. 134p.

This volume, which contains ten papers by various authors, is concerned with the impact on Malaysian women of the processes of modernization and development. Four principal aspects of this subject are considered: the economic and social position of women in Malaysia; the problems faced by women workers in manufacturing industries; health hazards faced by women; and violence against women. The majority of papers have an attached list of references.

368 **Wives and midwives. Childbirth and nutrition in rural Malaysia.**
Carol Laderman. Berkeley, California; London: University of California Press, 1983. 267p. map. bibliog.

This study is based on anthropological research in a district (Merchang) in Trengganu where traditional healers and midwives were active, and yet where access to cosmopolitan medicine was relatively easy. The main chapters consider: Malay beliefs and behaviour with respect to food; the Malay humoral system; conception and pregnancy; government midwife and traditional midwife; giving birth in a Malay village; and the postpartum period.

369 **Drug abuse in East Asia.**
C. P. Spencer, V. Navaratnam. Kuala Lumpur: Oxford University Press, 1981. 227p. bibliog.

This volume primarily considers: the historical origins of contemporary drug abuse in East Asia; contemporary patterns of drug abuse in the region; the profile of the adult and the adolescent drug user; the variety of preventive education, treatment and rehabilitation methods found in the region; and the variety of legal and enforcement responses to drug abuse in East Asia. Despite its title the study considers drug abuse throughout South Asia and South East Asia, as well as East Asia as more conventionally defined, and therefore gives considerable attention to the situation in Malaysia. The extensive bibliography is divided by country: there are approximately thirty references for Malaysia.

370 **Malnutrition, health resources and education in Peninsular Malaysia.**
Tan Loong-Hoe. Singapore: Maruzen Asia, under the auspices of the Institute of Southeast Asian Studies, 1982. 118p. map. bibliog. (Occasional Paper no. 69).

Tan is concerned primarily with two related questions. What is 'the appropriate nutrition education response specific to the malnutrition problem of the rural Malay communities in Peninsular Malaysia?' What would constitute 'a comprehensive and effective rural health care system which is accessible to and acceptable by the client-population', in the context of Peninsular Malaysia? In detail he considers: malnutrition in Peninsular Malaysia with special reference to the rural Malay communities; the causes of malnutrition; the traditional Malay medical health system; the existing modern medical health system; recommendations for a more responsive alternative health care system for the rural Malays;

and an appropriate nutrition education. In conclusion Tan considers 'how effective and to what extent nutrition education can contribute to overcoming the complex malnutrition problems amongst the rural Malay population'.

371 **Marriage and divorce among Malay peasants in Kelantan.**
Yoshihiro Tsubouchi. *Journal of Southeast Asian Studies*, vol. 6, no. 2 (Sept. 1975), p. 135-50.

This paper draws on statistical and descriptive data collected by the author in a rather remote Malay village in Kelantan in 1970-71. It presents a detailed, largely statistical, analysis of marriage, divorce, and remarriage patterns in that community. Particular attention is given to the very high, but recently declining, incidence of divorce among the Kelantan Malays.

372 **Urban low-income housing and development. A case study in Peninsular Malaysia.**
Emiel A. Wegelin. Leiden, The Netherlands; Boston, Massachusetts: Martinus Nijhoff Social Sciences Division, 1978. 347p. 4 maps. bibliog. (Studies in Development and Planning, vol. 6).

The core of this study consists of a sophisticated cost-benefit evaluation of several squatter rehousing schemes carried out by the Malaysian government in the Kelang valley area, (the main focus of urbanization in Peninsular Malaysia), taking account of the different impacts of the schemes on different ethnic and income groups. Particular attention is paid to the social impact of improved housing, such as those related to health, economic productivity, the incidence of crime, fire, and inter-racial attitudes.

Urbanization and the urban population in Peninsular Malaysia, 1970.
See item no. 58.

Public expenditure in Malaysia. Who benefits and why.
See item no. 520.

Malaysia. Growth and equity in a multiracial society.
See item no. 531.

Politics

General

373 As a matter of interest.
Tunku Abdul Rahman. Kuala Lumpur: Heinemann Educational Books (Asia), 1981. 268p.

In the mid-1970s, Tunku acquired an interest in a Penang newspaper, *The Star*. Part of his interest involved him in writing a weekly column in the paper, in which he would either comment on current issues or reminisce over events in Malaysia's recent history, (notably the independence campaign), and the prominent role which he had played in them. This volume brings together a collection of these articles, 'a collection of my thoughts and views on people, events and issues, past and present, with which in one way or the other I have been connected or which are of interest and concern to me'. The forty-three articles initially appeared between August 1977 and May 1980.

374 Contemporary issues in Malaysian politics.
Tunku Abdul Rahman. Petaling Jaya: Pelanduk Publications, 1984. 397p.

This volume consists of a selection of the Tunku's articles which originally appeared in *The Star*. They are grouped under the following four headings: The Malaysian constitution and the role of the Sultans; Malay politics; Islam; Britain and the Look East policy. A number of the articles have appeared in earlier collections of the Tunku's newspaper pieces.

375 **Lest we forget. Further candid reminiscences.**
Tunku Abdul Rahman Putra.   Singapore, Petaling Jaya: Eastern
Universities Press, 1983. 200p.

This is a further collection of articles from the Tunku's regular newspaper
column, originally published in 1980-81. The articles consist not only of candid
reminiscences but also contemporary comment.

376 **Looking back. Monday musings and memories.**
Tunku Abdul Rahman Putra Al-Haj.   Kuala Lumpur: Pustaka
Antara, 1977. 380p.

This volume brings together fifty-three of the Tunku's newspaper articles which
originally appeared between December 1974 and August 1976.

377 **The separation of Singapore from Malaysia. A study in political
involution.**
Robert Allan Andersen.   PhD thesis, The American University,
1973. 276p. bibliog. (Available from University Microfilms, Ann
Arbor, Michigan, order no. 74-13714).

A study which examines the separation of Singapore from Malaysia in 1965 and
subsequent events, 'in terms of both the international factors and the domestic
communal pressures and attitudes which affect[-ed] the leaders in both Singapore
and Malaysia'. There is consideration of: the creation of Malaysia; merger and
separation; the effect of the separation and other internal communal problems on
the international relations of both states; and continuing communal problems,
including the May 1969 riots. It is Andersen's view that there has been a tendency
for Malaysia to fragment into its components, rather than weld into a
homogeneous whole. The study explores 'the possibility of these Malaysian
components merging with neighbouring countries or being absorbed into a new
regional grouping'.

378 **The dynamics of coercion in the Malaysian political process.**
Simon Barraclough.   *Modern Asian Studies*, vol. 19, part 4 (Oct.
1985), p. 797-822.

'Coercion' is here defined as 'the conscious and deliberate application of legally-
sanctioned force by the [Malaysian] regime against those whom it perceives to be
in any way a source of threat to its authority or political primacy'. Barraclough's
essay includes a consideration of the principal coercive mechanisms employed by
the Malaysian authorities, and an examination of some specific examples of their
application. His conclusion challenges both the 'consociational' view of Malaysian
politics, and the radical left assessment of the role of coercion in the political life
of Malaysia: '. . . . the regime has always regarded the strategic application of
coercion as both legitimate and necessary in achieving its societal and economic
goals . . . Yet such coercion has been only one of many strategies to achieve
these ends'.

379 **Malaysia and Singapore. The building of new states.**
Stanley S. Bedlington. Ithaca, New York: Cornell University Press, 1978. 285p. map. bibliog.

Bedlington served in the colonial administration in Malaya from 1948 to 1957, and then in North Borneo until 1963. He then turned to an academic career. At the time he wrote this volume he was a political analyst in the US Department of State. The book falls into four parts. The first provides a survey of the history of Malaya and Singapore before 1945. The second and third parts consider the recent history; the contemporary setting; the political process; and major problems with respect to Malaysia and then Singapore. The final part discusses the history and future status of Brunei.

380 **Class, politics and race in modern Malaysia.**
Martin Brennan. *Journal of Contemporary Asia*, vol. 12, no. 2 (1982), p. 188-215.

As Brennan observes, from the mid-1970s many social scientists have called for 'a more sophisticated incorporation of both race and class' in analyses of contemporary Malaysia. 'Indeed the task facing us now appears to be one of identifying the intersection of race and class and of spelling out and clarifying the relationship between these two structural variables'. His paper thus attempts to 'identify the classes which intersect and occasionally coincide with racial groups in the Malaysian social formation'. He concludes that 'all racial conflict in the Malaysian social formation has its origins in the struggle between classes . . . [Moreover] that the contradictions between fractions of the power-bloc have given rise to a specific conjunctural context in which race is deployed both as a vehicle of legitimation and a mechanism of social control and domination'. This article has been reprinted in: *Southeast Asia. Essays in the political economy of structural change.* Edited by Richard Higgott and Richard Robison. (London: Routledge & Kegan Paul, 1985, p. 93-127).

381 **Class and communal conflict in Malaysia.**
B. N. Cham. *Journal of Contemporary Asia*, vol. 5, no. 4 (1975), p. 446-61.

Cham rejects 'conventional analyses of Malaysian politics and society' which focus largely on 'race' in explaining the perpetuation of racial cleavages and social inequality in Malaysia. Instead he argues that 'class relations' are the key to an understanding of 'the root of communalism and the whole context of Malaysia's social, political and economic development . . . Just as there exists a common [economic] interest between a Malay *Datuk* and a Chinese *Tun*, there is a unity of interests between a Chinese rubber tapper and a Malay fisherman.' Any viable approach to the task of economic and political development in the country must be directed to unite the lower-class members of Malaysian society in 'a common cause to eliminate exploitation and poverty and to fight against racialism'.

382 **Malaysian defence policy. A study in parliamentary attitudes 1963-1973.**
Chandran Jeshurun. Kuala Lumpur: Penerbit Universiti Malaya, under the auspices of the Institute of Southeast Asian Studies, Singapore, 1980. 147p. bibliog.
This is primarily 'an attempt to construct a tentative framework for the study of Malaysian defence policy and the military organization [in the period 1963-73] based essentially on the lengthy reports of the parliamentary debates in the Dewan Rakyat (House of Representatives)'. The main chapters consider: the study of the Malaysian military; the expansion of the armed forces; some important issues in the services; defence in the regional context; and an appraisal of Malaysian defence policy.

383 **Some observations on coalition politics in Penang.**
Chew Huat Hock. *Modern Asian Studies*, vol. 19, part 1 (Feb. 1985), p. 125-46.
As in the case of the Federal Government and the governments of the other states in West Malaysia, Penang is ruled by the Barisan Nasional coalition, comprising primarily the UMNO, MCA, Gerakan, and the MIC. However coalition politics in Penang differs from that at the federal level and from that in the other states, in that the central political role there is played by the Chinese. Chew is primarily concerned with the fierce political rivalry between the component parties of the Barisan Nasional in contemporary Penang, broadly between the UMNO and Gerakan on the one hand, and between MCA and Gerakan on the other. There is also a discussion of the influence of the Federal UMNO over coalition politics in Penang.

384 **The Communist Party of Malaya. Selected documents.**
Published by the South East Asia Documentation Group, 1979. 83p. 2 maps.
This volume brings together some twelve important statements by the Communist Party of Malaya, dating from the 1970s. They include: the new constitution of the party, published in May 1972; an analysis of the May 1969 riots; an exposition of party policies and programmes; and four lengthy statements on the history of the Malayan Communist Party (from 1930) and the Malayan Revolution. Materials used in this publication were 'gathered . . . from transcripts of the Voice of the Malayan Revolution, a clandestine radio of the Communist Party of Malaya'.

385 **Malaysia. Quest for a politics of consensus.**
Kiran Kapur Datar. New Delhi: Vikas Publishing House, 1983. 228p. bibliog.
This is a study of Malaysian politics from 1969 to the early 1980s. Its main chapters examine: the 1969 elections, the riots and their political consequences; a new political model, 1969-71; the National Front [Barisan Nasional]; the Opposition; foreign policy and Malaysian politics; and the 1978 elections.

386 **Tunku Abdul Rahman.**

A. M. Healy. St. Lucia, Australia: University of Queensland
Press, 1982. 36p. bibliog.

A very brief political biography of the man who led Malaya to independence in
1957, and who then became Malaya's first prime minister (until 1970).

387 **Class and communalism in Malaysia. Politics in a dependent**
capitalist state.

Hua Wu Yin. London: Zed Books, in conjunction with Matram
Books, 1983. 230p. map. bibliog.

Hua 'seeks to highlight the mechanisms of oppression that maintain the conditions
responsible for Malaysia's economic subordination to metropolitan capital'. He
argues that the political domination by the ruling class in Malaysia has been
established through communalism – through the denial of democratic rights to the
Chinese and Indians and through the deflection of the economic grievances of the
Malay masses into an ideological support of the Malay ruling class. He concludes
that only through recognition of the rights of the Chinese and Indian minorities
'can the masses be united on a democratic and equal basis, and the Malay workers
and peasants be freed from the ideology that ties it to its own ruling class'. He
pursues his analysis through a consideration of Malaysian history from pre-
colonial Malay society; colonial rule and the anti-colonial movement; the
Emergency; the 1969 riots; to the New Economic Policy.

388 **The Malays. Their problems and future.**

S. Husin Ali. Kuala Lumpur: Heinemann Educational Books
(Asia), 1981. 143p. bibliog.

This work seeks to analyse the major religious, social, economic, and political
problems confronting the Malay people; and to envisage the possible future for
the Malays. The author's central theme is that, although the Malay élite are now
enjoying very considerable political and economic privileges, the Malay masses
continue to suffer great disadvantage and deprivation. The author, a prominent
Malaysian sociologist, wrote this book whilst he was held in government
detention.

389 **Of race, class, and clientship in Malaysia.**

Roger Kershaw. *Journal of Commonwealth and Comparative*
Politics, vol. 14, no. 3 (Nov. 1976), p. 299-303.

This is a review article of Karl von Vorys [429], Margaret Clark Roff [465],
William R. Roff [445], and S. Husin Ali [552]. Kershaw is primarily concerned
with the relevance of a moderate class analysis of West Malaysian society and its
alternative, the communalist model of political identity and action. In a
concluding paragraph, where the discussion centres on S. Husin Ali, Kershaw
argues that 'in the best of circumstances the emergence of class-consciousness and
class leaders among the poor peasants must be a long drawn-out process . . .
Nevertheless, the rise of new, class-conscious leaders from among the landless
peasants is assisted, in the long run, by the widening economic gap in the villages
and the changing life-style of established village leaders'.

390 **Whither democracy? An analysis of the Malaysian experience.**
Edited by Khoo Yoke Kuan. [n.p.]: Aliran Publications, 1978.
88p.

Aliran is a non-communal, reformist pressure group formed in Malaysia in 1977.
This publication reproduces the speeches and subsequent discussions from a
forum on 'Democracy in Malaysia', organized by Aliran in December 1977. There
were three panels: democracy and the man-in-the-street; democracy for
development; and the future of democracy in Malaysia. The participants included
academics, trade unionists, politicians, parliamentarians, lawyers, journalists, and
leaders of interest groups.

391 **Communism in Malaysia and Singapore. A contemporary survey.**
Justus M. van der Kroef. The Hague: Martinus Nijhoff, 1967.
268p.

This study of communism in Malaysia and Singapore is primarily concerned with
the period from the formation of Malaysia in September 1963 through to 1967. It
focuses mainly on political developments, social and economic considerations
being noted only when an understanding of political change demands it. There are
separate chapters on Singapore, Peninsular Malaysia, Sarawak, and Sabah and
Brunei, although as communist activity in the mid-1960s appears to have been
strongest in Sarawak and Singapore, it is those two territories which receive major
attention. A further chapter considers the influences of Jakarta and Beijing on
communist activity in Malaysia and Singapore during the early and mid-1960s.

392 **Human rights in Malaysia.**
John A. Lent. *Journal of Contemporary Asia*, vol. 14, no. 4
(1984), p. 442-58.

This paper reviews the historical perspective behind 'repressive' legislation and
actions in Malaysia; considers in detail 'the recent inhibiting legislation, especially
acts that have amended the Constitution and have perpetuated a state of
emergency'; and examines 'repressive actions affecting societal institutions such as
the political system, press, labour and trade unions, academia and the legal
profession'.

393 **Time bombs in Malaysia. Problems of nation-building in Malaysia.**
Lim Kit Siang. Petaling Jaya: Democratic Action Party, 1978.
2nd ed. 346p.

Lim Kit Siang, Secretary-General of the Democratic Action Party, is probably the
most outspoken parliamentary critic of the Malaysian Government. This volume
brings together 41 of his speeches, grouped under the following main headings:
nation-building, democracy and corruption; the New Economic Policy, Malaysian
plans and budgets; human rights and constitutional guarantees; and education and
labour. The speeches are preceded by a number of articles, including a
'commentary' on the 1978 general election (which had taken place immediately
prior to the publication of this volume); and a statement of the charges under the
Official Secrets Act by which Lim had been arrested in April 1978.

394 **Ethnic and class relations in Malaysia.**
Lim Mah Hui. *Journal of Contemporary Asia*, vol. 10, nos 1 & 2 (1980), p. 130-54.

This paper attempts to analyse 'the interplay between class and ethnicity [in Malaysia] from an historical and structural perspective'. It argues that 'the fundamental dimension in ethnic relations is not found in cultural diversity; rather it is rooted in economic relations, specifically in the relations of production and exchange entered into by members of different classes who also happen to be members of different ethnic communities'. In brief, 'the interactions between class and ethnicity provide the crucial explanation for ethnic conflict'. The analysis is primarily historical, covering the pre-colonial period to the present.

395 **The political economy of state policies in Malaysia.**
Lim Mah Hui, William Canak. *Journal of Contemporary Asia*, vol. 11, no. 2 (1981), p. 208-24.

Lim and Canak observe that in contemporary Malaysia, the dominant class is divided into three fragments – 'the Malay governing class which has control of state power but without a strong economic base, the non-Malay (predominantly Chinese) capitalist class which constitutes the most developed segment of the local bourgeoisie, and the metropolitan or international bourgeoisie who still retain substantial ownership and control of Malaysia's economy but without direct control of state apparatus after independence in 1957'. No one fragment of the dominant class is able to achieve hegemony: and 'it is this crisis of hegemony which forms the basis of the different forms of social conflict, particularly ethnic, religious, and class conflicts in Malaysia'.

396 **The Malay dilemma.**
Mahathir bin Mohamed.   Singapore: Donald Moore for Asia Pacific Press, 1970. 188p.

In late 1969 Dr. Mahathir was expelled from the UMNO for his leading part in the strong criticism of the then prime minister, Tunku Abdul Rahman, which had arisen in the wake of the May racial riots. In this book – which is essentially an assertive statement of Malay rights – Mahathir seeks to explain the causes of the 1969 riots; the reasons for Malay economic backwardness (including the influence of heredity and environment, as well as the experience of colonial rule); and the Malay insistence that the immigrant populations must in time become 'real' Malaysians – abandoning their language and their culture, and speaking only Malay. Dr. Mahathir's analysis was felt by the authorities to be too provocative in the tense racial atmosphere of the post-riot years (for it also contains sharp criticisms of the Malays themselves), and the book was banned in Malaysia, even after Mahathir, readmitted to the UMNO, had become deputy prime minister under Hussein Onn. The ban was lifted after Mahathir became prime minister in 1981.

397 **Malaysia: what price 'success'?**
Southeast Asia Chronicle, no. 72 (April 1980), 28p.

This issue is designed to be an introduction to the political economy of West Malaysia. It contains three main articles: 1) Malaysian underdevelopment: which argues that 'the pattern of postwar Malaysian economic growth . . . has resulted in increasingly unequal distribution of income and the impoverishment of larger and larger numbers of workers and peasants'; 2) The power game in Malaysia: this includes a profile of a detainee, Syed Husin Ali; an examination of the restriction of the trade union movement; and a consideration of increasing American arms sales to Malaysia. In general this section provides an outline of Malaysian political history 'and a detailed examination of repression in various aspects of Malaysian life'; 3) Race and class in Malaysia: which argues that although 'the Malay élite manipulates tensions among the country's ethnic groups to enhance its own power . . . Malaysians of all races are coming to recognize that these tensions have economic roots'. This section also includes an article, by Judith Strauch, on Malaysia's response to the Boat People – the ethnic factor.

398 **Barisan Nasional. Coalition government in Malaysia.**
Diane K. Mauzy.   Kuala Lumpur, Singapore: Marican & Sons (Malaysia), 1983. 187p. bibliog.
This book is essentially concerned with the origins and nature of Malaysia's dominant political coalition. Its four main chapters discuss: the precursor of the Barisan Nasional, the Alliance; the political coalition-building which took place following the 1969 racial riots; the formation of the Barisan Nasional and the 1974 General Election; and the tensions and stresses within the coalition, as well as the Barisan Nasional's electoral performance in 1978 and 1982.

399 **The Mahathir administration in Malaysia: discipline through Islam.**
Diane K. Mauzy, R. S. Milne.   *Pacific Affairs*, vol. 56, no. 4 (winter 1983-84), p. 617-48.
At a general level, this article considers the extent to which the Mahathir administration (July 1981-) has pursued policies different from those of earlier Malaysian governments. In detail it considers: 1) 'the new administration's management of the parties in the Barisan Nasional, . . . political aspects of federal-state relations, and . . . the administration's policies on human rights'; 2) 'its drive for clean and efficient government and, in the economic context, its "Look East Policy" which seeks to learn from the experience of Japan and South Korea'; and 3) 'government policy as regards Islam'. Mauzy and Milne argue that while there has been little change under the first heading, 'under the others a new theme has emerged which links the promotion of discipline and the work ethic to appropriate Islamic moral values'.

400 **Malaysian politics.**
Gordon P. Means.   London: Hodder & Stoughton, 1976. 2nd ed. 483p. 2 maps. bibliog.
The most detailed and comprehensive chronological account of Malaysian politics to appear thus far. This work covers the period from the end of the Japanese occupation through to the mid-1970s. Among the twenty-two chapters are those concerned with: the colonial legacy; the Malayan Communist Party; the radical and conservative nationalists in the period 1945-48; communalism and the Emergency; the introduction of elections in the 1950s; the *Merdeka* Constitution; the Alliance Government; the creation of Malaysia; confrontation with Indonesia;

the politics of federalism in East Malaysia; the May 1969 riots; the restructuring of Malaysian politics in the early 1970s.

401 **Prince and premier. A biography of Tunku Abdul Rahman Putra al-Haj. First Prime Minister of the Federation of Malaya.**
Harry Miller. London: George G. Harrap, in association with Donald Moore, Singapore, 1959. 224p.

This is a congenial, uncritical biography of the Tunku, produced in the early years of independence. It was written with the full assistance of the subject, who indeed also provides a brief foreword.

402 **Government and politics in Malaysia.**
R. S. Milne. Boston, Massachusetts: Houghton Mifflin, 1967. 259p. 2 maps.

Milne provides an account and analysis of government and politics in Malaysia (and Singapore) essentially from 1945 to the mid-1960s. The main chapters are: Malaya and Singapore after 1945; the Borneo territories and the formation of Malaysia; federal-state relations; political parties, elections, and interest groups; the Federal Parliament and state legislatures; the federal and state executives and the conference of rulers; the civil service; local government and the judiciary; foreign policy and defence; Singapore, in and out of Malaysia; and national unity. The majority of chapters have an extensive list of suggested readings.

403 **Politics and government in Malaysia.**
R. S. Milne, Diane K. Mauzy. Singapore: Federal Publications, under the auspices of the Institute of Southeast Asian Studies, Singapore, 1978. 406p. bibliog.

This book was originally intended to be a revised edition of R. S. Milne's *Government and politics in Malaysia* (Boston, Massachusetts: Houghton Mifflin, 1967). In the event, this is essentially a new book. It is mainly concerned with the decade from 1969. In this respect it considers: '1969' and its consequences; federal-state relations; political parties and interest groups; the formal organs of government; foreign policy and security; economics and politics – the New Economic Policy; and the styles of politics – national unity and stability. Together with Gordon P. Means (q.v.), this is the best introduction to the contemporary politics of Malaysia. Unlike Milne's 1967 book, this study does not consider politics in Singapore, except where it influences politics in Malaysia.

404 **Hussein Onn. A tryst with destiny.**
J. Victor Morais. Singapore: Times Books International, 1981. 224p.

Morais' study of Malaysia's third premier (from January 1976 to July 1981), is concerned mainly with his years as prime minister, although it was in fact completed before Hussein Onn retired from office. The tone is uncritical, indeed almost adulatory. One half of the book is devoted to extracts from Hussein Onn's speeches and statements.

405 **Mahathir. A profile in courage.**
J. Victor Morais. Kuala Lumpur, Singapore: Eastern Universities
Press, 1982. 294p.

Dr. Mahathir has been Prime Minister of Malaysia since July 1981. Morais is concerned principally with Mahathir's administration as premier. The tone is uncritical, indeed almost adulatory. Approximately one-third of the book is devoted to reports on Mahathir's speeches and statements.

406 **The Malaysian predicament: towards a new theoretical frontier.**
Chris Mullard, Martin Brennan. *Journal of Contemporary Asia*,
vol. 8, no. 3 (1978), p. 341-54.

This article argues that 'both the model and the conceptual and analytical apparatus' provided by pluralism 'is not only inappropriate for a sociological analysis and reappraisal of Malaysian society but that it also forms a central part of the political ideology of the ruling racial or cultural bloc'. Mullard and Brennan thus suggest that 'rather than relying on an outmoded pluralist perspective which has become ideologized by those who wish to maintain power and control', there should be constructed a new analytical framework – 'one which embraces racial, cultural, and emerging class realities in Malaysian society'.

407 **Intellectuals, religion, and politics in a divided society: Malaysia.**
Daniel Regan. PhD thesis, Yale University, New Haven,
Connecticut, 1977. 331p. bibliog. (Available from University
Microfilms, Ann Arbor, Michigan, order no. 77-27456).

This dissertation reviews 'the religio-cultural and political orientations of Malaysian intellectuals in the light of prevailing theories about intellectual life'. It draws on interviews with 133 people. It indicates 'major differences in religious commitment along ethnic lines'. In addition, Malaysian intellectuals are said to be 'more integrated into than alienated from their society', and to be pragmatists rather than ideologists.

408 **The report of the International Mission of Lawyers to Malaysia.**
London: Marram Books, 1983. 66p.

This is a report of a mission of international lawyers to Malaysia in early August 1982 whose primary aim was 'to examine the working of the national security legislation as it is related to those charged with offences under the Internal Security Act 1960, the mandatory nature of the death sentences for certain of those offences, and the trial procedures in security cases which lead to the mandatory death sentence [under the Essential (Security Cases) (Amendment) Regulations 1975] . . . The mission also investigated the position of those detained without trial under the Internal Security Act 1960 (ISA)'.

409 **Capitalist development and the formation of the bureaucratic bourgeoisie in Peninsular Malaysia.**
T. Salem. *Kajian Malaysia* (Journal of Malaysian Studies), vol. 1, no. 2 (Dec. 1983), p. 71-104.

A paper which seeks to understand 'the particular historical circumstances which have allowed for the transformation of a bureaucratic governing stratum into a bureaucratic bourgeoisie in Peninsular Malaysia'. The major part of the paper involves a discussion of 'those aspects of class formation under colonial rule that are essential to understanding the recent ascendance of a bureaucratic capitalist class'; an analysis of post-colonial society, in which 'a relatively free hand was given to the Malay bureaucratic stratum to use the state machinery to satisfy its interests'; and a consideration of the 'self-conscious transformation of the Malay bureaucratic stratum into a fraction of the bourgeoisie' since the early 1970s.

410 **Political ideology in Malaysia. Reality and the beliefs of an elite.**
James C. Scott. Kuala Lumpur: University of Malaya Press; New Haven, Connecticut: Yale University Press, 1968. 302p.

This work is concerned with the political beliefs of the Malaysian administrative élite in the middle 1960s, for example their attitudes towards Western political ideology, institutions and practices; their level of political cynicism; their degree of attachment to formal ideology. The analysis is based principally on extensive interviews with seventeen Malaysian civil servants. The interview guide used to structure the conversations with the informants, and the questions used to measure their attitudes, are reproduced in appendixes. However it should be noted that Scott is concerned less with 'the unique and particular character of the Malaysian experience' than with drawing out those political beliefs and experiences which would be common to many newly independent and relatively poor states.

411 **Tun Razak. His life and times.**
William Shaw. Kuala Lumpur: Longman Malaysia, 1976. 267p. 2 maps. bibliog.

An essentially political biography of Malaysia's second prime minister, who was premier from September 1971 to January 1976. It does not concentrate unduly on his final years of power, but gives considerable attention to his early years and education, and in particular to his political career from the early 1950s through to 1971. The tone is uncritical and rather reverential.

412 **The advocacy of Malaysia – before 1961.**
Mohamed Noordin Sopiee. *Modern Asian Studies*, vol. 7, part 4 (Oct. 1973), p. 717-32.

It is commonly argued that the idea for a Federation of Malaysia (to include Peninsular Malaya, Singapore, Sabah, and Sarawak) was launched by the Malayan Prime Minister, Tunku Abdul Rahman, in a speech to foreign correspondents in May 1961; and that in making this proposal, the Tunku was guided mainly by a desire to ensure Kuala Lumpur's control over the internal security of Singapore, in view of the 'seemingly perpetual leftward movement of Singapore politics'. According to this view, the Borneo territories were to be included in the federation as a racial counter-balance to Singapore's overwhelmingly Chinese population. Mohamed Noordin Sopiee challenges this orthodox explanation, arguing first that the Tunku had been considering a Malaysia federation from the mid-1950s; and second, that he envisaged at that early stage the inclusion in the federation of the Borneo territories, but not Singapore; 'but was informed [by the British Government] that the Federation could not have these territories *unless* she agreed also to take Singapore off Whitehall's hands. This the Tunku was not prepared to do till 1961'.

413　**Class and race in West Malaysia.**
Michael Stenson. *Bulletin of Concerned Asian Scholars*, vol. 8, no. 2 (April-June 1976), p. 45-54.

Stenson calls for a 'more critical analysis of the sources and significance of class as well as racial conflict' in writings on Malaysian history and on contemporary Malaysia. For example he argues that the race riots of May 1969 had their roots in intra-Malay class conflict: 'the youthful rioters were unconsciously warning the too-complaisant, too accommodatory UMNO élite which had for so long collaborated with the urban non-Malays while failing to uplift its own racial group'. Stenson gives main consideration to such intra-Malay polarization: will it lay 'the foundations for multi-racial peasant-worker alliances against the power of the ruling Malay élite . . . or is Malay radicalism more likely to remain channeled along racial lines, seeking solutions to the Malay dilemma in demands for further Malay special privileges and assistance?' In a postscript he notes: 'there is [as yet] little or no hint to the outside observer of multi-racial class alliances'. There is abundant evidence [in the mid-1970s] 'of a continuing polarization on racial lines'.

414　**Without fear or favour.**
Tan Chee Khoon.　Singapore, Petaling Jaya: Eastern Universities Press, 1984. 339p.

Tan Chee Khoon was a very prominent opposition member of the Malaysian Parliament from 1964 to 1978. Following his retirement from active politics he became a political columnist, primarily for *The Star* newspaper. This volume contains a collection of his articles, along with several previously unpublished pieces. They are grouped under the following headings: the constitution and the laws; the leaders (this section includes transcripts of interviews with a number of political leaders, including Mahathir); the cabinet and the government; political parties; elections; and education and language. Tan's views are notably outspoken.

415　**Ethnic politics in Malaysia.**
R. K. Vasil.　New Delhi: Radiant Publishers, 1980. 234p. bibliog.

Vasil argues that since independence, Malaysia, which 'was founded on the principles of multi-racialism and representative democracy', has 'tragically declined into a virtually authoritarian *Malay* Malaysia controlled and managed largely by the indigenous Malays to promote their sectional interests'. His analysis covers the period from the final years of British rule to the early 1970s and considers, for example: the constitution of independent Malaya; the Alliance and Malay political paramountcy from 1957; the political parties of the non-Malays;

the threat to Malay political paramountcy from 1963; and the end of the Alliance – the trend towards Malay rule.

416 **Politics in a plural society. A study of non-communal political parties in West Malaysia.**
R. K. Vasil. Kuala Lumpur: Oxford University Press, 1971. 338p. bibliog.

This study considers the history and position in the mid-1960s of the principal non-communal political parties in West Malaysia – notably the Independence of Malaya Party and the Party Negara; Labour Party; Party Raayat; Malayan People's Socialist Front; People's Progressive Party; and the United Democratic Party. A postscript provides a brief survey of political developments in West Malaysia from 1967 through to 1970, and therefore includes consideration of the formation of the Democratic Action Party and the Gerakan Rakyat Malaysia. An opening chapter discusses communalism and the political process in West Malaysia.

417 **Military-civilian relations in South-East Asia.**
Edited by Zakaria Haji Ahmad, Harold Crouch. Singapore: Oxford University Press, 1985. 368p. bibliog.

This volume contains an essay [p. 118-35], by Zakaria Haji Ahmad, on military-civilian relations in Malaysia. It is primarily concerned with explaining why the Malaysian Armed Forces has not intervened in the political processes of the country since independence: this largely involves a consideration of the 'institution-building' of the military. Zakaria notes that the military is Malay-dominated and therefore could be expected to support the Malay régime in power: but he argues that its apolitical stance is more important than its ethnic composition.

418 **Violence at the periphery: a brief survey of armed communism in Malaysia.**
Zakaria Haji Ahmad, Zakaria Hamid. In: *Armed communist movements in Southeast Asia.* Edited by Lim Joo-Jock, Vani S. Aldershot, England: Gower Publishing, issued under the auspices of the Institute of Southeast Asian Studies, Singapore, 1984, p. 51-65.

Provides a survey of the main features of the two armed communist movements in contemporary Malaysia – the Communist Party of Malaya; and the North Kalimantan Communist Party. The analysis considers: the objectives and approaches of the two parties; leadership and organizational changes; strategy and tactics; ethnic composition and following; ideological orientations; and international implications.

Class, race and colonialism in West Malaysia. The Indian case.
See item no. 227.

Nation-building in Malaysia 1946-1974.
See item no. 264.

Contemporary issues on Malaysian religions.
See item no. 336.

Public policy toward religion in Malaysia.
See item no. 342.

Malaysian politics and the 1978 election.
See item no. 432.

Politics and business. A study of Multi-Purpose Holdings Berhad.
See item no. 534.

Ethnicity, class and development. Malaysia.
See item no. 551.

Communal politics

419 **May 13: before and after.**
Tunku Abdul Rahman Putra Al-Haj. Kuala Lumpur: Utusan
Melayu Press, 1969. 207p.
This is the Tunku's own account and analysis of the racial riots of May 1969,
written in their immediate aftermath. He argues that the communists and their
supporters were the principal instigators of the racial violence: but he also has
harsh words for his critics within the UMNO itself.

420 **13 May 1969. A historical survey of Sino-Malay relations.**
Leon Comber.   Kuala Lumpur: Heinemann Educational Books
(Asia), 1983. 134p. 2 maps. bibliog.
Comber provides an account (spread over six chapters), of Sino-Malay relations
from the time of the earliest Chinese settlements through to the racial riots of
May 1969. Just one chapter is devoted to an account of the riots themselves; and
one concluding chapter considers the aftermath of the riots through to the
resumption of parliamentary business in February 1971.

421 **Multi-ethnic politics: the case of Malaysia.**
Cynthia H. Enloe. Berkeley, California: Center for South and
Southeast Asia Studies, University of California, 1970. 172p.
bibliog. (Research Monograph no. 2).
This study of multi-ethnic politics in Peninsular Malaysia is concerned with the
period 1950-67. It concentrates on government policy-making, and on one policy
area in particular – that of education. There is consideration of the emergence of
education policy as an ethnic issue; the issue of national language; and of the

activities of voluntary associations concerned with education. This is a valuable study of ethnic divisions and communal bargaining in Malaysia in the period prior to May 1969.

422 The May thirteenth incident and democracy in Malaysia.
Goh Cheng Teik. Kuala Lumpur: Oxford University Press, 1971. 76p.

Goh's principal concern is not to describe the racial riots of May 1969 (only nine pages are devoted to an account of the events themselves), but to provide an analysis of the causes of the riots, and to consider their possible effects 'on the future of democratic government in Malaysia'. There are, in a glossary, brief descriptions of the political parties and party personalities involved; and statistical appendixes containing the MCA's federal election results and the Selangor state election results in 1969.

423 An analysis of the distribution of rewards in the Malaysian Alliance coalition (1959-1973).
Patrick Martin Mayerchak. PhD thesis, The American University, 1975. 230p. bibliog. (Available from University Microfilms, Ann Arbor, Michigan, order no. 76-11466).

This study focuses on the distribution of rewards (in practice, cabinet portfolios) among the members of the Alliance (UMNO, MCA, MIC) between 1959 and 1974. Mayerchak argues that in this period, an Alliance party frequently placed different values on different cabinet posts: moreover, any two parties may have valued the same cabinet post differently. In these circumstances, it is argued, the nature of the distribution of rewards among Alliance members would be determined by which, rather than how many, portfolios were acquired. This is not a detailed study of Malaysian politics as such, but is rather a contribution to political coalition theory, drawing on the Malaysian experience.

424 'Special Rights' as a strategy for development. The case of Malaysia.
Gordon P. Means. *Comparative Politics*, vol. 5, no. 1 (Oct. 1972), p. 29-61.

Means seeks to explain how the strategy of providing 'special privileges' to the Malays has evolved and been applied in Malaysia; examines the consequences and effectiveness of this strategy; and considers the longer-range implications of the policies being pursued under this strategy. His analysis includes consideration of: colonial rule and Malay special rights; educational special rights under colonial rule; post-war politics and Malay special rights; the psychological effects of Malay special rights in contemporary Malaysia; the contemporary political effects of special rights; the national ideology – *rukunegara*; and the New Economic Policy. In a conclusion, Means asks: 'will the concentration of government effort to induce social change in one racial community only tend to perpetuate a new form of communally defined functional compartmentalization? Such a possibility is more likely if special rights are viewed as permanent policy rather than as appropriate transitional strategy.'

425 **The May 13 tragedy. A report.**
National Operations Council, Kuala Lumpur. October, 1969. 96p.
This is the official government report on the May 1969 racial riots, prepared by
the National Operations Council under the directorship of Tun Razak. The major
part of the report provides an account and analysis of the events, both short- and
long-term, leading to the riots, and of the riots themselves. There is also a brief
outline of the historical background, and an outline of 'the tasks ahead'.

426 **Race and politics in urban Malaya.**
Alvin Rabushka. Stanford, California: Hoover Institution Press,
1973. 148p. bibliog.
This volume examines 'the values, attitudes, and social and political behaviour of
the man in the street' in Kuala Lumpur and George Town (Penang), to determine
'how these two urban populations view the racial question', both in its political
context and at the level of personal (social) interaction. The analysis draws
principally on a survey conducted in Kuala Lumpur and George Town in early
1967.

427 **Communalism and the political process in Malaya.**
K. J. Ratnam. Kuala Lumpur: University of Malaya Press, 1965.
248p. map. bibliog.
This work is concerned with the communal problem in Malaya in the period from
1945 to the early 1960s, a period in which the Chinese and Indian communities
became firmly part of the settled population of the country. Ratnam concentrates
on those issues which were the source of communal disagreement, including,
notably, the issue of rights to Malayan citizenship, and the terms of the
independence settlement. There is analysis of the special position of the Malays,
(which involves a consideration of religion and language issues); a review of the
main political parties in this period; and an analysis of the 1955 and 1959 general
elections.

428 **The Kuala Lumpur riots and the Malaysian political system.**
Anthony Reid. *Australian Outlook*, vol. 23, no. 3 (Dec. 1969),
p. 258-78.
This is essentially a personal record, prepared without access to official reports, of
the origins and, in particular, the course of the 1969 racial riots. It was written
soon after those events by an expatriate lecturer in history at the University of
Malaya.

429 **Democracy without consensus. Communalism and political stability
in Malaysia.**
Karl von Vorys. Princeton, New Jersey: Princeton University
Press, 1975. 443p. 2 maps.
The author provides a detailed description and analysis of West Malaysian politics
from the Japanese occupation through to the early 1970s: however, the major part
of the study covers the period from independence in 1957, through the communal
crisis of 1969, to the restoration of political stability in the post-riot years. The

author argues that Malaysia's independence and post-independence leaders were, and are, influenced by two principal considerations: first, the realization that a viable political system in Malaysia would have to come to terms with the country's deeply ingrained communal cleavages; and second, their own preference for democratic politics. Consequently Malaysian leaders 'set out to establish a viable, democratic system not based on a national community, but on the cooperation of discrete communal groups': in other words, democracy without consensus.

430   **Race relations in Malaysia.**
      Wan Hashim.   Kuala Lumpur: Heinemann Educational Books
      (Asia), 1983. 127p. bibliog.

This study has two principal aims: to examine race relations or communalism in Malaysia over the period from the early 1900s to the early 1970s; and to examine, in the context of Malaysia, 'the paradox where increased economic development and social change heighten and exacerbate communal cleavages rather than diminish them'. In detail this study considers: the formation of a plural society under British colonial rule; the origins and development of nationalism in pre-independence Malaya, which in turn 'gave rise to the formation of communal socio-political organizations which intensified communal tension and brought about racial polarization'; the demographic, economic, socio-cultural, and political impediments to national integration; and attempts by the Malaysian government to achieve integration and unity after May 1969. The study is concerned only with Peninsular Malaysia.

Race, politics and moderation. A study of the Malaysian electoral process.
See item no. 433.

Elections

431   **Malaysia's 1982 general election.**
      Harold Crouch.   Singapore: Institute of Southeast Asian Studies,
      1982. 70p. (Research Notes and Discussion Paper no. 34).

Crouch provides a general overview of the 1982 Malaysian general election, written in the month following the poll. He discusses: the political parties which contested the election; the contest within the Barisan Nasional; the contest between the government and the opposition; and the new federal and state governments.

432   **Malaysian politics and the 1978 election.**
      Edited by Harold Crouch, Lee Kam Hing, Michael Ong.   Kuala
      Lumpur: Oxford University Press, 1980. 330p.

This volume is concerned not only with the 1978 national election in Malaysia, but also with providing an analysis of the main Malaysian political parties and of recent political developments in important regions of the country. The twelve papers by various authors include discussion of: the UMNO (United Malays National Organization) crisis of 1975-1977; PAS (Parti Islam se Malaysia) and the 1978 election; the UMNO-PAS contest in Kedah; the communal parties and the urban Malay vote; the DAP and the 1978 election; the peninsular non-Malay parties in the Barisan Nasional; a view of the election from a Chinese New Village; and Sarawak at the polls. There is also a very brief analysis of the actual results of the 1978 election, as well as a substantial statistical break-down of the poll. Five political cartoons used by the parties during the campaign are reproduced.

433 **Race, politics and moderation. A study of the Malaysian electoral process.**
Ismail Kassim. Singapore: Times Books International, 1979. 143p. bibliog.

This is a study of racial and political accommodation in contemporary Malaysia, using the example of the 1978 general election which Ismail Kassim covered as a journalist working for the Singapore newspaper, *New Nation*. The major part of the book, therefore, provides an account of the 'prenomination manoeuvrings', the electoral campaign itself, and the results of the 1978 poll. This is preceded by a discussion of the political framework and electoral setting; and is followed by an examination of the racial factor in Malaysian politics. There is a postscript which surveys political developments from the election in July to the end of 1978.

434 **The Malayan parliamentary election of 1964.**
K. J. Ratnam, R. S. Milne. Singapore: University of Malaya Press, 1967. 467p. 2 maps.

The major part of this book is devoted to an account of political issues and party activities during the 1964 Malayan parliamentary election campaign; the role of the press and of radio in that campaign; and an analysis of the election results. There is also a survey of Malayan politics in the period 1959-64; a consideration of the district elections held in Sarawak in 1963 and in Sabah at various times between 1962 and 1964; and a consideration of the Singapore Assembly election of 1963. The study is essentially descriptive: some tentative hypotheses and speculations are reserved for a concluding chapter.

435 **The 1969 parliamentary election in West Malaysia.**
K. J. Ratnam, R. S. Milne. *Pacific Affairs*, vol. 43, no. 2 (summer 1970), p. 203-26.

This article provides a very detailed analysis of the actual results of the May 1969 parliamentary election in West Malaysia. 'What did the actual results show about support or lack of support, and by what groups, for the Alliance government as opposed to the interpretations later placed upon the results?' The article is not concerned with the violent events and political upheaval which succeeded the declaration of the results.

436 **The Malaysian general election of 1969: a political analysis.**
Martin Rudner. *Modern Asian Studies*, vol. 4, part 1 (Jan. 1970), p. 1-21.
A consideration of the 1969 Malaysian general election which examines: the political parties; the candidates; the results, by party count, by states, by urban-rural pattern, by racial community, and by popular vote. A brief conclusion provides a political evaluation of the 1969 election.

Malay political activity

437 **Malay politics in Malaysia. A study of the United Malays National Organization and Party Islam.**
John Funston. Kuala Lumpur: Heinemann Educational Books (Asia), 1980. 326p. bibliog.
This work traces the history of the two major Malay political parties, focusing principally on the period 1945-69. The first three chapters present an overview of the pre-1969 Malaysian political system, and an analysis of Malay politics from the colonial period through to the late 1960s. There follows an account of the early development of UMNO (United Malays National Organization) and PAS (Parti Islam Se Malaysia); an analysis of the backgrounds of the party leaders; an examination of party ideologies; and an account of their formal organization, internal politics, and mobilization of support. The final two chapters consider developments from 1969 to the death of Tun Abdul Razak in January 1976 – involving the suspension of parliamentary government after the May 1969 riots, and the restructuring of the political system after 1971.

438 **The origins of Parti Islam Se Malaysia.**
John Funston. *Journal of Southeast Asian Studies*, vol. 7, no. 1 (March 1976), p. 58-73.
This article considers the origins of the Parti Islam Se Malaysia (PAS) in the late 1940s and early 1950s; and offers an interpretation of the various ideological forces that gave rise to the formation of this party. Material from this article also appears in Funston's *Malay politics in Malaysia. A study of the United Malays National Organization and Party Islam* (Kuala Lumpur, 1980).

439 **The 'East Coast' in Malayan politics: episodes of resistance and integration in Kelantan and Trengganu.**
Roger Kershaw. *Modern Asian Studies*, vol. 11, part 4 (Oct. 1977), p. 515-41.
Kershaw is primarily concerned with politics – mainly electoral politics – in the east coast states of Kelantan and Trengganu in the period from independence to the mid-1970s. He thus focuses mainly on the electoral conflicts in those states between UMNO, which as the principal component of the Alliance maintained

control of the central government, and PAS. Kershaw's main theme is that 'resistance [in Kelantan and Trengganu] to centralizing pressures has rarely had separatist overtones but has tended to express rejection of particular developments in the west coast polity from a standpoint of moral superiority. Resistance [thus] . . . should not be interpreted as a failure of national integration'. A series of appendixes provides extracts from PAS and UMNO, as well as Parti Sosialis Rakyat Malaysia and United Independents, electoral manifestos (in 1969 and 1974) for Kelantan and Trengganu.

440 Islam and politics in a Malay state. Kelantan 1838-1969.

Clive S. Kessler. Ithaca, New York: Cornell University Press, 1978. 274p. 4 maps. bibliog.

Kessler's work is principally a community study of a market township in Kelantan (Jelawat), and its surrounding villages, although it also provides a brief social and political history of Kelantan as a whole from the early 19th century to the Japanese occupation. It focuses on the Pan-Malayan Islamic Party (Parti Islam), an essentially populist movement which secured political power in the state at the end of the 1950s, in competition with parties led by the leading noble families in the state, and held that power for more than a decade. More specifically there is analysis of, for example: the impact of colonial rule upon Kelantanese society and politics; and the background to and conduct of political rivalry between the Pan-Malayan Islamic Party (PMIP) and the United Malays National Organization (UMNO) in Jelawat from the early 1950s. Finally there is a consideration of the political significance of Kelantanese Islam, 'as a powerful social institution commanded by the old families and . . . as an ideological and cultural force wielded against them by the peasant-backed PMIP'.

441 Islam, society and political behaviour: some comparative implications of the Malay case.

Clive S. Kessler. *The British Journal of Sociology*, vol. 23, no. 1 (March 1972), p. 33-50.

This study rests upon the argument that Islam is not, as has so often been maintained, 'qualitatively special and different [from other universalistic religions], but special only in the diminished sense that it presents, in a revealingly accentuated form . . . the tensions between a religious morality and social experience'. Kessler draws on his research in Kelantan, which was directed towards examining 'the relation between the political behaviour of Muslims and the Islamic intellectual heritage of ideas about the way in which societies ought ideally to be constituted and power exercised within them'. Specifically he seeks to explain the electoral success in Kelantan of the opposition Pan-Malayan Islamic Party (PMIP) from 1959. He argues that the Islamic vision of society, manipulated and put forward by the PMIP, 'has been the means of a morally-informed criticism and rejection of the Alliance's policies for the creation of a new national society; while that same vision of the just society . . . has provided the behavioural rhetoric in which a peasantry, whose mundane lives are far from being principled and unmaterialistic, become momentarily in their own eyes the kind of people who would populate the envisaged just society of Islam'.

442 **Muslim identity and political behaviour in Kelantan.**
Clive S. Kessler. In: *Kelantan. Religion, society and politics in a Malay state.* Edited by William R. Roff. Kuala Lumpur: Oxford University Press, 1974. p. 272-313.

The aim of this essay is twofold. It seeks to provide an explanation, 'in the context of the overall development of Kelantanese society from precolonial times, of the electoral successes of the Pan-Malayan Islamic Party, or PMIP, in Kelantan since 1959'. It also seeks to examine the causes of the PMIP's popularity among the predominantly peasant population. On the one hand, it seeks to locate the PMIP 'within an antecedent pattern of relations between religion and elite politics in Kelantan; on the other, it attempts to indicate the manner in which the PMIP has succeeded in articulating widespread peasant grievances by means of a largely implicit Islamic theory of society and politics. Both dimensions of the argument are directed towards indicating the complexity, both historical and contemporary, of the sources of support for the PMIP'.

443 **A woman's place: Malay women and development in Peninsular Malaysia.**
Lenore Manderson. In: *Issues in Malaysian development.* Edited by James C. Jackson, Martin Rudner. Singapore: Heinemann Educational Books (Asia), for the Asian Studies Association of Australia, 1979. p. 233-71.

Manderson considers the ways in which Malay women have participated and are participating in the development effort in Peninsular Malaysia, and discusses the direction of their participation. She concludes that women's participation in development can be considered as 'indirect, subordinate, subsidiary, and ignored'.

444 **Women, politics, and change. The Kaum Ibu UMNO, Malaysia, 1945-1972.**
Lenore Manderson. Kuala Lumpur: Oxford University Press, 1980. 294p. 5 maps. bibliog.

The Pergerakan Kaum Ibu UMNO is the women's section of the United Malays National Organization. After a consideration of the traditional roles of Malay women, this volume examines the structure, activities, membership, leadership and interests of the Kaum Ibu from 1945, when it was created from a number of women's associations, to 1972, a period in which Malay women had come to play an increasingly visible role in the political life of Malaysia. Manderson is concerned to analyse the nature of their political participation, by examining the role of women within UMNO and in electoral politics, and by considering their appointment to public office. She concludes that despite the important political changes which occurred in Malaysia in the period from 1945, in essence the role of women in Malaysian politics had altered little.

445 **Kelantan. Religion, society and politics in a Malay state.**
Edited by William R. Roff. Kuala Lumpur: Oxford University
Press, 1974. 371p. 2 maps. bibliog.
This volume contains twelve papers by various authors on the Kelantan
Malays – their history, social organization and religious life, and their politics.
Among the papers are those which consider: a Thai view of Kelantan in the 19th
century; political developments involving the state between 1891 and 1910; the
To' Janggut rebellion of 1915; the origins and early years of the Majlis Ugama (a
Council of Religion and Malay Custom); theological debates in the state
principally in the first half of the 20th century; Kelantan village magic; the social
organization of Islam in the state; and Muslim identity and political behaviour in
Kelantan. The bibliography aims to provide a comprehensive list of books and
articles published in Western languages, Malay and Thai dealing, in whole or in
part, with Kelantan.

446 **The politicization of Malay villagers. National integration or**
disintegration?
Marvin L. Rogers. *Comparative Politics*, vol. 7, no. 2 (Jan.
1975), p. 205-25.
Rogers argues that a major cause of 'political decay' in Malaysia from and
including May 1969 'has been the nature of the extensive politicization of Malay
society during the past three decades'. He is concerned with 'the process of
politicization in a rural Malay community in northwestern Johore [Sungai Raya,
where Rogers undertook fieldwork in 1965-67] and the implications of the
villagers' increasing political involvement'. He suggests that his analysis helps to
explain 'the frustrations underlying the rioting of May 1969 and the Malay
communal pressures confronting Malaysian leaders' in the mid-1970s. In a
conclusion he argues that 'whereas before the war most villagers in Sungai Raya
thought of themselves as subjects of the Sultan of Johore, today they regard
themselves as members of the Malay race living in the land of the Malays'.
Politicization has fostered a sense of identity and common concern with national
Malay leaders, but it has also 'accentuated cleavages between Malays and
Chinese'.

447 **The Islamic Party of Malaysia. Its formative stages and ideology.**
Safie bin Ibrahim. Kelantan, Malaysia: Nuawi bin Ismail, 1981.
161p. bibliog.
This study divides into two main parts. The first considers the formative years of
the Parti Islam Se Malaysia (PAS) in the early 1950s. The second examines the
ideology of the party. Particular attention is paid to the main foundations of PAS
ideology – Malay nationalism and Islam; and to the principal features of the
Islamic state as it is advocated by the party.

448 **Malay religion, society and politics in Kelantan.**
Robert Winzeler. PhD thesis, University of Chicago, 1970. 250p.
bibliog.
Winzeler is concerned primarily with the relationship of Malay religion to the
various processes of social and political change in Kelantan, 'probably the major

heartland of traditional Malay culture in the peninsula'. Field research was conducted in 1966-67, mainly in the district capital of Pasir Mas. There is analysis of, for example: Islam, *adat* and traditional Malay society; religion in traditional Kelantan; contemporary religion and society in town – the fast and the *haj* (pilgrimage to Mecca); aspects of religious-political conflict in Pasir Mas; and the nature of religious-political factionalism in a Kelantanese village.

449   **The social organization of Islam in Kelantan.**
      Robert L. Winzeler. In: *Kelantan. Religion, society and politics in a Malay state.* Edited by William R. Roff. Kuala Lumpur: Oxford University Press, 1974. p. 259-71.

The author is concerned with the 'traditional' side of Islamic social organization in Kelantan – notably the more important forms of religious institution and religious leadership; and 'the effects that various processes of change have had, particularly the effects of the rise of modern party politics'. The study draws on fieldwork conducted in and around the town of Pasir Mas in 1966-67.

Islamic revivalism and the political process in Malaysia.
See item no. 337.

Malaysia: Islamic revivalism and political disaffection in a divided society.
See item no. 341.

The new fundamentalism: Islam in contemporary Malaysia.
See item no. 344.

The reflowering of Malaysian Islam. Modern religious radicals and their roots.
See item no. 345.

Religious ideology and social change: the Islamic revival in Malaysia.
See item no. 346.

Chinese political activity

450   **Politics in Perak 1969-1974: some preliminary observations with particular reference to the non Malay political parties.**
      Lee Kam Hing. Kuala Lumpur: Department of History, Universiti Malaya, 1977. 34p. map.

This brief, but valuable, study of politics in Perak in the late 1960s and early 1970s pays particular attention to the causes and course of a major reform movement within the Perak MCA [the Perak 'task force']. Consideration is also given to the restructuring of the Alliance in Perak towards the end of this period, to allow the formation of a coalition government in the state.

451 **The politics of Chinese unity in Malaysia: reform and conflict in the Malaysian Chinese Association 1971-73.**
Loh Kok Wah.   Singapore: Maruzen Asia, issued under the auspices of the Institute of Southeast Asian Studies, 1982. 99p. map. (Occasional Paper no. 70).

Loh is concerned primarily with the reorganization undertaken by the MCA (Malaysian Chinese Association) in the early 1970s which was directed principally at bringing into the party younger, professional Chinese, as well as strengthening the party's mass support. Particular attention is paid to 'the activities of the Perak Task Force which ventured down to the Chinese in the rural areas so as to mobilize them to support the party'. Consideration is also given to the expulsion in 1973 of the younger, reformist Chinese leaders within the MCA who, as a result of the reorganization and reform movements of the immediately preceding years, had begun to challenge the old leadership for control of the party.

452 **Chinese village politics in the Malaysian state.**
Judith Strauch.   Cambridge, Massachusetts: Harvard University Press, 1981. 187p. map. bibliog.

A study of the social and political life of a Chinese new village in southern Perak in the early 1970s, 'as it is played out . . . in the context of a Malay- dominated bureaucratic state'. There is consideration of, for example: the local leadership in the community; the formal structures of administration and politics; and factional rivalry within the Perak MCA, and its impact on the political life of the new village community, again in the early 1970s.

453 **Multiple ethnicities in Malaysia: the shifting relevance of alternative Chinese categories.**
Judith Strauch.   *Modern Asian Studies*, vol. 15, part 2 (April 1981), p. 235-60.

This paper examines 'the shifting relevance of segmentally ordered "levels" of ethnicity among Chinese in Malaysia, revealing some of the diversity possible among the several related meanings of the single conceptual term ethnicity'. There is consideration of: ethnicity as a concept; overseas-Chinese ethnicity; the special condition of the Chinese of West Malaysia; the Chinese sub-ethnic structure and social relations within a small rural market town/'new village' in southern Perak; and sub-ethnic categories among Chinese and Malays – contrasting forms and meanings. Strauch argues that 'sub-ethnic boundaries separating culturally and linguistically distinct groups within the wider Chinese-Malaysian community appear to be declining in salience . . . At the same time, a conscious ethnic identification with a more broadly defined "Chineseness" has become heightened'.

454 **The socialization of the Chinese into Malaysian politics: some preliminary observations.**
Robert O. Tilman. *Studies on Asia* (Nebraska), vol. 7 (1966), p. 107-20.

This article outlines 'the major contours of the socialization processes among the Malaysian Chinese community of the peninsula'. Political socialization is defined as 'the process by which children and adults are introduced to various roles in the political game'. Tilman examines the political socialization of the Malaysian Chinese, achieved primarily through the influence of the family, and the influence of the school. He suggests that [in the mid-1960s] the Chinese of the peninsula divided into: a small segment which, 'while acknowledging with pride their Chinese heritage . . . are also outspokenly Malaysian in the political sense'; a small core of Chinese chauvinists who believe firmly in 'the innate superiority of the Chinese community'; and the large majority of Chinese who are apathetic and confused – 'physically and emotionally they are Chinese, but culturally and spiritually they are neither Chinese nor English nor Malay'.

Ethnicity, class and development. Malaysia.
See item no. 551.

Indian political activity

455 **Indians in Southeast Asia.**
Edited by I. J. Bahadur Singh. New Delhi: Sterling Publishers, 1982. 232p. bibliog.

This collection of essays contains two which consider, in part, Indian political activity in contemporary Malaysia: Indians in Malaysia – the neglected minority [V. Suryanarayan]; Indians in Peninsular Malaysia – communalism and factionalism [R. Rajoo]. As the sub-titles indicate, these two papers seek to explain the relative political weakness and fragmentation of the Malaysian Indians.

Politics in East Malaysia

456 **The emergence of towkay leaders in party politics in Sabah.**
Edwin Lee. *Journal of Southeast Asian History*, vol. 9, no. 2 (Sept. 1968), p. 306-24.

Lee considers the background, role and influence of prominent commercial Chinese in party politics in Sabah, from the emergence of political parties in the territory following the Malaysia proposal of May 1961.

457 **Is there development in Sarawak? Political goals and practice.**
Michael Leigh. In: *Issues in Malaysian development.* Edited by
James C. Jackson, Martin Rudner. Singapore: Heinemann
Educational Books (Asia), for the Asian Studies Association of
Australia, 1979. p. 339-74.
Leigh's paper has two principal concerns. First it questions whether economic
development is really taking place in Sarawak: attention is drawn, in particular, to
the government's relative neglect of the rural sector, and to the heavy
subsidization of the urban areas. Second, and more important, it relates the
pattern of economic growth in Sarawak to a series of political developments in the
1970s. Leigh argues that the government 'has institutionalised a pattern of
operating that eschews popular participation in decision-making and substitute[s]
the use or threat of force'. He further suggests that the benefits of existing
development policies 'accrue to an ever-increasing degree to the urban rich'.

458 **The rising moon. Political change in Sarawak.**
Michael B. Leigh. Sydney: Sydney University Press, 1974. 232p.
4 maps. bibliog.
This study of political change in Sarawak covers the period from the late 1950s
through to the early 1970s. It considers: the formation of political parties in the
years 1959-63; the entry of Sarawak into Malaysia in 1963 and the formation of
the first fully-elected state government; political developments in the period 1963-
66; the Malaysianization of Sarawak politics between 1966 and 1970; and coalition
government in Sarawak after 1970. There are two appendixes. The first is a
lengthy analysis of the main characteristics of the elected leadership of Sarawak in
this period; the second reproduces the results of the 1970 Sarawak election.

459 **Parties, personalities and crisis politics in Sarawak.**
Craig A. Lockard. *Journal of Southeast Asian History*, vol. 8,
no. 1 (March 1967), p. 111-21
Lockard provides a brief survey and analysis of the 'confusion, disunity, and
repeated crisis' which characterized political life in Sarawak in the years
immediately following the formation of Malaysia in 1963.

460 **Political parties in Sarawak and Sabah.**
R. S. Milne. *Journal of Southeast Asian History*, vol. 6, no. 2
(Sept. 1965), p. 104-17.
Much of the information and analysis presented in this article was gathered by
Milne during a visit to Sarawak and Sabah in October-November 1964. The
author focuses on three issues: 1. the way in which the, largely communal, party
system had taken shape in the two territories in the preceding few years; 2. the
extent to which it was a 'developed' party system; 3. the presence of 'a
troublesome Opposition in Sarawak and the, possibly troublesome, absence of an
open Opposition in Sabah'.

461 **Malaysia – new states in a new nation. Political development of Sarawak and Sabah in Malaysia.**
R. S. Milne, K. J. Ratnam. London: Frank Cass, 1974. 501p. map. bibliog.

This volume is concerned with political developments in Sarawak and Sabah over the period 1963-70. There is consideration of, for example: the formation of Malaysia and the consequent conflict between state nationalism and Malaysian nationalism in Sarawak and Sabah; the formation and functioning of political parties; the 1967 state election in Sabah, and the 1969-70 state and parliamentary elections in Sarawak; the cabinet crises of 1965 and 1966 in Sarawak; the evolution of local government councils and the machinery for rural development; and the political process in detail – including the strategies and 'rules' of politics, and the relation between money and power in the two territories. Interviews with, in particular, politicians, administrators, and journalists was the most important source for the study.

462 **The Sarawak elections of 1970: an analysis of the vote.**
R. S. Milne, K. J. Ratnam. *Journal of Southeast Asian Studies*, vol. 3, no. 1 (March 1972), p. 111-22.

This paper provides a detailed analysis of the voting at the Sarawak elections of 1970, 'particularly at the state, as opposed to the parliamentary, election'.

463 **The Borneo response to Malaysia 1961-1963.**
James P. Ongkili. Singapore: Donald Moore Press, 1967. 148p. 2 maps. bibliog.

A consideration of the various and changing responses of the three territories of Sarawak, Brunei, and Sabah to the Malaysia proposal. It covers the period from May 1961, when Tunku Abdul Rahman launched the proposal, until September 1963 when Sarawak and Sabah, but not Brunei, entered the federation. Ongkili seeks, in particular, to explain the influences which eventually reconciled Sarawak and Sabah to Malaysia, within two years of their initial rejection of the proposal. The study draws largely on official publications and newspaper reports.

464 **Modernization in East Malaysia 1960-1970.**
James P. Ongkili. Kuala Lumpur: Oxford University Press, 1972. 123p. map. bibliog.

In this work Ongkili analyses the principal administrative, defence, political, social and economic developments in East Malaysia during the 1960s, and relates them to 'the overall policy of the Federal Government in Kuala Lumpur'. There is also a consideration of the influence on federal policy towards East Malaysia of 'Confrontation' with Indonesia, and the Philippine claim to Sabah. Finally there is a discussion of the impact of federal administrative, political and socio-economic programmes on Sarawak and Sabah. A glossary contains brief biographies of the principal personalities referred to in the text.

465   **The politics of belonging. Political change in Sabah and Sarawak.**
Margaret Clark Roff.   Kuala Lumpur: Oxford University Press,
1974. 202p. map. bibliog.
This study examines the processes of political change in Sabah and Sarawak over
the decade from 1963, the year in which the Bornean states achieved
independence from Britain and were brought into the new Federation of
Malaysia. She concentrates on the most important political development in the
two states in this period – 'the rapid growth of political parties and the
unprecedented participation of the population in elections'. There is also
consideration of the progress made in this decade in the direction of incorporating
Sabah and Sarawak 'as entities into the framework of the Malaysian nation-state'.

466   **The rise and demise of Kadazan nationalism.**
Margaret Clark Roff.   *Journal of Southeast Asian History*, vol. 10,
no. 2 (Sept. 1969), p. 326-43.
Roff considers the growth from the late 1950s 'of what might be termed a self-
conscious Kadazan nationalism' among the Dusun and Murut peoples of North
Borneo – an emerging identity of distinct social and political interests which
would set them apart from both the Malayo-Muslim peoples and the Chinese. She
also recounts and analyses the decline of Kadazan nationalism (and the ideal of
multi-racial politics), in Sabah in the later 1960s.

467   **The politics of federalism. Syed Kechik in East Malaysia.**
Bruce Ross-Larson.   Singapore: Bruce Ross-Larson, 1976. 240p.
2 maps.
Syed Kechik bin Syed Mohamed is a Malay lawyer and businessman who was the
political adviser to Tun Mustapha (the Chief Minister of Sabah from 1967 to 1975)
and his United Sabah National Organization (USNO). This study provides an
account of political events in Sabah (and to a lesser extent, in Sarawak), from
1965 to the fall of the USNO from power in 1976, 'from the viewpoint of Syed
Kechik – a viewpoint distinct from the reportage in the Malaysian press, from the
interpretations in other books written on East Malaysian politics, and from that of
the public personalities involved'. The book is based mainly on interviews, and
analysis of government documents, personal files and newspaper reports. An
appendix includes brief biographical sketches of the principal personalities.

468   **Politics in Sarawak 1970-1976. The Iban perspective.**
Peter Searle.   Singapore: Oxford University Press, 1983. 243p.
8 maps. bibliog.
This book seeks to examine political developments in Sarawak in the period 1970-
76 from a 'grass-roots perspective', that of 'the Iban longhouse dwellers who
constitute the largest single native group in the state'. Part one explains why, until
the early 1970s, the Ibans were divided in their political loyalties; and then
considers the subsequent development of Iban political unity. In order to explain
more fully this process of political change, there are detailed case studies of
long-house politics in three districts in this period. Part two opens with a
description of the development of Sarawak politics at the state level from 1970-74,
particular attention being paid to the reasons for and significance of the survival

of the Sarawak National Party (SNAP), the more 'modernist' of the two Iban parties, and the associated failure of the predominantly Chinese political parties in Sarawak to retain their former Iban support. Finally there is a consideration of the more significant changes within SNAP following the 1974 general elections; the Ibans and the development of Sarawak politics at the state level between 1974 and 1976; and the decision of SNAP in March 1976 to join the National Front (Barisan Nasional) Government.

The towkays of Sabah. Chinese leadership and indigenous challenge in the last phase of British rule.
See item no. 136.

Leadership and power within the Chinese community of Sarawak: a historical survey.
See item no. 220.

Constitution, Legal System

469 The law of the Straits Settlements. A commentary.
Roland St. John Braddell, with an introduction by M. B.
Hooker. Kuala Lumpur: Oxford University Press, 1982. 3rd ed.
278p.

Sir Roland St. John Braddell (1880-1966) was a member of colonial Malaya's most prominent legal family. This work was originally published in Singapore in 1915. It comprises four chapters: legal history; modifications of English law; institutions of government; and the judiciary and the bar – which together 'constitute the first comprehensive descriptions of English legal history in the Straits'. It also includes five appendixes: treaties; Acts of Parliament; letters patent, instructions and standing orders; cases on Straits Ordinances; and the applicability of English Statutes – which together 'provide the essential data of Straits legal history'.

470 An introduction to the Federal Constitution.
R. H. Hickling. Kuala Lumpur: Federation of Malaya Information
Services, 1960. 80p.

This is a valuable, clearly-presented introduction to the *Merdeka* constitution, intended to explain its provisions and practices to the citizens of the newly-independent Malaya.

471 A concise legal history of South-East Asia.
M. B. Hooker. Oxford, England: Clarendon Press, 1978. 289p.
bibliog.

This outline of the history of South East Asian legal thought contains two chapters which are notably concerned with Malaysia: 1. the Islamic legal world: the law texts of island South-East Asia; 2. the English legal world: the Straits Settlements, Federated and Unfederated Malay States, British Borneo, and Burma.

139

472 **Islamic law in South-East Asia.**

M. B. Hooker. Singapore: Oxford University Press, 1984. 330p. bibliog.

Hooker seeks to outline the main characteristics of Islamic law in South East Asia. An introductory chapter considers Islamic legal history in the region as a whole, but for the remainder of the study the analysis proceeds country-by-country. Thus there are separate chapters for: the Straits Settlements and Singapore; the Malay States and Peninsular Malaysia; and Sarawak and Sabah. The analysis has a pronounced historical emphasis: and it does not deal with law later than December 1978.

473 **The personal laws of Malaysia. An introduction.**

M. B. Hooker. Kuala Lumpur: Oxford University Press, 1976. 276p. bibliog.

In Malaysia, personal laws – those 'which apply to specific groups of people who are defined according to race or religion or, occasionally, both' – are primarily confined to family law matters and, in the case of the *adats* (customary laws), to some aspects of landownership. This volume has chapters on: Islamic law; the Malay *adat* laws; the Dayak *adat* laws; Chinese law; Hindu law; the Orang Asli. There is also discussion of the conflict between personal laws and common law in Malaysia; and of personal laws and the nation state. An appendix reproduces the Law Reform (Marriage and Divorce) Bill, 1972. See also: *Adat laws in modern Malaya. Land tenure, traditional government and religion*, by M. B. Hooker (Kuala Lumpur: Oxford University Press, 1972. 294p. 5 maps. bibliog.).

474 **Malaysian customary laws and usage.**

Haji Mohtar bin H. Mohamed Dom. Kuala Lumpur: Federal Publications, 1979. 74p. (Federal Cultural Series).

In the majority of states in Peninsular Malaysia, Malays abide by a patriarchal system of traditional law known as 'Adat Temenggung'. This slim volume is mainly concerned with the matriarchal system of customary law, 'Adat Perpatih', which is followed by the Malays in Negeri Sembilan. It also includes a number of appropriate stories from Negeri Sembilan; and a chapter on the customs of Malaysians. The book is intended for the general reader.

475 **The constitution of Malaysia.**

L. A. Sheridan, Harry E. Groves. Singapore: Malayan Law Journal (Pte), 1979. 3rd ed. 545p. bibliog.

An exhaustively detailed account of, and commentary upon, the constitution of Malaysia 'in the light of materials available to the end of 1978'. Articles and schedules of the constitution; and sections of the Malaysia Act are produced in full.

476 **The law of contract in Malaysia and Singapore. Cases and commentary.**
Visu Sinnadurai. Kuala Lumpur: Oxford University Press, 1979. 764p. bibliog.

This volume provides a scholarly compilation of cases, together with commentaries, on the law of contract as applied in Malaysia and Singapore. It is intended not only for the law student and legal practitioner, but also for those accountants, bankers, engineers and businesssmen whose work brings them into contact with contract law in the two countries.

477 **The constitution of Malaysia. Its development: 1957-1977.**
Edited by Tun Mohamed Suffian, H. P. Lee, F. A. Trindade. Kuala Lumpur: Oxford University Press, 1978. 425p.

This volume contains fifteen papers, written either by academics who teach law, or by law officers in the Malaysian government. Among the contributions are: an overview of constitutional changes in Malaysia, 1957-77; fundamental liberties in the constitution of the Federation of Malaysia; the position of Islam in the constitution of Malaysia; the citizenship laws of Malaysia; ministerial responsibility in Malaysia; the constitutional position of the Yang Di-Pertuan Agong; the Malaysian parliament; the judiciary during the first twenty years of independence; emergency powers in Malaysia; and the process of constitutional change in Malaysia.

478 **An introduction to the Malaysian legal system.**
Wu Min Aun. Kuala Lumpur: Heinemann Educational Books (Asia), 1982. 3rd rev. ed. 196p. bibliog.

This is an excellent introduction to the Malaysian legal system, 'designed for students preparing for professional and sub-professional examinations, and for the interested general reader'. It has the following chapters: Malaysian legal history; the sources of Malaysian law; legislation and subsidiary legislation; the federal and state constitutions; the administration of justice; civil procedure; and criminal procedure. The law is stated as it stood on 1 June 1981. Extensive references both to important legal cases and to major source materials facilitate further study.

479 **The commercial law of Malaysia.**
Wu Min Aun, Beatrix Vohrah. Kuala Lumpur: Heinemann Educational Books (Asia), 1979. 264p.

This is a general survey of the commercial law of Malaysia, designed for students preparing for professional examinations as well as for those already working in industry and commerce. The book divides into three parts: Law of Contract; Agency and Partnership; and the principal types of contracts.

Adat and Islam in Malaya.
See item no. 339.

Administration and Local Government

480 **The district. A study in decentralization in West Malaysia.**
J. H. Beaglehole. London: Oxford University Press, 1976. 122p. map. bibliog. (Hull Monographs on South-East Asia, no. 6).

This study is concerned with local administration – notably the role of the district officer – in contemporary Kelantan, the overwhelmingly Malay east coast state in which the opposition Parti Islam long held dominance. Beaglehole concentrates on three themes: 'the district officer and the general administration of the district, including a separate treatment of land administration and problems of enforcement; local government [in Kelantan] based on an examination of the work of selected councils; [and] some aspects of the interaction of politics and administration' in local government in Kelantan. The study emphasizes the changing role of the district officer as a result of 'the development of administrative specialization and the related problem of co-ordination, the growth of local government and the politicization of administration'.

481 **Local government in Peninsular Malaysia.**
M. W. Norris. Westmead, England: Gower Publishing Company, 1980. 121p. 5 maps. bibliog.

Norris provides a succinct study of the historical evolution and current (late 1970s) situation of local government in Peninsular Malaysia, 'particularly directed to those involved in local government affairs, to students of government, and those interested in comparative local government'. There is discussion of: the work and recommendations of two Royal Commissions, first on the workings of local authorities in West Malaysia, and second on the remuneration and conditions of service in local authorities and statutory authorities in the later 1960s and early 1970s; the restructuring of local authorities between 1973-75; and the Local Government Act of 1976 and its aftermath.

482   **The politics of administration. The Malaysian experience.**
Mavis Puthucheary.   Kuala Lumpur: Oxford University Press,
1978. 170p. bibliog.
In this work Puthucheary examines the working of the Malaysian bureaucracy
within its political, social and economic environment. There is analysis of the civil
service in its historical setting; and of the political interests and involvement of the
bureaucracy from the colonial period through to the present. The socio-economic
background of civil servants, their language of education, regional background,
and their attitudes towards authority, democracy and political neutrality are each
examined. Finally there is consideration of morale and job satisfaction within the
bureaucracy, and an attempt to examine 'what civil servants themselves consider
to be the most serious obstacles to achieving the tasks that they have to perform'.
The lengthy questionnaire, which was sent to about 1,500 civil servants as the
major part of the research for this study, is reproduced in full in an appendix.

483   **The abolition of elective local government in Penang.**
Paul Tennant.   *Journal of Southeast Asian Studies*, vol. 4, no. 1
(March 1973), p. 72-87.
Penang was the only state in the post-independence federation to attain fully
developed elective local government: it was 'the only state in which every local
authority consisted entirely of elected members and the only state in which every
local authority was financially autonomous of the state government'. In 1966 the
George Town Council was suspended; and in 1971 the remaining local authorities
in Penang state were suspended. Tennant provides a detailed account, analysis,
and an intricate explanation for this abolition of elective local government in
Penang.

484   **Bureaucratic transition in Malaya.**
Robert O. Tilman.   Durham, North Carolina: Duke University
Press; London: Cambridge University Press, 1964. 175p. bibliog.
Tilman is concerned with the changing character and composition of the Malayan
bureaucracy from the first arrivals of British officials through to 1963. There is
consideration of: the colonial bureaucracy and the Malayan colonial experience;
the Malayanization of the bureaucracy in the late 1950s and early 1960s; and the
institutional and administrative legacy of colonial rule for the Malayan
bureaucracy.

Political ideology in Malaysia. Reality and the beliefs of an elite.
See item no. 410.

143

Foreign Relations

485 **A collection of treaties and other documents affecting the states of Malaysia, 1761-1963.**
Edited by J. de V. Allen, A. J. Stockwell, L. R. Wright. London: Oceana Publications, 1981. 2 vols.

This collection is designed to provide as complete a record as possible of 'all treaties, engagements, agreements and other documents official and semi-official, which are relevant to the relations of the States that were part of Malaysia at the time of its formation both with each other and with external powers between the late eighteenth century and 1963'. The editors provide extensive introductory notes for each treaty/document, or for each coherent group of treaties/documents.

486 **The Philippines' claim to Sabah. Its historical, legal and political implications.**
M. O. Ariff. Kuala Lumpur: Oxford University Press, 1970. 76p. 5 maps. bibliog.

At the time he wrote this monograph, Ariff was a senior legal officer in the Malaysian administration. His study attempts an objective examination of the Malaysian and Philippine views with respect to Sabah, 'based on the historical, legal and political aspects of the dispute'. There is consideration of: the British claim to Sabah based on historical treaty, international law, and on account of possession and consolidation; the legal basis of the Philippine claim to Sabah; and the bases of Sabah's independence and integration within Malaysia. The analysis covers the period until the end of 1969.

487 **Malaysia and Singapore in international diplomacy. Documents and commentaries.**
Peter Boyce.   Sydney: Sydney University Press, 1968. 268p. map.
The 174 documents reproduced in this book 'are meant to focus attention on Malaysia's diplomatic quest for acceptance in the world community of sovereign states'. The documents, the majority of which are from official sources, cover the period from independence to the beginning of 1967. They are concerned with such aspects as: the formation of Malaysia; confrontation with Indonesia; the Philippine claim to Sabah; the British military presence; China relations; relations with the Commonwealth; relations with the USA; defence arrangements with Australia and New Zealand; and relations with the USSR and eastern Europe.

488 **The defence of Malaysia and Singapore. The transformation of a security system 1957-1971.**
Chin Kin Wah.   Cambridge, England: Cambridge University Press, 1983. 219p. bibliog.
Following Malayan independence in 1957, provision for the external security of Malaya and Singapore was set by the Anglo-Malaysian Defence Agreement (AMDA), a defence system which 'contained one anchor power (Britain), two principal consumers of alliance security (Malaysia and Singapore), and two associate powers (Australia and New Zealand) which were both providers and consumers of alliance security'. Chin is concerned primarily with the transformation of that defence guarantee into a loose five-power arrangement under which, from 1971, Malaysia and Singapore became primarily responsible for their own external security. Particular attention is thus paid to the policy of withdrawal of British forces east of Suez undertaken by the Labour Governments of the later 1960s.

489 **The separation of Singapore from Malaysia.**
Nancy McHenry Fletcher. Ithaca, New York: Cornell University, 1969. 98p. bibliog. (Southeast Asia Program, Data Paper no. 73).
This slim volume examines the varied and inter-related economic, political, and ethnic tensions between Malaysia and Singapore which led to the separation of the latter from the newly-created Federation on 9 August 1965. The author insists that this is a preliminary, incomplete study: but it provides a most valuable introduction to this complex issue. It includes the full text of Tunku Abdul Rahman's speech to the Malaysian House of Representatives on 9 August 1965.

490 **The undeclared war. The story of the Indonesian confrontation 1962-1966.**
Harold James, Denis Sheil-Small.   London: Leo Cooper, 1971. Reprinted, Kuala Lumpur: University of Malaya Co-operative Bookshop, 1979. 201p. 5 maps.
This is primarily an account of the military operations conducted by British and Commonwealth forces in Borneo between 1962 and 1966 in response to the Brunei Revolt and then Indonesian 'Confrontation'.

145

491 **The Sarawak-Indonesian border insurgency.**
Justus M. van der Kroef. *Modern Asian Studies*, vol. 2, part 3 (July 1968), p. 245-65.

This article considers the political and social origins of the Sarawak-Indonesian border insurgency of the 1960s, the operations of the border rebels, and the measures taken by the Malaysian and Indonesian governments to combat the insurgency.

492 **Malaysia-Singapore relations: crisis of adjustment, 1965-68.**
Lau Teik Soon. *Journal of Southeast Asian History*, vol. 10, no. 1 (March 1969), p. 155-76.

Lau considers the further deterioration which occurred in relations between Malaysia and Singapore in the three years immediately following separation in August 1965; and briefly examines the prospects for either economic and political reintegration or economic co-operation.

493 **Malacca, Singapore, and Indonesia.**
Michael Leifer. Alphen aan den Rijn, The Netherlands: Sijthoff & Noordhoff, 1978. 217p. 6 maps. (Series: International Straits of the World, no. 2).

In November 1971 Malaysia and Indonesia issued a joint statement which asserted that the Straits of Malacca no longer enjoyed the status of International Straits. The maritime powers reacted strongly to this claim, and sought by diplomatic means to sustain the traditional principle of 'freedom of the seas', as applied to the Straits. Leifer first provides an analysis of the background to this dispute, by examining: historical conflict over the Straits; the physical nature of the Straits; and the legal régime of straits. He then traces the course of the dispute, which involved not only Malaysia, Singapore and Indonesia, and the major maritime powers (US, USSR, and Japan), but also a number of governmental and non-governmental international bodies, as well as the UN Conference on the Law of the Sea. It should be added that the study also examines at length the comparable dispute which has arisen with regard to the major navigation straits in the Indonesian archipelago: consequently the study as a whole focuses primarily on Indonesian, rather than Malaysian, perceptions and policies.

494 **The Philippine claim to Sabah.**
Michael Leifer. Hull, England: University of Hull, Centre for South-East Asian Studies (Inter Documentation Company AG Zug Switzerland), 1968. 75p. (Hull Monographs on South-East Asia, no. 1).

This study is concerned with the political and non-legal aspects of the presentation of the Philippine claim to Sabah by President Macapagal, and the subsequent progress of the Philippine suit through to the early years of the Marcos presidency.

495 **The Wilson Government and the British defence commitment in Malaysia-Singapore.**
Derek McDougall. *Journal of Southeast Asian Studies*, vol. 4, no. 2 (Sept. 1973), p. 229-40.

McDougall outlines certain factors relevant to the formulation of British foreign policy under the first Wilson governments and 'describes how these factors influenced the rundown of the British defence commitment in Malaysia-Singapore' in the later 1960s. Britain's straitened economic circumstances provided the 'initial impetus for a revision of the [defence] commitment' to Malaysia-Singapore; and was of very considerable importance in determining the scale of the future British participation in the defence of the area.

496 **Konfrontasi. The Indonesia-Malaysia dispute 1963-1966.**
J. A. C. Mackie. Kuala Lumpur: Oxford University Press, 1974. 368p. 2 maps. bibliog.

The formation of Malaysia in 1963 provoked a severe response – less than outright war but certainly more than a simple diplomatic protest – from Indonesia. This volume considers principally the causes and course of this confrontation, in relation to Indonesia's internal politics – specifically the relative influence of President Sukarno, the Indonesian Communist Party, and the army leadership, in the opposition to Malaysia. The course of the dispute – its propaganda, military, economic, and diplomatic aspects; and its abandonment in August 1966, are each considered in very great detail. Considerable attention is also paid to important related issues such as the Brunei revolt of 1962; the Philippine claim to Sabah; and the separation of Singapore from Malaysia in 1965.

497 **Philippine policy toward Sabah. A claim to independence.**
Lela Garner Noble. Tucson, Arizona: University of Arizona Press, 1977. 267p. map. bibliog.

This study is mainly concerned with a detailed analysis of the international dispute arising from the Philippine claim to Sabah, from the time it was officially announced by President Macapagal in June 1962 to the early 1970s when the pursuit of the claim was discontinued. The focus of the study is on the 'perceptions of people affecting policy toward the claim in the Philippines'; the perceptions of those outside the Philippines who were affected by the claim (Malaysia and Britain); and the way in which those changing perceptions and the policies which arose from them, interacted with each other during the course of the dispute.

498 **Singapore and Malaysia.**
Milton E. Osborne. Ithaca, New York: Cornell University, 1964. 115p. 2 maps. bibliog. (Southeast Asia Program, Data Paper no. 53).

In 1959 the People's Action Party came to power in Singapore, with the objective of merger with Malaya as a major part of its party platform. In 1964, with merger achieved, the party attempted to extend its power beyond Singapore and to secure representation in the Federal Parliament in Kuala Lumpur. This latter ambition posed a major strain on the new Federation, and was an important contributory factor in the expulsion of Singapore from Malaysia in August 1965. Osborne provides primarily an account and analysis of the events between 1959 and 1964. Written in the latter year, it is inevitably only a preliminary study: but nevertheless it provides a valuable, immediate, insight into these crucial events.

499 **The dilemma of independence. Two decades of Malaysia's foreign policy 1957-1977.**
J. Saravanamuttu.   Penang: Penerbit Universiti Sains Malaysia, for the School of Social Sciences, 1983. 206p. bibliog.

This work seeks to provide an analysis of the content and course of Malaysian foreign policy in the two decades following independence. The treatment is essentially chronological. The four principal empirical chapters examine: foreign policy in the immediate post-independence years; 'confrontation', turmoil and change in the period 1964-69; the move towards the consolidation of South East Asian regional relationships in the period 1970-75; and the re-inforcement of that new direction in foreign policy in 1976-77. Each of these main chapters divides the discussion under the headings: defence and security; development and trade; and international co-operation and diplomacy. The principal treaties, declarations, and agreements from this period are reproduced in a series of appendixes.

Malaysia. Prospect and retrospect. The impact and aftermath of colonial rule.
See item no. 109.

The separation of Singapore from Malaysia. A study in political involution.
See item no. 377.

Economics

General

500 Inequality and poverty in Malaysia. Measurement and decomposition.
Sudhir Anand. New York: Oxford University Press, for the
World Bank, 1983. 371p. map. bibliog.

An analysis of the primary data on income distribution in Malaysia collected in
the 1970 Post-Enumeration Survey, 'a very large sample survey covering some
135,000 individuals, or approximately 1.5 percent of the population of Peninsular
Malaysia'. There is consideration of: inequality in levels of living; the definition
and measurement of poverty in Peninsular Malaysia; rural poverty; inequality in
personal income distribution; and 'the empirical relations among age, education,
and income of urban employees'. The concluding chapter is mainly concerned
with an assessment of the New Economic Policy, in terms of that policy's main
objectives of the eradication of poverty and the restructuring of employment.
There are six technical appendixes concerned with the measurement of income
inequality.

501 Malaysian economic development and policies.
Edited by Stephen Chee, Khoo Siew Mun. Kuala Lumpur:
Malaysian Economic Association, 1975. 280p.

There are sixteen papers in this volume, divided under four headings: the New
Economic Policy and the restructuring of society; development in an inflationary
environment; land development; and regional (i.e., regional within West
Malaysia) economic development. The papers were originally presented at a
convention organized by the Malaysian Economic Association which examined
Malaysia's economic development and policies within the framework of the New
Economic Policy.

502 **Malaysia. Some contemporary issues in socioeconomic development.**
Edited by Cheong Kee Cheok, Khoo Siew Mun, R.
Thillainathan. Kuala Lumpur: Malaysian Economic Association,
1979. 313p. map.

This volume contains twenty-two papers divided into the following eight sections: distribution of income and wealth; housing, landownership and urban development; financing the Third Malaysia Plan; manufacturing, industrialization and entrepreneurship; management of public enterprises; agricultural policy and rural development; population policy in national development; and unemployment and manpower planning. Some of the papers review the achievements and shortfalls of the Second Malaysia Plan (1971-75); others consider the likely implications of the Third Malaysia Plan (1976-80) targets and policies on growth and income equality; the remaining papers are concerned with more specific contemporary problems and policy issues in Malaysian society which have not been explicitly dealt with in the Plans.

503 **The Malaysian balance of payments 1960-1970.**
Chew Fook Yew, Alan. Kuala Lumpur: University of Malaya
Press, 1975. 284p. bibliog.

A study of the Malaysian balance of payments in the 1960s which considers, for example: the current balance (for the separate territories of Peninsular Malaysia, Sabah, and Sarawak) and the capital account; the foreign exchange reserves and exchange rate policy (including an examination of the case for not devaluing the new Malaysian dollar when sterling was devalued in 1967); the possible use of monetary policies to bring about adjustments in the balance of payments; the effects of import substitution on the Malaysian balance of payments; and alternative policies – including the imposition of restrictions on transfer payments, the introduction of separate trade policies for manufactured and primary exports, and the development of the potential of the tourist industry.

504 **The economic development of Malaya.**
Baltimore, Maryland: Johns Hopkins Press, for the International
Bank for Reconstruction and Development, 1955. 707p. 11 maps.

This is a report of an IBRD mission to Malaya in the first half of 1954 to assess the resources available for future development, to consider how these resources might best contribute to the economic and social development of Malaya, and to make recommendations for practical measures to further such development. The report is in five parts: 1. a general introduction to the economy of Malaya and a discussion of the problems and prospects of Malaya's development; 2. the productive sectors – agriculture, forestry, and fisheries; mining and power; transport and communications; industry and entrepôt trade; 3. the social service sectors, including education; 4. the mission's proposed public investment programme for 1955-59, 'based upon its appraisal of the public financial resources which may be expected to be available for development during that period'; and 5. twelve technical reports on: agriculture and forestry; irrigation, drainage and river conservancy; land tenure; fisheries; mining; power; transport and communications; industrial development; education; public health and medical care; social welfare; and currency and banking. The report covers the Federation of Malaya (Peninsular Malaysia) and the Crown Colony of Singapore.

505 **Public finances in Malaya and Singapore.**
C. T. Edwards. Canberra: Australian National University Press, 1970. 386p. bibliog.

This work has two main objects: first, to outline and analyse the main features of public finances in Malaya and Singapore; second, to make suggestions 'designed to raise more revenue, to achieve a more equitable distribution of the tax burden, and to enhance the contribution of the fiscal system to economic stabilization and growth'. There are chapters on: the government sector; income taxation – general considerations; company income taxation; personal income taxation; import and excise taxation; a value added tax; export taxation; domestic borrowing; external finance; state and local government finance; federal-state financial relations; and the fiscal system and the economy. The analysis concentrates on developments since 1945.

506 **Underdevelopment and economic nationalism in Southeast Asia.**
Frank H. Golay, Ralph Anspach, M. Ruth Pfanner, Eliezer B. Ayal. Ithaca, New York; London: Cornell University Press, 1969. 494p.

This is a study of the impact of economic nationalism on economic policy and development in post-war Southeast Asia. An important term used in the analysis is 'indigenism', which is used to describe 'the structure of policies and institutions created to transform the racial dimensions of the colonial-type economies inherited by Southeast Asian societies . . . [and] the process by which control over wealth and sources of income is transferred to members of the national society'. The chapter on Malaya (p. 341-89), written by Golay, is concerned with the indigenism of the Malays rather than that of Malaysians. A major part of the discussion is concerned with the nature of Malayan [Malay] indigenism: this involves an analysis of citizenship, naturalization, and immigration; the special Malay position; Malay participation in business; natural resource policy; manufacturing and public utilities; foreign and domestic commerce; banking, credit, and finance; and the bureaucracy, professions and labour. It should be noted that the analysis covers the period only to the mid-1960s.

507 **Capital, labour and the state: the West Malaysian case.**
Fatimah Halim. *Journal of Contemporary Asia*, vol. 12, no. 3 (1982), p. 259-80.

This paper seeks to assess the role of the state in the achievement of the Malaysian 'economic miracle'. It is mainly concerned with the post-colonial state, and more precisely, 'with the ruling bourgeoisie presiding over capital accumulation'. The author attempts 'to characterize the relationship of the Malaysian state *vis-à-vis* various sectors of capital and labour in order to understand the significance of the state for the advancement of labour and capital, and the extent to which state power is used to cater to the material interests of the various fractions of the capitalist and labouring classes'. In a conclusion she notes 'it is ironic that government agencies set up to bolster the rights of the Bumiputras – the underprivileged community – are now turned against the Bumiputra masses, including the peasants organized by Felda, by MADA and the workers labouring in productive enterprises owned by the state'.

508 **Ethnic and social stratification in Peninsular Malaysia.**
Charles Hirschman. Washington, DC: American Sociological
Association, 1975. 115p. bibliog. (The Arnold and Caroline Rose
Monograph Series).

Hirschman is concerned with the socio-economic inequalities which exist among
the ethnic communities of Peninsular Malaysia – the magnitude of ethnic
inequality; how it has changed over time; and the degree to which 'ethnic
differentials in socioeconomic levels can be accounted for by differences in social
origins'. The analysis draws principally on census data for the period 1911-67; the
Malaysian socioeconomic sample survey of households, 1967-1968; and the *1966-
1967 West Malaysian family survey*.

509 **Industrial and occupational change in Peninsular Malaysia,
1947-70.**
.Charles Hirschman. *Journal of Southeast Asian Studies*, vol. 13,
no. 1 (March 1982), p. 9-32.

A detailed analysis of 'the changes in the industrial and occupational structure of
Peninsular Malaysia during the post-war era, using the population censuses of
1947, 1957, and 1970'. He also considers the relative changes in economic roles of
the ethnic communities in Peninsular Malaysia. In this article, the term 'industrial'
is apparently used in its wider sense, to mean 'form of economic activity', or
'economic sector'. And indeed Hirschman draws attention to the continuous
decline in the agricultural sector and the decrease in agricultural employment for
the Malays and particularly for the Chinese, as being the dominant trend of the
post-war occupational structure for those communities.

510 **Retail development in Third World cities: models and the Kuala
Lumpur experience.**
James C. Jackson. In: *Issues in Malaysian development*. Edited by
James C. Jackson, Martin Rudner. Singapore: Heinemann
Educational Books (Asia), for the Asian Studies Association of
Australia, 1979. p. 273-303.

An examination of some of the recent attempts which have been made 'to
conceptualise relationships between urban retail systems and the development
process mainly in the light of evidence from Kuala Lumpur'. He demonstrates
how particular consumer preferences have induced different forms of food
marketing in the federal capital. Jackson further argues that there are economic
and socio-cultural considerations operating in Kuala Lumpur (indeed in Third
World cities as a whole), which favour the persistence, and even growth, of
traditional food-retailing systems – the fresh-food market, the shop-houses, and
the hawker-stalls.

511 **Recession and the Malaysian economy.**
Khor Kok Peng. Penang: Institut Masyarakat, 1983. 89p. bibliog.

Khor analyses 'the roots, manifestations, effects and implications of recession in
the Malaysian economy as it developed from 1980 to early 1983'. He argues that
the recession has at least brought into focus the heavy dependence of the

Malaysian economy on the developed world, and he therefore advocates an alternative development strategy – one which would reduce external dependence and increase economic self-reliance for Malaysia.

512 **Economic growth and the public sector in Malaya and Singapore 1948-1960.**
Lee Soo Ann.   Kuala Lumpur: Oxford University Press, 1974.
192p. bibliog.

In this study Lee seeks to describe the inter-relationships between the growth of the economy and the growth of the public sector in Malaya and Singapore between 1948 and 1960 – to examine 'the post-war role of the government in the development of the Malayan-Singapore economy'. Particular attention is paid to: the growth in income in the economy in that period; political and constitutional elements which affected government policy; the principal features of the tax system – an assessment of the resources available to government; current and capital government expenditures; and overall fiscal policy, particularly in relation to the annual budget and the deployment of funds.

513 **Fiscal policy and political transition: the case of Malaya, 1948-1960.**
Lee Soo Ann.   *Journal of Southeast Asian Studies*, vol. 5, no. 1
(March 1974), p. 102-14.

Lee considers whether the movement towards national independence in Malaya caused any change in government fiscal policy, or was 'the phenomenon of political transition totally independent of fiscal policy determination'. He examines this question in the light of data on Federal government revenue and expenditure pattern in the period 1948-60; and concludes that during the period when Malaya was moving to political independence, 'the pursuit of fiscal policy did not deviate much from the pattern set by colonial practice'.

514 **Economic growth and development in West Malaysia 1947-1970.**
David Lim.   Kuala Lumpur: Oxford University Press, 1973. 346p.
map. bibliog.

This book is concerned with 'the diversification of the West Malaysian economy over the period 1947-70'. It is divided into four main parts. The first examines some of the major factors calling for diversification: the decline in prospects for rubber and tin; economic instability; political pressures; and demographic pressures. The second part considers the impact of these four factors on the form of the diversification programme pursued, and on the rate of its implementation. The third part discusses the extent of structural change in the Malaysian economy in this period, and 'the degree to which the overall objectives of development planning had been achieved'. The final substantial part examines the role of the agricultural and industrial sectors in the diversification programme.

515 **Export instability and economic development in West Malaysia, 1947-1968.**
David Lim. *Malayan Economic Review*, vol. 17, no. 2 (Oct. 1972), p. 99-113.

Lim seeks to examine the extent of economic instability in West Malaysia over the period 1947-68, 'and to test the hypothesis that instability has been detrimental to the process of economic growth' in those years. He concludes that 'there is a fairly high degree of economic instability in West Malaysia resulting mainly from fluctuations in the export earnings of rubber and tin . . . however, the transmission of instability from the export sector to the rest of the economy is smaller than is commonly believed'. Furthermore he finds little evidence of three of the alleged consequences of economic instability – a speculative mentality, inflation, and frequent disruptions to planning. In short he finds it difficult to argue that 'economic instability had been detrimental to economic growth in West Malaysia on the available statistical evidence'. See also K. A. Mohamed Ariff, entry no. 577.

516 **Further readings on Malaysian economic development.**
Edited by David Lim. Kuala Lumpur: Oxford University Press, 1983. 309p. bibliog.

This collection of twenty-six readings follows the same format as Lim's *Readings on Malaysian economic development* (q.v.). The sub-headings here are: the New Economic Policy; agricultural development; industrial development; internal migration; the unemployment problem; foreign investment; and fiscal policies. Together with Lim [517], this volume provides the most valuable introduction to the contemporary Malaysian economy, and, primarily through the annotated bibliographies, the most useful introduction to the literature in this field. But it might also be noted that the readings in both volumes are concerned almost exclusively with West Malaysia. Among the papers included are: David Lim, 'The political economy of the New Economic Policy in Malaysia', p. 3-22; R. Thillainathan, 'Discriminatory allocation of public expenditure benefits for reducing inter-racial inequality in Malaysia – an evaluation', p. 23-39. Reprinted from: *The Developing Economies*, vol. 18, no. 3 (Sept. 1980); Yukon Huang, 'Tenancy patterns, productivity, and rentals in Malaysia', p. 43-52. Reprinted from: *Economic Development and Cultural Change*, vol. 23, no. 4 (July 1975); David Lim, 'Actual, desired and full levels of capital utilization in Malaysian manufacturing', p. 81-88. Reprinted from: *The Journal of Development Studies*, vol. 14, no. 1 (Oct. 1977); Charles Hirschman, 'Recent urbanization trends in Peninsular Malaysia', p. 111-24. Reprinted from: *Demography*, vol.13, no. 4 (Nov. 1976); Colin MacAndrews and Kazumi Yamamoto, 'Induced and voluntary migration in Malaysia: The Federal Land Development Authority role in migration since 1957', p. 125-39. Reprinted from: *Southeast Asian Journal of Social Science*, vol. 3, no. 2 (1975); Amos H. Hawley, Dorothy Fernandez and Harbans Singh, 'Migration and employment in Peninsular Malaysia, 1970', p. 196-206. Reprinted from: *Economic Development and Cultural Change*, vol. 27, no. 3 (April 1979); Charles Hirschman, 'Ownership and control in the manufacturing sector of West Malaysia', p. 209-20. Reprinted from: *UMBC Economic Review*, vol. 7, no. 1 (1971); Gerald Tan, 'Foreign investment, employment generation and the profit-wage ratio in the manufacturing sector of West Malaysia', p. 225-28. Reprinted from: *UMBC Economic Review*, vol. 14, no. 2 (1978); K. von

Rabenau, 'Trade policies and industrialization in a developing country: the case of West Malaysia', p. 257-76. Reprinted from: *Malayan Economic Review*, vol. 21, no.1 (April 1976).

517 **Readings on Malaysian economic development.**
Edited by David Lim. Kuala Lumpur: Oxford University Press, 1975. 421p. bibliog.

This volume contains twenty-nine articles grouped under the following sub-headings: development perspectives; the export sector; agricultural development; industrial development; the unemployment problem; distribution of income and wealth; human factors in economic development; and money and finance. The majority of the articles were previously published in professional journals and specialized monographs, and are here reprinted in full; there are also a number of previously unpublished articles. The editor has provided an introduction for each group of papers, in order to give continuity and direction to the discussion; and each group of papers is followed by a brief annotated bibliography relevant to that theme. Among the papers are: David Lim, 'The economic, political and social background to development planning in Malaysia', p. 2-9; J. T. Thoburn, 'Exports and economic growth in West Malaysia', p. 12-27. Reprinted from: *Oxford Economic Papers*, vol. 25 (1973), p. 88-111; J. T. Thoburn, 'Exports and the Malaysian engineering industry: a case study of backward linkage', p. 28-46. Reprinted from: *Oxford Bulletin of Economics and Statistics*, vol. 35, no. 2 (May 1973); Martin Rudner, 'The Malayan quandary: rural development policy under the first and second five-year plans', p. 80-88. Reprinted from: *Contributions to Asian Studies*, vol. 1 (1971); Yukon Huang, 'Some reflections on padi double-cropping in West Malaysia', p. 89-96. Reprinted from: *Malayan Economic Review*, vol. 17, no. 1 (April 1972); C. P. Brown, 'Rice price stabilization and support in Malaysia', p. 97-110. Reprinted from: *The Developing Economies*, vol. 11, no. 2 (June 1973); R. Wikkramatileke, 'Federal land development in West Malaysia 1957-1971', p. 111-123. Reprinted from: *Pacific Viewpoint*, vol. 13, no. 1 (May 1972); Wolfgang Kasper, 'A new strategy for Malaysia's economic development in the 1970s?', p. 126-36. Reprinted from: *UMBC Economic Review*, vol. 9, no. 1 (1973, revised); Lutz Hoffmann and Tan Tew Nee, 'Pattern of growth and structural change in West Malaysia's manufacturing industry 1959-68', p. 137-55. Reprinted from: *Kajian Ekonomi Malaysia*, vol. 8, no. 2 (Dec. 1971); B. L. Johns, 'Import substitution and export potential – the case of manufacturing industry in West Malaysia', p. 156-71. Reprinted from: *Australian Economic Papers*, vol. 12, no. 21 (Dec. 1973); J. T. Purcal, 'Employment pattern in the rice growing areas of West Malaysia', p. 195-212; David Lim, 'Industrialization and unemployment in West Malaysia', p. 213-24; Lutz Hoffmann and Tan Siew Ee, 'Employment creation through export growth: a case study of West Malaysia's manufacturing industries', p. 225-47; D. R. Snodgrass, 'Trends and patterns in Malaysian income distribution, 1957-70', p. 251-68; R. Thillainathan, 'Planning for economic equality and the role of the public sector: the West Malaysian case', p. 309-17; Martin Rudner, 'The state and peasant innovation in rural development: the case of Malaysian rubber', p. 321-31. Reprinted from: *Asian and African Studies*, vol. 6 (1970); Brien K. Parkinson, 'Non-economic factors in the economic retardation of the rural Malays', p. 332-40. Reprinted from: *Modern Asian Studies*, vol. 1, part 1 (Jan. 1967); William Wilder, 'Islam, other factors and Malay backwardness: comments on an argument', p. 341-46. Reprinted from: *Modern Asian Studies*, vol. 2, part 2 (April

1968); Brien K. Parkinson, 'The economic retardation of the Malays – a rejoinder', p. 346-49. Reprinted from: *Modern Asian Studies*, vol. 2, part 3 (July 1968); and Anders Olgaard, 'Monetary policy in Malaysia as part of policies towards economic development', p. 362-74. Reprinted from: *UMBC Economic Review*, vol. 5, no. 2 (1969).

518 **The Malaysian economy at the crossroads: policy adjustment or structural transformation.**
Edited by Lim Lin Lean, Chee Peng Lim.   Kuala Lumpur: Malaysian Economic Association, and Organizational Resources Sdn. Bhd., 1984. 478p.

This is a collection of nineteen papers and an introduction concerned with two major, and related, problems facing the present-day Malaysian economy: the current global recession; and the task of transforming the basic structure of the economy. The papers are grouped under the following headings: the global economic crisis and domestic repercussions; Malaysian financial developments, public and private; the nature, role and performance of public enterprises; and reforming Malaysia's economic structure. Some of the papers have a list of references. The contributors include a number of prominent Malaysian academics, bankers (from the public sector), and government officials.

519 **The urban labor market and income distribution. A study of Malaysia.**
Dipak Mazumdar.   New York: Oxford University Press, for the World Bank, 1981. 375p.

This is a detailed case study of the working of the labour market in the urban sector of Peninsular Malaysia and of the factors which affect the distribution of income in this sector. Its primary focus is on 'income distribution at the lower end of the earnings scale, [unemployment], and on the determinants of poverty'. An important policy conclusion of the study is that 'efforts to reduce the burden of dependency among poor households, either through family planning programs or through policies to increase the employment opportunities of females and nonprime-age males, may help to alleviate relative poverty; the principal objective of policy, however, should be to tackle problems associated with low individual earnings'. The main sources for this study are two surveys conducted in Malaysia by the World Bank in 1973 and 1975.

520 **Public expenditure in Malaysia. Who benefits and why.**
Jacob Meerman.   New York: Oxford University Press, for the World Bank, 1979. 383p. map. bibliog.

This study develops two sets of data: information on the costs of government programmes in education, medical care, public utilities (electricity, water and sewage), and agriculture; and second, a sample survey of the use of those services by households. From this data an estimate of government spending on households divided by income, region, race and other variables is derived. The study relates solely to West Malaysia and draws on material relating to 1973-74. It is primarily an exercise in the measurement of the distributive effects of public expenditures. Analysis of policy issues receives less attention.

521   Malaysia. Development pattern and policy, 1947-1971.
V. V. Bhanoji Rao.   Singapore: Singapore University Press, 1980.
267p. bibliog.

An attempt to assess the development pattern and policy of the Malaysian economy during 1947-71 through an analysis of 'macroeconomic data from national accounts, population censuses and surveys, industrial censuses and surveys, and other sources'. The methods of analysis are drawn from the pioneering contributions of Clark, Kuznets, Chenery, Leontief, and several other scholars. The chapters are titled: analysis of economic growth; structure of output and employment; inter-industry structure and structural change; industrialization and import substitution; review of economic planning; and the employment problem and related issues.

522   Changing planning perspectives of agricultural development in Malaysia.
Martin Rudner.   *Modern Asian Studies*, vol. 17, part 3 (July 1983), p. 413-35.

Rudner notes in an introductory paragraph that although Malaysia remains 'a staunchly market-oriented, open, and predominantly private enterprise economy', government economic planning is highly institutionalized. His article considers the evolution of development planning in Malaysia from the mid-1950s; and, more particularly, the changing official perception of, and planning perspectives for, agricultural development (mainly concerning rubber and rice) over the same period.

523   Nationalism, planning, and economic modernization in Malaysia: the politics of beginning development.
Martin Rudner.   Beverly Hills, California; London: Sage Publications, 1975. 85p. bibliog.

This volume is intended as 'an interpretative essay on the economic and political dynamics of Malayan development planning during the First and Second Five-Year Plans, 1956-1960 and 1961-1965, respectively'. The two most substantial chapters provide a detailed examination of the two Plans themselves; briefer chapters consider: the political setting of independence; the Malayanization of the bureaucracy; development strategies and planning machinery; and the dimensions of economic modernization.

524   The political economy of independent Malaya – a case study in development.
Edited by T. H. Silcock, E. K. Fisk. London: Angus & Robertson; Canberra: The Australian National University, 1963. 306p.

This collection of eleven papers provides an analysis of the principal features of the economy of Malaya [Peninsular Malaysia and Singapore] in the early years of the Federation's independence. The opening three contributions examine the social, political, and demographic context: the succeeding papers consider specific aspects of the Malayan economy (for example: export prospects; the balance of payments; rubber supply conditions; rural development policy; financial developments since independence; industrialization). The concluding paper provides a general review of Malayan economic policy in that period.

525 **Readings in Malayan economics.**
Edited by T. H. Silcock. Singapore: Eastern Universities Press, 1961. 501p.

This volume brings together twenty-four articles previously published in various journals in the period from the end of the Pacific War to the late 1950s. The articles are divided into five groups, concerned with: economic growth; macroeconomic analysis; rubber; tin; currency and credit. The contributors include: R. W. Firth; M. G. Swift; M. Freedman; P. T. Bauer; Ooi Jin-Bee; Sir Sydney Caine; F. C. Benham; and T. H. Silcock himself.

526 **Inequality and economic development in Malaysia.**
Donald R. Snodgrass. Kuala Lumpur: Oxford University Press, 1980. 326p. bibliog.

In this work the author examines the origins, nature, extent and possible rectification of economic inequality (particularly that which is related to an ethnic group), in Peninsular Malaysia. The first part of the volume considers, with reference to the Malaysian experience, the historical origins of inequality, and the social science theories as to how such inequality arises and is maintained. There is also an analysis of the patterns and trends in economic inequality in Malaysia over the period 1957-70, and an assessment of the extent of inequality around 1970. The second part of the book discusses the policies and programmes which have been introduced to reduce economic inequality – fiscal redistribution; rural and urban development policies; and educational, health and family planning programmes. The Malaysian Government's efforts to reduce economic inequality are analysed; and the achievements of the New Economic Policy up to the late 1970s are assessed.

527 **Some development implications of political integration and disintegration in Malaysia.**
Donald R. Snodgrass. In: *Government and economic development.* Edited by Gustav Ranis. New Haven, Connecticut; London: Yale University Press, Economic Growth Center, Yale University, 1971. p. 30-50.

The author asks what is the effect on the economic development prospects of Malaysia's three main components (West Malaysia, Sarawak, Sabah) of 'their integration into a single, federally structured state?'. He considers, for example: economic integration 1963-65; economic integration and disintegration 1965-68; and the potential and actual economic effects of the federation as of the late 1960s. Snodgrass concludes that firstly, Malaysian GNP and its growth rate are relatively unaffected in either direction by the federation; and secondly, with respect to the welfare judgement – whether economically Malaysia is 'a good thing'; it clearly is from the point of view of Sabah and Sarawak, but from the point of view of West Malaysia, it is not. There are some concluding remarks by Van Doorn Ooms.

528 **Income distribution and determination in West Malaysia.**
Tan Tat Wai.   Kuala Lumpur: Oxford University Press, 1982.
364p. map. bibliog.

Provides a description of income distribution, and an analysis of the origins of
income inequality and wealth in Peninsular Malaysia. It is divided into two parts.
The first considers the distribution of income, and the factors which determine
that distribution. It includes analysis of: the income of padi farmers and
fishermen; the income of rubber and coconut small-holders; the income of the
salaried and urban workers, and the rise of the Malaysian middle class. The
second part considers the distribution of wealth and its impact on income, and
includes analysis of: ownership and control of the largest corporations; the
earnings of firms and the income of their owners; the monopoly-monopsony
position of middlemen; and the origins, nature, and outlook of Malaysian
businessmen. Data is drawn mainly from the period 1965-70.

529 **Primary commodity exports and economic development. Theory,
evidence and a study of Malaysia.**
John T. Thoburn.   London: John Wiley & Sons, 1977. 310p. map.
bibliog.

The focus of this book is on 'the role primary commodity exports can play as a
source of economic growth and development'. The book is divided into three
parts, of which the second is a case study of commodity exports and development
in Malaysia. This includes consideration of the three principal Malaysian primary
commodity exports – tin, rubber, and palm oil; the technology and organization
of the tin industry; the structure and technology of the rubber industry; the
linkage effects of tin and rubber; tin-mining and rubber-estate capital payments;
and palm oil in comparison to rubber. This is followed by analysis of: final
demand linkages and the development of the local market for consumer goods;
exports and the Malaysian engineering industry as a case study of backward
linkage; and technology, employment creation, income distribution, and poverty
in Malaysia.

530 **ASEAN economies in perspective. A comparative study of
Indonesia, Malaysia, the Philippines, Singapore and Thailand.**
John Wong.   London: Macmillan, 1979. 217p. map. notes and
references.

Wong does not provide a collection of country studies, but treats the ASEAN
(Association of South-East Asian Nations) economies 'as an integral whole'. His
four main chapters consider: foreign trade; industrialization; agricultural and rural
development; and the socioeconomic framework of development. This book
offers a perceptive general introduction to the main features of the contemporary
Malaysian economy, within the context of the ASEAN economies as a whole.
Approximately one-third of the book is given over to an appendix of statistical
tables.

531 **Malaysia. Growth and equity in a multiracial society.**
Co-ordinating authors Kevin Young, Willem C. F. Bussink, Parvez
Hasan. Baltimore, Maryland; London: Johns Hopkins University
Press, 1980. 345p. map. (A World Bank Country Economic
Report).

This volume draws on the findings of World Bank missions to Malaysia in the
1970s. It reviews the performance of the Malaysian economy from 1960 to 1976,
and assesses future prospects through to 1990. It focuses on the Malaysian
government's New Economic Policy, introduced in the early 1970s, which aims to
reduce poverty and racial economic imbalances. The study argues that 'sustained
industrial growth, and the employment opportunities it would engender, are of
particular importance in reducing poverty and increasing the participation of
Malays in the modern sectors of the economy'; it therefore emphasizes the
importance of providing 'a policy framework conducive to a high rate of
investment in the manufacturing sector'. It also suggests that there is a need to
accelerate the pace of rural development, although it admits that in this case 'the
main constraint is the capacity of the public sector to design projects that can
affect large numbers of rural poor'. The volume contains nine papers, each by a
different author. The issues covered include: employment and income distribution; the access of the poor to basic services; monetary and fiscal issues; industrial
policies; agriculture and rural poverty; and exports. The study is concerned
primarily with West Malaysia.

**Demographic impact on socio-economic development. The Malaysian
experience.**
See item no. 283.

**Population and development: theory and empirical evidence. The
Malaysian case.**
See item no. 286.

**Malaysia: patterns of population movement to 1970; Malaysia: a
demographic analysis of internal migrants; Malaysia: migration and
development: a regional synthesis; Malaysia: population distribution and
development strategies.**
See item no. 287.

Is there development in Sarawak? Political goals and practice.
See item no. 457.

Ministry of Finance Malaysia. Economic report.
See item no. 641.

National accounts of West Malaysia 1947-1971.
See item no. 643.

The New Economic Policy

532 The Second Malaysia Plan 1971-1975: a critique.

Syed Hussein Alatas. Singapore: Institute of Southeast Asian
Studies, 1972. 16p. (Occasional Paper, no. 15).

Alatas mounts a vitriolic attack on the Second Malaysia Plan. The Plan, as a
document, is 'relatively incomplete, inconsistent, and unintelligent in presentation'.
Among his comments: the Plan aims to create a Malay capitalist class, but 'what
shall take place in reality is that a group of present Malay in power shall seize the
opportunity of transforming themselves with government aid to become
capitalists. Thus we shall have an artificial group of capitalists who shall only be
able to function as a parasitic minority because they have been deprived of a
natural history of growth . . . [the] Alliance government . . . wishes to act worse
than a slave to a group of Malay capitalists'.

533 Malaysia and Singapore: the political economy of multiracial development.

Stephen Chee. *Asian Survey*, vol. 14, no. 2 (Feb. 1974),
p. 183-91.

This brief survey of Malaysia (and Singapore) in 1973 is mainly concerned with
the government's recently-introduced policy of restructuring society under the
New Economic Policy, so as to reduce and then eliminate racial economic
predominance. There are also sections on government and politics, and on the
foreign policy of Malaysia during 1973.

534 Politics and business. A study of Multi-Purpose Holdings Berhad.

Bruce Gale. Singapore, Petaling Jaya: Eastern Universities Press,
1985. 244p.

Multi-Purpose Holdings Berhad is the investment arm of the Malaysian Chinese
Association. It began operations in 1977, and is currently one of the largest
companies in Malaysia with important interests in plantations, property, trading,
insurance, and finance. This detailed study considers the establishment and
subsequent very rapid expansion of Multi-Purpose Holdings Berhad; its relations
with the Chinese community; and its relations with the UMNO and with
government agencies charged with attaining Malay corporate objectives under the
NEP. This study provides a valuable insight into the increasingly politicized
economic structures of contemporary Malaysia.

535 Politics and public enterprise in Malaysia.

Bruce Gale. Singapore, Kuala Lumpur: Eastern Universities
Press, 1981. 246p. bibliog.

Gale presents a history of three major public enterprises in Malaysia – the
Perbadanan Nasional (National Corporation), Majlis Amanah Rakyat (Council of
Trust for the Indigenous People), and the Perbadanan Pembangunan Bandar
(Urban Development Authority). He analyses their activities in terms of the
social and political contexts in which they operate. Each of these enterprises was

161

'committed to opening opportunities for Malay businessmen in a commercial sector that was dominated by an immigrant Chinese community'. They were 'quintessentially political organizations in origin, status, policies and operational codes'. A final concluding chapter considers public enterprises and the New Economic Policy; in this, the author argues that government agencies are not necessarily the most efficient or equitable instruments for achieving the NEP's targets.

536 **The politics of planning: Malaysia and the new Third Malaysia Plan (1976-1980).**
Colin MacAndrews. *Asian Survey*, vol. 17, no. 3 (March 1977), p. 293-308.

This article examines the Third Malaysia Plan, 'the forces that have moulded it, and the objectives it is trying to achieve, looks at both its strengths and weaknesses, and finally tries to assess as far as possible the likelihood of its success'. The introductory discussion considers the major factors affecting 'the formulation of national planning in Malaysia since 1957 . . . and the development of planning as an important policy mechanism to meet internal and changing political demands'. In a conclusion MacAndrews argues that with the Third Plan, 'the government's intervention has been refocused to lessen the excessive concentration of the Second Malaysia Plan on rapid Malay participation in the economy and Malay poverty, and is aimed at all Malaysians, irrespective of race. The emphasis is also on the Malays using their own initiative to develop entrepreneurial skills'.

537 **Communalism, industrial policy and income distribution in Malaysia.**
Fred R. von der Mehden. *Asian Survey*, vol. 15, no. 3 (March 1975), p. 247-61.

An analysis of some aspects of Malaysia's efforts to meet the problem of communal economic disparities. Consideration is first given to the pattern of economic inequality, particularly with respect to employment, ownership in the modern sector, and income distribution. The major part of the article discusses the problems attendant upon the Malaysian government's policies aimed at reducing communal disparities, with emphasis given to those problems which are communally based. Here attention is given to three major issues which have arisen in the implementation of the New Economic Policy: the involvement of Malays in employment in the modern sector; the increase in Chinese ownership; and increased state ownership of the modern sector, and the implications of this for politics and for the management of the economy.

538 **The politics of Malaysia's New Economic Policy.**
R. S. Milne. *Pacific Affairs*, vol. 49, no. 2 (summer 1976), p. 235-62.

This article is concerned with the political aspects of the NEP (New Economic Policy), especially those arising 'from measures designed to increase the percentage of Malays employed in non-agricultural occupations, particularly at managerial level, and to increase the Malay share of ownership of the national wealth'. It considers, for example: the provisions and implementation of the NEP; ethnic reactions to the NEP; the NEP and UMNO leadership; ethnic competition and co-operation under the NEP; relations between Malays – the possibility of class cleavages.

539 **The Fourth Malaysia Plan: economic perspectives.**
Edited by Jomo Kwame Sundaram, R. J. G. Wells.   Kuala
Lumpur: Persatuan Ekonomi Malaysia (Malaysian Economic
Association), 1983. 185p.

This volume, which contains fourteen papers, provides a critical analysis of the Fourth Malaysia Plan (1981-85). The papers are grouped under the following headings: the philosophy of planning; growth and public finance; the primary and manufacturing sectors; and the tertiary sector. Contributors include some of the most prominent academic commentators on the political economy of contemporary Malaysia: David Lim, S. Husin Ali, R. Thillainathan, Tan Siew Ee, and the editors themselves.

540 **Ideology, politics and economic modernization: the case of the Malays in Malaysia.**
Tham Seong Chee.   *Southeast Asian Journal of Social Science*,
vol. 1, no. 1 (1973), p. 41-59.

Tham argues that attempts made so far in the early 1970s to encourage greater Malay participation in the entrepreneurial and manufacturing sectors of the Malaysian economy 'have not been significantly successful principally because traditional values and groups continue to dominate the action and value consciousness of the Malays. By value consciousness is meant the tendency to evaluate prestige and honour by reference to traditional structural groups, that is, the aristocracy and the bureaucracy at both state and federal levels. The crux of the matter is to evoke an ideology of achievement based on success acquired in entrepreneurship. This can only be done if there is a changing awareness in cultural evaluation in the area of prestige and status as they relate to the Malay status system which heavily favours the political and bureaucratic élites'. In a conclusion it is further noted that 'the encroachment of both political and bureaucratic control in the economy has only strengthened the prevailing attitude of dependence on the government for ensuring their [Malay] success in entrepreneurship'.

541 **Inter-racial balance in Malaysian employment and wealth: an evaluation of distributional targets.**
R. Thillainathan.   *The Developing Economies* (Tokyo), vol. 14,
no. 3 (Sept. 1976), p. 239-60.

The author provides a critical analysis of the objectives set out in the Second Malaysia Plan for the restructuring of the ownership of wealth and employment composition in favour of the Malays. In a conclusion he notes that according to the plan, 'the share of Malays in employment and wealth in the modern sector of the economy is to be raised to the targeted level, not by redistributing what is available but by giving them a larger share of increments arising from growth. Even if the target of employment composition by sector is attained over a twenty-year time horizon, it will require a substantial rural-urban migration of Malays and an equally significant reverse movement of non-Malays. On the other hand, if the target is to be attained in a shorter period, unemployment of non-Malays can rise above tolerable limits. The target for wealth ownership is far from attainable, if it is left to the Malay-owned private sector'; but recent research has pointed up 'the glaring inadequacies of the Malaysian public sector in its new found role as an entrepreneur'. Econometric techniques are mainly employed.

542 **The Second Malaysia Plan. Notes on the objectives of balanced distribution of wealth and employment.**
R. Thillainathan. *Kajian Ekonomi Malaysia* (Malaysian Economic Studies), vol. 7, no. 2 (Dec. 1970), p. 57-71.
This paper considers critically the objectives of effecting an ethnically balanced distribution of wealth and employment as set out in the Second Malaysia Plan. The discussion 'pertains to the distribution of wealth and employment in the modern sector in West Malaysia'. The author casts doubt on the feasibility of the targets set for the restructuring of employment and the ownership of corporate assets in the modern sector in favour of the Malays. The article mainly employs econometric techniques.

543 **The twenty-year plan for restructuring employment in Peninsular Malaysia: a quarterly assessment.**
R. Thillainathan. *Kajian Ekonomi Malaysia* (Malaysian Economic Studies), vol. 14, no. 2 (Dec. 1977), p. 49-62.
On the basis of data given in the Third Malaysia Plan, this paper evaluates the actual implementation and progress achieved in attaining the employment composition target of the New Economic Policy over the period 1970-75. In a conclusion, Thillainathan suggests that the actual proportions of the new jobs in the various sectors and occupations that have accrued to the different ethnic groups over this period, diverge rather significantly from the required proportions for attaining the target over the period 1970-90. Given this divergence, the proportion of new jobs that must be taken up by the different ethnic groups over the 1975-90 period 'to attain the sectoral and occupational targets in employment by the terminal year 1990' appears to be a little unrealistic. It requires 'a more substantial movement of Malays from rural to urban areas and of non-Malays in the reverse direction than what would have been required in the absence of this divergence'. He also argues that 'the actual implementation of the employment restructuring objective have led to some displacement of existing workers in certain sectors and occupations which appears to be in conflict with the declared aim of the NEP . . . The incidence of unemployment, in proportionate terms, has increased among non-Malays whereas that among Malays has declined'.

Colonialism, dualistic growth and the distribution of economic benefits in Malaysia.
See item no. 222.

'Special Rights' as a strategy for development. The case of Malaysia.
See item no. 424.

Rural poverty and development

544 **The sociology of production in rural Malay society.**
Conner Bailey.   Kuala Lumpur: Oxford University Press, 1983.
226p. 4 maps. bibliog.

Bailey is concerned with the following basic questions: how does the manner in which people earn a living affect patterns of social interaction in both economic and non-economic relationships? To what extent can we trace the basis of social structure through analysis of the material basis of a society's existence? He pursues these questions through an examination of three rural Malay communities, 'each of which is engaged in different environmental and economic adaptations'. These are villages engaged in rice farming (in Trengganu), rubber tapping (Kedah), and fishing (Trengganu). Fieldwork was carried out in the later 1970s. Bailey suggests that 'by focusing on production processes and relationships in a comparative context, it is hoped to present a richer portrayal of rural Malay society than has been possible through previous studies'.

545 **The cultural ecology of a Chinese village: Cameron Highlands, Malaysia.**
James D. Clarkson.   Chicago: University of Chicago, Department of Geography, 1968. 174p. 4 maps. bibliog. (Research Paper, no. 114).

This study considers, in the context of cultural ecology, three overlapping sets of events: the vegetable production and distribution system of the Chinese in the Cameron Highlands of Malaysia; the history of settlement and resettlement of a part of that population; and the conflicting attitudes and values of this Chinese community and of the members of various state and national government agencies. The first part of the book provides the background, mainly historical,

165

necessary for an understanding of the contemporary (mid-1960s) man-land system of the Chinese agriculturalists in the Cameron Highlands. The second part describes and analyses three aspects of this scene: the crop ecology of the vegetable industry; the settlement history of the Bertam Valley population; and the conflicts engendered by divergent local and state/national agency views with regard to land use.

546 **The persistence of poverty: rural development policy in Malaysia.**
Lorraine Corner. *Kajian Malaysia* (Journal of Malaysian Studies), vol. 1, no. 1 (June 1983), p. 38-61.

Corner observes that 'despite large investments in rural development during the seventies directed, amongst other objectives, towards the goal of improving rural living standards, rural poverty remains perhaps the single most significant and most intractable development problem for Malaysia in the eighties'. She provides a critical analysis of the Malaysian government's development programmes from the 1960s which, she argues, have failed 'to make significant inroads into the income gap between the poor in traditional, especially rural areas of economic activity and the rest of the rapidly expanding Malaysian economy'. In particular, Corner suggests that 1) there has been a misplaced, overly optimistic, dependence in development policy (even under the NEP) on an indirect, 'trickle-down' strategy to distribute the benefits of development to the poorest strata of society; and 2) that a disturbing contradiction has emerged between a development model which will involve the contraction of the agricultural sector relative to the rest of the economy, and a political tenet which equates the preservation of the peasantry with the preservation of Malay culture.

547 **Malay fishermen. Their peasant economy.**
Raymond Firth. London: Routledge & Kegan Paul, 1966. 2nd ed. 398p. 6 maps. bibliog.

Provides a detailed analysis of production, marketing and distribution in a Malay fishing community in Kelantan, 'related to community structure and values'. The major field research was carried out in 1939-40, with the first edition of this book being published in 1946. This second, revised and enlarged, edition incorporates the results of further fieldwork in 1947 and, in particular, in 1963. The main body of the book consists, in effect, of 'an historical case study in economic anthropology' of the Malay fishing community studied in detail at the end of the 1930s; this is followed by an account, in the final chapter, of developments in the same community through to the early 1960s, 'to bring out some of the underlying social and economic forces that have been at work during the past generation'. One brief appendix considers problems and technique in a field study of a peasant economy.

548 **Housekeeping among Malay peasants.**
Rosemary Firth. London: Athlone Press; New York: Humanities Press, 1966. 2nd ed. 242p. 2 maps.

The major part of the research for this study of housekeeping in a Malay coastal village in Kelantan was undertaken in 1939-40. There are chapters on: the conditions of housekeeping; the position of women; divorce and polygyny; the importance of rice in the economy; how money is spent daily; the child's place in the household; shopping and marketing; and larger-scale household planning (i.e. saving, private ceremonial obligations, and public ceremonial occasions). Two final chapters consider some of the main changes in housekeeping practices in the village which were observed by the author during a brief return in 1963. An appendix includes a number of cooking recipes commonly employed in the village.

549   **Differentiation of the peasantry: a study of the rural communities in West Malaysia.**
Fatimah Halim.   *Journal of Contemporary Asia*, vol. 10, no. 4 (1980), p. 400-22.

This article provides a detailed characterization of the principal class divisions in the rural communities of contemporary West Malaysia, drawn from extensive fieldwork in three communities in the northeast of the peninsula.

550   **Land ownership and economic prospects of Malayan peasants.**
Robert Ho.   *Modern Asian Studies*, vol. 4, part 1 (Jan. 1970), p. 83-92.

Ho first considers the evolving pattern of agricultural development and land ownership in a part of Kuala Kangsar District in Perak since 1890. This analysis is then supplemented with data from two other areas of Malaysia to show typical features of land ownership in the Malayan peasant sector in the 1960s. Ho's concern is to explain the overcrowding on the land and the frustration of ambitions to acquire land which is characteristic of contemporary rural Malaysia; and his explanation places considerable emphasis on Malay cultural values and attitudes towards, notably, the modern monetary economy. 'To set the Malay peasant on the road to economic progress requires changes in his habits of thought and attitudes as much as alterations in land codes or economic policies'.

551   **Ethnicity, class and development. Malaysia.**
Edited by S. Husin Ali. Kuala Lumpur: Persatuan Sains Sosial Malaysia [Malaysian Social Science Association], 1984. 382p.

This volume brings together nineteen papers under the following headings: ethnicity and class; politics; socio-culture; education; economics; overviews. Some of the papers are in Bahasa Malaysia. Among the contributions in English: 'Social relations – the ethnic and class factors' [S. Husin Ali]; 'The growth of the worker class and its implications for social relations' [Lim Teck Ghee]; 'The socio-economic basis of ethnic consciousness – the Chinese in the 1970s' [Loh Kok Wah]; 'Malaysian Indians – ethnic and class loyalties' [P. Ramasamy]; 'Ethnic representation and the electoral system' [Sothi Rachagan]; 'Acculturation, assimilation and integration – the case of the Chinese' [Tan Chee Beng]; 'Caste, ethnicity, class and national unity – the dilemma of the Indians' [R. Rajoo]; 'Education as a vehicle for reducing economic inequality' [Toh Kin Woon]; 'Schooling as a dead end – education for the poor, especially the estate children' [T. Marimuthu]; 'Capitalist development, class and race' [Hing Ai Yun]; 'the New Economic Policy and "national unity" – development and inequality 25 years after independence' [Ishak Shari and K. S. Jomo]; 'Has the communal situation worsened over the last decade? Some preliminary thoughts' [Chandra Muzaffar].

552 **Malay peasant society and leadership.**
S. Husin Ali. Kuala Lumpur: Oxford University Press, 1975.
192p. 4 maps. bibliog.

The main objectives of this study of society and leadership among the rural Malays are 'to examine the nature of society within which the leadership exists, to identify the various types of leaders existing in the different communities, to discover their positions and functions in the context of their own social, economic and political environments and to assess their effectiveness in providing leadership to the people'. The analysis derives mainly from fieldwork undertaken through the 1960s in three rural communities in West Malaysia, each with a different predominant economic occupation – fishing, rice-growing, and rubber-tapping. The author argues that since independence, as new political and administrative institutions penetrated the village communities, the traditional rural leadership of elders and religious figures had partially given way to a new type of leadership which had little or no traditional roots – that of the landlord, party functionary, and the government official.

553 **Patterns of rural leadership in Malaya.**
S. Husin Ali. *Journal of the Malaysian Branch of the Royal Asiatic Society*, vol. 41, part 1 (July 1968), p. 95-145.

This lengthy article considers the pattern of Malay rural leadership and its transformation within the context of the rural society and its own transformation. The main sections of the article discuss: traditional Malay rural society; traditional leadership patterns in rural Malay society – kinship leaders, magico-religious leaders, political leaders; and contemporary (mid-1960s) leadership patterns among the rural Malays. The article draws on fieldwork conducted in two rural communities (in Pahang and Johor) and, for comparative purposes, one urban community (Kampung Baru in Kuala Lumpur). The author is mainly concerned to draw out the transformation of some aspects of traditional leadership in Malay rural society, involving either a diminution of importance or a change of substance; and the emergence of new forms and types of leadership to meet the needs of modern development and change.

554 **Poverty and landlessness in Kelantan, Malaysia.**
S. Husin Ali. Saarbrücken, GFR; Fort Lauderdale, Florida: Breitenbach, 1983. 128p. bibliog. (Bielefeld Studies on the Sociology of Development, vol. 20).

S. Husin Ali's examination of poverty and landlessness in the state of Kelantan is set against a major objective of contemporary Malaysian development planning – 'the eradication of poverty'. Two opening chapters consider various definitions of poverty, and then present a general view of the economic and social structure of Kelantan. The major part of the analysis, drawn mainly from the author's surveys in Kota Bharu and two rural areas, considers access to land, employment and income in the state, as well as social status; access to education; patterns of leadership in both urban and village communities; and political trends (most notably, the conflict and cooperation of the PMIP and the UMNO in Kelantan). Finally there is a critical examination of the government's development efforts as to whether they assist in the eradication of poverty. His analysis is notably radical: 'The most effective efforts towards eradicating or at least reducing poverty are those which are conducive to the weakening and finally replacing [of] the laissez-faire socio-economic system, which is a fertile breeding ground for the diseases of inequality, exploitation and poverty'.

555 **Some case studies on poverty in Malaysia. Essays presented to Professor Ungku A. Aziz.**
Edited by B. A. R. Mokhzani, Khoo Siew Mun. Kuala Lumpur: Persatuan Ekonomi Malaysia (Malaysian Economic Association), 1977. 262p.

This volume contains fourteen papers grouped under the following headings: definitions and measurement of poverty; poverty in selected sectors; poor groups; socio-psychological implications of poverty; and strategies for eradicating poverty. Some of the papers have a list of references.

556 **Bureaucracy and rural development in Malaysia. A study of complex organizations in stimulating economic development in new states.**
Gayl D. Ness. Berkeley, California: University of California Press; London: Cambridge University Press, 1967. 257p. 2 maps. bibliog.

The author begins with the view that all new states of the world have created national development plans and often new organizations to implement those plans. Of these countries, 'only the Federation of Malaysia and Singapore have achieved any success in their development programs'. Malaysia and Singapore alone appear 'to have made serious and sustained attempts to translate their development programs into action'. His study seeks to understand Malaysia's 'unique' experience in this respect. It is mainly concerned with the Ministry of Rural Development (and its autonomous authorities, FELDA and RIDA), and examines: the character of the society in which the Ministry emerged; the organizational experience that preceded the formation of the Ministry and helped to shape its goals and structure; and the Ministry's operations and functions. Ness' central argument is that 'the delicate demographic balance of the country . . . is the basic moving force behind [the] success in public investment'. His study is based mainly on fieldwork in Malaysia carried out in 1961-64, and which included, most importantly, 'interviews with the officers concerned with the programs, and with other observers in Malaysia'.

557 **Non-economic factors in the economic retardation of the rural Malays.**
Brien K. Parkinson. *Modern Asian Studies*, vol. 1, part 1 (Jan. 1967), p. 31-46.

In seeking to explain the relative economic backwardness of the rural Malays, Parkinson emphasizes an alleged resistance on the part of the Malays to radical change, unless that change can be incorporated within established patterns. Thus, for example, the Malays are alleged to have resisted major changes in agricultural techniques (which, if adopted, would have raised rural incomes), in large part because they simply preferred to work in the old ways. Parkinson probes the cultural and religious origins of these Malay values, emphasizing that they are in no way irrational. But he concludes that there is a serious conflict between the values of the rural Malays and the values required for capitalism, such that, if the values of the Malays remain basically unaltered, 'economic advance for them will remain relatively slow'. Reprinted in: *Readings on Malaysian Economic Development*, edited by David Lim (Kuala Lumpur, 1975, p. 332-40).

558 **The economic retardation of the Malays – a rejoinder.**
Brien K. Parkinson. *Modern Asian Studies*, vol. 2, part 3 (July 1968), p. 267-72.

In this brief paper, Parkinson replies to criticisms by Wilder (q.v.) of his original article (q.v.), restating and developing his basic argument that, as a general tendency, the rural Malays have not been receptive to change in the past and continue to show signs of resistance to change in the present. Reprinted in: *Readings on Malaysian Economic Development*, edited by David Lim, (Kuala Lumpur, 1975, p. 346-49).

559 **The failure of rural development in Peninsular Malaysia.**
Frank Peacock. In: *Issues in Malaysian development*. Edited by James C. Jackson, Martin Rudner. Singapore: Heinemann Educational Books (Asia), for the Asian Studies Association of Australia, 1979. p. 375-96.

Peacock is concerned with the persistence, indeed relative worsening of poverty in Malaysia, despite the rapid growth of Gross National Product in recent decades. He suggests that 'the failure of poverty groups to benefit from high growth rates can be explained by the concentration of growth in certain limited sectors of the economy'. Peacock argues that until the mid-1970s the government sought to combat poverty directly 'through increased productivity within the traditional and poor agricultural sector'. However the Third Malaysia Plan (1976-80) 'seeks to alleviate poverty largely through shifting the poor into the more productive, high income, modern sector of the economy'. But Peacock doubts whether the Third Plan's proposals will, in fact, make much impact on poverty in Malaysia.

560 **The development of the underdevelopment of the Malaysian peasantry.**
Shamsul Amri Baharuddin. *Journal of Contemporary Asia*, vol. 9, no. 4 (1979), p. 434-54.

This paper has two objectives: 1. to consider the impact of British colonial rule on the Malaysian peasantry – the historical process that led to the underdevelopment of the Malaysian peasantry; and 2. to analyse the present underdevelopment of the Malaysian peasantry, specifically the Malay rice-growers and the Malay peasant rubber smallholders. The author suggests that the successive development plans launched from the 1950s to alleviate the problems faced by the majority of the rural population have, in fact, been of benefit only to the rural élite, and have left most of the peasants 'in similar or even worse circumstances'.

561 **Capital, saving and credit in a Malay peasant economy.**

M. G. Swift. In: *Capital, saving and credit in peasant societies. Studies from Asia, Oceania, the Caribbean and Middle America.* Edited by Raymond Firth, B. S. Yamey. London: George Allen & Unwin, 1964. p. 133-56.

A consideration of the roles of capital, saving and credit in a mixed farming (rubber, fruit and rice) peasant economy, as studied in Jelebu, in Negeri Sembilan.

562 **Economic concentration and Malay peasant society.**

M. G. Swift. In: *Social organization. Essays presented to Raymond Firth.* Edited by Maurice Freedman. London: Frank Cass, 1967. p. 241-69.

Swift seeks 'to make a *prima facie* case for a generalization about recent trends in Malay peasant economy'; that is, that important areas of peasant economic activity show a change from a fairly equal distribution of wealth to one where a small number of peasants are set off from their fellow villagers by substantially greater income and possessions; and a 'related tendency for ownership of village assets to pass from the peasants to other groups in society'. His analysis focuses mainly on concentration of ownership in rice cultivation, but there is also discussion of: rubber growing; the fishing industry; and the social implications of the process of economic concentration.

563 **Malay peasant society in Jelebu.**

M. G. Swift. London: Athlone Press; New York: Humanities Press, 1965. 181p. map. bibliog.

This study of Malay peasant social organization in Jelebu (a district in Negeri Sembilan), focuses on two aspects – the matrilineal kinship system and the economy. Swift began fieldwork (in the mid-1950s) with the hypothesis that the introduction of rubber had led 'to an individualization of the economy, and therefore to opposition to the traditional ownership of land by women as representatives of the matri-kin, and also to kinship restrictions on the rights of landowners. Furthermore that these changes had spread into a general decline of the traditional kinship organization'. In detail there is discussion of such aspects as: the nature of the economy; saving and capital; the decline of the traditional political organization; *adat* disputes; and the village, status and social stratification.

564 **Poverty and rural development in Malaysia.**

Ungku A. Aziz. *Kajian Ekonomi Malaysia* (Malaysian Economic Studies), vol. 1, no. 1 (June 1964), p. 70-105.

This article, by the present Vice-Chancellor of the University of Malaya, provides a broad introduction to the problem of rural poverty in Malaysia and its alleviation. Ungku Aziz provides a number of measures of the socioeconomic characteristics of rural poverty, including nutritional levels, mortality rates, and the per capita ownership of *sarongs*. There is a brief discussion of the historical context within which poverty has evolved in Malaysia. But the major interest of the paper focuses on the proposals for the alleviation of rural poverty. Ungku

Aziz discusses land reform; legislation to improve the conditions of rural labour; and, most important, the creation of rural co-operatives in selected districts to undertake such activities as marketing, the provision of credit, processing, and the distribution of consumer goods in the rural communities. Ungku Aziz notes with scepticism 'a strong political desire in some quarters to secure an increase in the number of Malay capitalists or traders as some kind of solution to the problem of Malay rural poverty'.

565 **A Malay peasant community in Upper Perak. Integration and transformations.**
Wan Hashim. Bangi, Malaysia: Penerbit Universiti Kebangsaan Malaysia, 1978. 192p. 4 maps. bibliog.

This study, drawn primarily on fieldwork in a Malay village, Kampong Ulu Kenderong, in Upper Perak, examines the changes introduced into traditional Malay rural social organization 'consequent to the introduction of cash cropping and the integration of the village into a national political system based on democratically elected legislatures and competition between parties'. Wan Hashim argues that the introduction of rubber has partly eroded the relatively egalitarian basis of traditional Malay rural organization, and that the introduction of modern politics and administration has undermined traditional village loyalties. He also discusses the changes in 'peasant value systems pertaining to new employment opportunities available' to villagers; and the problem that modern Islam faces in a world of rapid change.

566 **Communication, social structure and development in rural Malaysia. A study of Kampung Kuala Bera.**
William D. Wilder. London: Athlone Press; New Jersey: Humanities Press, 1982. 234p. 3 maps. bibliog.

A consideration of the social communications systems in a Malay peasant village in Pahang. The opening chapters analyse domestic and marriage groups, before considering 'more complex face-to-face units knitted together primarily by the spoken word – the kinship categories, the village-kindred, and the local community at large'. Finally there is analysis of the various media systems 'beyond the spoken word which are instrumental in the formation of larger groupings – mass media, commerce, administration, and associations'.

567 **Islam, other factors and Malay backwardness: comments on an argument.**
William Wilder. *Modern Asian Studies*, vol. 2, part 2 (April 1968), p. 155-64.

This study provides a severely critical analysis of Parkinson's argument (q.v.) that rural Malay society is economically backward primarily because of alleged Malay resistance to radical change; and his view that there exist among the rural Malays 'fatalistic attitudes towards life which arise from adherence to Islam'. Wilder takes issue with virtually all Parkinson's observations; and in conclusion argues from his own empirical research in rural Malaysia that adherence to Islam produces some practices, notably the *haj* (pilgrimage to Mecca), which, he suggests, encourage rather than deter capitalistic values among Malay villagers. Reprinted in:

Readings on Malaysian Economic Development, edited by David Lim, (Kuala Lumpur, 1975, p. 341-46).

568   A Malay village and Malaysia. Social values and rural development.
Peter J. Wilson.   New Haven, Connecticut: Human Relations Area Files Press, 1967. 171p. 2 maps. bibliog.

This work is concerned with 'the conduct of Malay villagers in their relationships with their outside world and the values and attitudes that underlie this conduct'. More specifically it considers: Malay villager stereotypes of the people with whom they come into contact; 'villager reaction to outside events and processes which in various ways form part and parcel of Malaysian development'; the economics of the village, and more specifically the nature of social relations arising out of economic activities; and 'the basis of social relations among villagers and the structure of village social life'. The study draws primarily on fieldwork conducted in the village of Jendram Hilir, in Selangor.

569   Differentiation among padi households in the Muda region: a village case study.
Diana Wong.   *Kajian Malaysia* (Journal of Malaysian Studies), vol. 1, no. 2 (Dec. 1983), p. 124-42.

Presents data on differentiation between households in a Malay village located in the Muda region. From this data Wong argues 'that social differentiation between the village households is to be found, but that these differences are not yet indicative of *class* differentiation within the village. This is because the dynamics of household formation in the Malay peasant context is governed as much by the needs of subsistence reproduction as by production. Also, it is questionable whether village boundaries form the limits within which class formation is taking place within the present Malaysian context'.

570   Perspectives towards investigating Malay peasant ideology and the bases of its production in contemporary Malaysia.
Zawawi Ibrahim.   *Journal of Contemporary Asia*, vol. 13, no. 2 (1983), p. 198-209.

The author argues that almost all of the existing anthropological studies on the Malay peasantry have touched on 'the issue of peasant ideology as an adjunct to the wider analysis of the village or peasant society being studied rather than as a problematic in its own right'. His article 'represents an attempt to pioneer theoretical explorations into [the] area of ideological production among Third World peasantries', and discusses such aspects as: the bases of ideological production and modes of interpellation in the Malay peasantry; and theoretical principles and strategies in investigating peasant ideology.

Malay reservations and Malay land ownership in Semenjih and Ulu Semenjih *mukims* Selangor.
See item no. 233.

Common efforts in the development of rural Sarawak, Malaysia.
See item no. 313.

173

Economics. Rural poverty and development

Modernization among the Iban of Sarawak.
See item no. 322.

Malaysia. Growth and equity in a multiracial society.
See item no. 531.

Rules for agrarian change: Negri Sembilan Malays and agricultural innovation.
See item no. 600.

Mobility and modernisation. The Federal Land Development Authority and its role in modernising the rural Malay.
See item no. 602.

Three Malay villages: a sociology of paddy growers in West Malaysia.
See item no. 616.

Income distribution among farm households in the Muda irrigation scheme: a developmental perspective.
See item no. 617.

Finance and Banking

571 **The history and development of the Hongkong and Shanghai Banking Corporation in Peninsular Malaysia.**
Chee Peng Lim, Phang Siew Nooi, Margaret Boh. In: *Eastern Banking. Essays in the history of the Hongkong and Shanghai Banking Corporation.* Edited by Frank H. H. King. London: Athlone Press, 1983. p. 350-91.

This paper considers the early history of the HSBC in Malaya from the establishment of its first branch, in Penang, in 1884; the role of the bank in the early economic development of Malaya under colonial rule, and its influence on the evolution of the financial and monetary system of Malaya in that period; the expansion of the HSBC's activities in Malaya through to independence; and the responses of the bank to the changing financial, banking, and political circumstances of Malaysia since independence – in particular, to the requirements of the New Economic Policy. The paper also examines 'the present relative standing of the HSBC [in Malaysia], in terms of deposit base, loans and growth potential'.

572 **Financial development in Malaya and Singapore.**
P. J. Drake. Canberra: Australian National University Press, 1969. 253p. map.

A study of the financial system of Singapore and West Malaysia which is divided into two parts. The first is concerned with the money supply – with analysis of the evolution of money in Malaya; the working of the currency board; the formation and management of the money supply; and the dismantling of the currency union in 1967. The second part considers the allocation of credit – with analysis of the commercial banks, Post Office savings banks, development finance institutions, insurance companies and provident funds, and money and securities markets. The study concentrates on developments in the 1950s and 1960s through to mid-1967, 'when the common Malayan dollar gave way to the individual currencies of

Malaysia, Singapore, and Brunei'. An addendum considers the devaluation of the old Malayan dollar in November 1967.

573 **The monetary and banking development of Malaysia and Singapore.**
Lee Sheng-Yi.   Singapore: Singapore University Press, 1974.
404p. bibliog.

This volume is divided into four parts. The first considers the monetary development of Malaysia and Singapore from 1786 through to 1972 – notably the evolution of the currency board system; and the balance of payments and money supply. The second part is concerned with banking development: it first considers the development of commercial and merchant banks from the 1840s, before discussing such aspects as the function and attitude of banks in the more modern period; sources of bank funds; the interest rate structure of commercial banking; and the recent development of money and capital markets, and the financial systems in Malaysia and Singapore. The third part considers monetary and exchange rate issues from the late 1950s; whilst the final part is primarily concerned with an analysis of money, quasi-money and the income velocity of circulation in Malaysia and Singapore between 1947 and 1965.

574 **Bank Negara Malaysia: the first 25 years 1959-1984.**
Supriya Singh.   Kuala Lumpur: Bank Negara Malaysia, 1984.
405p.

This is a popular history of Malaysia's central bank during its first twenty-five years. It focuses primarily on the personalities involved rather than on technical aspects of money and central banking.

575 **Financial institutions and markets in Malaysia.**
Zeti Akhtar Aziz. In: *Financial institutions and markets in Southeast Asia. A study of Brunei, Indonesia, Malaysia, Philippines, Singapore and Thailand.* Edited by Michael T. Skully.   London; Basingstoke, England: Macmillan, 1984, p. 110-66.

Malaysia's financial system has experienced a remarkable expansion from the early 1970s. This paper seeks to provide a detailed analysis of recent developments and of the contemporary structure of the country's financial institutions (both the banks and non-bank institutions) and financial markets. Works of related interest are: 1. *Merchant banking in ASEAN. A regional examination of its development and operations.* Michael T. Skully (Kuala Lumpur: Oxford University Press, 1983. 200p. bibliog). This volume includes a directory of Malaysian merchant banks (p. 109-14); and 2. *ASEAN financial co-operation. Developments in banking, finance and insurance.* Michael T. Skully (London; Basingstoke, England: Macmillan, 1985. 269p. map. bibliog). Both these volumes contain considerable discussion of developments and structures in Malaysia, but no specific Malaysian chapters.

The Malaysian economy at the crossroads: policy adjustment or structural transformation.
See item no. 518.

Trade

576 **Primary commodity control.**
C. P. Brown. Kuala Lumpur: Oxford University Press, 1975. 292p. bibliog.

An authoritative analysis of international and national devices designed to regulate production/trade in certain primary commodities. The focus is on contemporary control devices. Although econometric techniques are employed in the substantial appendixes, the main part of the text is not beyond the reach of readers familiar with the basic principles of economics. There are a substantial number of references to the control agreements for rubber and tin, and thus to Malaysia.

577 **Export trade and the West Malaysian economy – an enquiry into the economic implications of export instability.**
K. A. Mohamed Ariff. Kuala Lumpur: Faculty of Economics and Administration, University of Malaya, 1972. 246p. bibliog. (Monograph Series on Malaysian Economic Affairs).

Ariff is concerned with the causes of West Malaysia's export instability, and with the manner and magnitude of the repercussions on the domestic economy of export fluctuations. His evidence suggests that both the short- and long-term adverse effects of export instability are not as serious as *prima facie* portrayed. In general, the West Malaysian economy is relatively immune to export oscillations. His analysis focuses primarily on the period from the late 1940s to the late 1960s. There is a substantial statistical appendix. See also David Lim entry no. 515.

578   Malaysia's foreign trade 1968-80. Trends and structures.
      Edited by Gerhard Schmitt-Rink. Bochum, GFR: Studienverlag
      Brockmeyer, 1982. 299p. bibliog.

This collection of essays, volume 4 in a series 'Contributions to Quantitative
Economics', includes the following contributions: 'The development of the
commodity and regional composition of Malaysia's imports 1970-77' [Klaus
Nobel]; 'Commodity and regional composition of Malaysia's exports 1968-77'
[Karl-Heinz Leuchten]; 'The trend of Malaysian exports to several regional
market groupings 1970-78' [Mahani bt. Zainal Abidin]; 'Trade effects of foreign
direct investment in Malaysia 1968-80' [Manfred Busch]; 'Estimation of
substitution and income elasticities of Malaysia's ten most important export
commodities 1962-77' [Rainer Zimmermann].

579   Malaysia-Japan trade: issues and prospects for the 1980s.
      Zakaria Haji Ahmad, K. C. Cheong. In: *ASEAN-Japan relations.
      Trade and development.* Edited by Narongchai Akrasanee.
      Singapore: Institute of Southeast Asian Studies, 1983. p. 57-78.

This essay considers, in three inter-related sections: the pattern of Malaysia's
external trade and its economic growth in the 1970's; the public policy issues
involved in the conduct of Malaysia-Japan trade; and the theoretical and policy
issues raised by, and the prospects for, that trade in the 1980s.

**Primary commodity exports and economic development. Theory, evidence
and a study of Malaysia.**
See item no. 529.

Malaysia. Growth and equity in a multiracial society.
See item no. 531.

International commodity control – the tin experience.
See item no. 619.

Industry

580 **Industrial growth, employment, and foreign investment in Peninsular Malaysia.**
Lutz Hoffmann, Tan Siew Ee.   Kuala Lumpur: Oxford University Press, for the Institut für Weltwirtschaft, Kiel, 1980. 322p. bibliog.

This study includes consideration of the following: the growth of manufacturing in Peninsular Malaysia during the 1950s and 1960s; government policy towards industry from the time of independence, and its impact; Malaysian manufacturing in the early 1970s; the sources of industrial growth in the 1960s and 1970s; industrial growth and the absorption of primary factors; the impact of foreign direct investment; and the conditions and prospects for further export expansion in manufactures.

581 **Multinational corporations and development in Malaysia.**
Lim Mah Hui.   *Southeast Asian Journal of Social Science*, vol. 4, no. 1 (1975), p. 53-76.

Lim is mainly concerned with the impact of the operations of multinational corporations in Malaysia – their impact on economic growth; effects on employment and labour; their influence on social and economic inequalities; their impact on the balance of payments and the supply of capital; and their contribution to the transfer of technology. There is a substantial statistical appendix. Lim concludes that other than their positive contribution to economic growth, multinational corporations tend to retard the other aspects of development. 'The benefits they generate are enjoyed by themselves and by a small segment in the host country. The rest of the population are kept in perpetual impoverishment. The local economy continues to be a satellite of the metropolis. A similar parasitical relationship exists between the national bourgeoisie and the people. In short it is more appropriate to recognize the multinational corporations as a continued source of underdevelopment in Malaysia'. This article should be compared closely with that by Lewis Mann (q.v.), published two years later in the *Bulletin of Concerned Asian Scholars*. A critical review of this article by Gerald Tan was published in the *Southeast Asian Journal of Social Science* in 1978 (q.v.).

582 **Ownership and control of the one hundred largest corporations in Malaysia.**
Lim Mah Hui.   Kuala Lumpur: Oxford University Press, 1981. 190p. bibliog.

The central aim of this study is the investigation of the nature of ownership and control of Malaysia's corporate economy in the mid-1970s and 'the implications it has on social, economic and political structures'. There is consideration of, for example: the economic dominance within Malaysia of large corporations; concentration of stock ownership and concentration of control; intercorporate relationships (interlocking stock ownership and interlocking directorates); the social and economic background of the directors of the top corporations in Malaysia, and their relationship to the polity; the separation of ownership and control in Malaysia's top corporations; and cliques and interest groups among the top corporations in Malaysia. There are ten mainly methodological and statistical appendixes.

583 **Some effects of foreign investment: the case of Malaysia.**
Lewis Mann.   *Bulletin of Concerned Asian Scholars*, vol. 9, no. 4 (Oct.-Dec. 1977), p. 2-14.

This work is primarily concerned with the impact of foreign investments in the manufacturing sector of Malaysia: the impact on economic growth; the effects on employment and labour; the influence on social and economic inequalities; the implications for the balance of payments and the supply of capital; and the effect on the transfer of technology. The article provides substantial statistical information, referring mainly to the early 1970s. Mann concludes that, apart from a contribution to the gross national product, foreign investments 'tend to retard all other aspects of development' in Malaysia. 'The benefits they generate are enjoyed by the multinationals, by the investors, and by a small segment in the host country. The rest of the population remains in perpetual impoverishment. The local economy continues to be a satellite of the metropolis, and a parasitical relationship exists between the national bourgeoisie and the people . . . Foreign investments are a continued source of *under*development in Malaysia'.

584 **Ownership and control in the Malayan economy.**
J. J. Putchucheary.   Kuala Lumpur: University of Malaya Co-operative Bookshop, 1979. 187p.

A reprint of a book first published in 1960 (Singapore: Donald Moore, for Eastern Universities Press). The author was a founder member of the Peoples Action Party in Singapore, and later a leader of the Barisan Socialis (Socialist Front). For a number of years in the 1950s he was imprisoned in Changi by the British administration in Singapore. This present study was written during his imprisonment. It is an examination of the structure of ownership and control and 'its effects on the development of secondary industries and [on] economic growth in Malaya and Singapore'. The first part focuses specifically on ownership and control, and includes an examination of the European agency houses, mining companies, secondary industries in Singapore, and the economic role of the Chinese. The second part examines the problems of capital supply for development in the light of the earlier analysis of ownership and control in the Malaya-Singapore economy. The main year of study is 1953.

585 **British industrial investment in Malaysia 1963-1971.**
Junid Saham.   Kuala Lumpur: Oxford University Press, 1980.
353p. bibliog.

Concerned with the role of British industrial firms in the Malaysian economy from 1963 through to early 1972, this is a study of a period during which the government began in earnest to attract foreign investors into the manufacturing sector. There is consideration of, for example: Malaysia's share of British overseas investment; the Malaysian climate for investment in manufacturing; the motivation of British firms for investing in Malaysia; the role of the agency houses in promoting British industrial investment; the structure and organization of British investment in Malaysian manufacturing; the role of British-based multinationals in Malaysia; the profitability of British industrial companies in Malaysia; and the direct and indirect effects of British investment on Malaysia – including the effect of British industrial investment on the economic goals and policy of the Malaysian government.

586 **Foreign investment and employment generation in Malaysia.**
Gerald Tan.   *Kajian Ekonomi Malaysia* (Malaysian Economic Studies), vol. 15, no. 1 (June 1978), p. 19-24.

Tan takes issue with a criticism which is frequently laid against foreign investment in less-developed countries that compared with locally-owned firms, foreign-owned firms do not generate as much employment on account of their higher capital intensity. His conclusion, drawn from the Malaysian experience: 'whether considered in terms of employment per firm, employment growth or employment per unit of investment, the available data suggest that foreign-owned firms in most industries generate more, rather than less, employment compared with locally-owned firms'.

587 **Multinational corporations and development in Malaysia: a comment.**
Gerald Tan.   *Southeast Asian Journal of Social Science*, vol. 6, no. 1-2 (1978), p. 27-36.

This is a critical review of Lim (581). Tan examines Lim's analysis with respect to: the rates of profits of multinational corporations operating in Malaysia; their exploitation of low-cost labour; their effects on employment and labour; their influence on social and economic inequalities; and their impact on the balance of payments and the supply of capital. Tan argues that although Lim's conclusions about the unfavourable effects of foreign investment in Malaysia may be correct, 'they do not necessarily follow from the analysis of the data he presents. The reason for this is that the available data are usually too aggregative and too imprecise to justify the inference of general statements about the effects of foreign investment on Malaysian economic development'.

Further readings on Malaysian economic development.
See item no. 516.

Readings on Malaysian economic development.
See item no. 517.

Malaysia. Growth and equity in a multiracial society.
See item no. 531.

Agriculture

General

588 **Food and agriculture Malaysia 2000.**
Edited by H. F. Chin, I. C. Enoch, Wan Mohamad
Othman. Serdang, Malaysia: Faculty of Agriculture, Universiti
Pertanian Malaysia, 1978. 522p.

This is the proceedings of a conference held at the Universiti Pertanian Malaysia
in July 1977. Although the majority of papers are concerned with food production
(primarily in Malaysia) at the present time, they do provide 'a stimulus for the
generation of ideas on achieving food sufficiency [for Malaysia] by the year 2000'.
There are forty-four papers grouped under the following headings: agriculture,
population and policies; climate and soils; crop production; animal production,
losses in food production; food utilization and consumption; and agricultural
development. Each paper has a list of references.

589 **The diversification of Malaysian agriculture, 1950-80: objectives
and achievements.**
P. P. Courtenay. *Journal of Southeast Asian Studies*, vol. 15, no.
1 (March 1984), p. 166-81.

It is the purpose of this paper to examine critically 'the concept of agricultural
diversification in Malaysia and to attempt to identify the theoretical bases on
which it has been founded'. Courtenay provides a brief survey of the references to
agricultural diversification in the seven Malaysian development plans since 1950,
and an analysis of the apparent objectives of agricultural diversification in
Malaysia. He concludes that with the major exception of the shift in emphasis of
the export sector from rubber alone to rubber and palm oil, 'agricultural
diversification has provided very limited opportunities for economic advance,
especially for the mass of the rural poor'.

184

590 **The plantation in Malaysian economic development.**
P. P. Courtenay. *Journal of Southeast Asian Studies*, vol. 12,
no. 2 (Sept. 1981), p. 329-48.
Courtenay provides a detailed analysis of some of the major characteristics of the
plantation in contemporary Malaysia. With respect to Kedah he presents
considerable information on: plantation size and distribution; ownership and
management; labour; the provision of facilities on plantations; and the patterns of
plantation purchases. Courtenay seeks to demonstrate the substantial contribution
which the plantation system of agricultural organization, increasingly under
Malaysian ownership, can make to Malaysian economic development, including
most notably the modernization of the rural districts.

591 **Some trends in the Peninsular Malaysia plantation sector
1963-1973.**
P. P. Courtenay. In: *Issues in Malaysian development.* Edited by
James C. Jackson, Martin Rudner. Singapore: Heinemann
Educational Books (Asia), for the Asian Studies Association of
Australia, 1979. p. 131-65.
The major aspects of the plantation sector in Peninsular Malaysia between 1963
and 1973 which are examined in this paper are: the number and area of
plantations and the crops produced; ownership of plantations; replanting of
rubber plantations with high-yielding material; productivity on plantations; and
labour on plantations.

592 **Forest resource exploitation in Malaysia.**
K. C. Goh. *Kajian Malaysia* (Journal of Malaysian Studies), vol.
1, no. 1 (June 1983), p. 116-31.
Recent decades have seen rapid changes in the forest ecosystem of Peninsular
Malaysia, 'both in terms of depletion of total acreage due to large scale land
development, and deterioration of its quality due to extensive logging activities in
lowland and upland areas'. This paper examines the effects on the peninsula's
forest resources of land use policy, technological improvements in timber
extraction, and market trends of timber products; it analyses the biological
implications of these rapid changes for the forest ecosystem; and considers the
future commercial implications for the timber industry and for timber exports.

593 **The modern plantation in the Third World.**
Edgar Graham with Ingrid Floering. London, Sydney: Croom
Helm, 1984. 231p. bibliog.
Edgar Graham was at one time a Director of Unilever, and had long experience
of that company's plantations in West Africa, Zaire, Malaysia and the Pacific.
This study argues that the modern plantation in Africa and Asia bears little
resemblance to the plantations of the colonial past: indeed that the modern
plantation offers host governments in the Third World 'possibly the most efficient
way of utilising available factors of production to provide a maximum social
return'. There are a substantial number of references to Malaysia, including an
extended consideration [by Ingrid Floering] of FELDA, as a variant of the
modern plantation.

594 **The politics of land: comparative development in two states of Malaysia.**
Dorothy Guyot. *Pacific Affairs*, vol. 44, no. 3 (fall 1971), p. 368-89.

In an introduction, Guyot notes that in the early 1970s Malaysia had more arable land uncultivated than in production: moreover that 'expanding agriculture is a particularly attractive means for combatting unemployment in Malaysia since the capital-labor ratio for land development is estimated at one-third the ratio for industry'. Her article contrasts the relatively more successful land development programme of Johor from independence and through the 1960s, compared with that of Trengganu over the same period. She identifies three main considerations to explain this contrasted performance: 1. In Trengganu a higher proportion of land was distributed on the basis of political criteria; 2. In Trengganu 'a strong man hoarded power and was unwilling to tolerate land development which might give power to others, thus weakening his grasp'; and 3. Johor's administration is far more competent than Trengganu's in executing land policies. The administration in Trengganu is 'hampered by total political domination and its own inertia, while Johore's civil service has taken initiative in both political and bureaucratic matters'.

595 **Agriculture in the Malaysian region.**
R. D. Hill. Budapest: Akadémiai Kiadó, 1982. Research Institute of Geography, Hungarian Academy of Sciences. 234p. 35 figs. bibliog. (Geography of World Agriculture, no. 11).

The Malaysian region is here defined as Malaysia, with Singapore and Brunei. After a number of introductory chapters which consider such general aspects as land use and environment, and the area distribution of crops in the Malaysian region, there is discussion of the five major agricultural forms found in the area: shifting cultivation; semi-commercial peasant rice-growing; perennial crop small-holder agriculture; plantation agriculture; and intensive market-gardening and livestock rearing. Considerable emphasis is given to the historical evolution of these different forms of agriculture in the Malaysian region.

596 **Land settlement projects in Malaya: an assessment of the role of the Federal Land Development Authority.**
Robert Ho. *The Journal of Tropical Geography*, vol. 20 (June 1965), p. 1-15.

This assessment was written when the initial FELDA (Federal Land Development Authority) settlements were on the point of producing their first cash crops. Ho considers: the governmental infrastructure within which FELDA operated; the financial aspects; and the Authority's actual operations in land development. In a conclusion Ho suggests that the achievements of the Authority have been distinctly impressive. But he also argues that some doubts persist as regards the impact it might have on the rural sector and on the evolution of the national socio-economic environment. For example by allocating most places to Malays, the Authority 'perpetuates the ethnic gulf between Malay primary producers and the wealthier immigrant communities engaged in commercial and industrial pursuits'. Moreover, the schemes will help 'to preserve Malay cultural values, mainly through land ownership and the status it confers. But this sociological achievement may not be compatible with economic objectives.'

597 **Land development strategies in Malaysia: an empirical study.**
Syed Hussain Wafa. *Kajian Ekonomi Malaysia* (Malaysian Economic Studies), vol. 9, no. 2 (Dec. 1972), p. 1-28.

The main objective of this paper is 'to evaluate, compare, and analyze two contrasting strategies in agricultural development' as undertaken by the Federal Land Development Authority and the Kelantan State Land Development Authority [KSLDA], particularly with respect 'to costs, benefits and methods of operations'. The evaluation and comparison of strategies is made from the point of view of the settlers themselves (who seek to increase their earning capacity and improve their standard of living); and from that of the government (which is interested not only in economic viability but also financial viability, so as to avoid having the projects become a financial burden). This paper is primarily concerned with methodological considerations and the results are presented in Wafa's work noted below [598].

598 **Land development strategies in Malaysia: an empirical study.**
Syed Hussain Wafa. *Kajian Ekonomi Malaysia* (Malaysian Economic Studies), vol. 10, no. 2 (Dec. 1973), p. 1-50.

This is a continuation of Wafa's study (see above), and presents the results of the analysis outlined in that earlier paper. Among the conclusions are: 'the settler-oriented approach of the KSLDA strategy seems to be more economically viable than the management-oriented FELDA strategy'; FELDA settlers in the east coast region are 'generally better off than their KSLDA counterparts if the government provides them with interest-free loans. However, under any other loan considerations, the KSLDA settlers derived greater annual incomes'. It is finally argued that 'a modified strategy of land development, incorporating the favourable features of FELDA and the KSLDA scheme, should be developed for Malaysia. The adoption of a settler-oriented strategy and the development and establishment of settler-oriented schemes seems indicated.' This article, and its companion (q.v.), provide an extremely detailed and valuable analysis of the land development policies pursued in Peninsular Malaysia since independence.

599 **The oil palm industry of Malaysia: an economic study.**
Harcharan Singh Khera. Kuala Lumpur: Penerbit Universiti Malaya, 1976. 354p. map. bibliog.

This is the standard introductory work on the economic aspects of the modern oil palm industry of Malaysia. Chapters include: historical development and contribution of the oil palm industry to the economy of Peninsular Malaysia; commercial and social rates of return from investment in oil palm; the economics of palm oil production; economic structure and organization of production; demand for palm oil and prospects; marketing; policy recommendations. See also: *A social cost benefit analysis of the Kulai oil palm estate. West Malaysia*, by I. M. D. Little and D. G. Tipping (Paris: Development Centre of the Organisation for Economic Co-operation and Development, 1972. 95p. bibliog. Series on Cost-Benefit Analysis, Case Study no. 3).

600 **Rules for agrarian change: Negri Sembilan Malays and agricultural innovation.**
Diane K. Lewis. *Journal of Southeast Asian Studies*, vol. 7, no. 1 (March 1976), p. 74-91.
Lewis explores 'receptivity to agrarian change in a Malay rice farming village in Negri Sembilan in 1958-59'. In this period the villagers were experiencing substantial population growth and an increased reliance on cash crops to buy food, as well as facing government attempts to introduce new techniques in food production. Lewis attempts to explain why the villagers were, in these circumstances, highly selective in their acceptance of new agricultural techniques; and the basis of their selectivity. She concludes that an understanding of the villagers' reaction 'to agricultural innovation, particularly their selective acceptance of new techniques, requires consideration of the complex interaction of cultural, ecological and demographic factors'.

601 **Land development schemes in Peninsular Malaysia: a study of benefits and costs.**
Lim Sow Ching. Kuala Lumpur: Rubber Research Institute of Malaysia, 1976. 386p. map. bibliog.
Using original data secured through extensive fieldwork in 1970-71, Lim assesses 'the relative merits of the three main types of [rubber] land development' schemes found in Peninsular Malaysia – those of the Federal Land Development Authority (FELDA); state schemes; and Fringe Alienation schemes, 'in which projects are established by individual state governments to supplement the income of small-holders already farming uneconomic units in nearby areas'. The assessment is made in terms of commercial criteria (the profitability of investment in land development on the basis of actual market prices); the return to Malaysian society as a whole; and effectiveness in raising settlers' income.

602 **Mobility and modernisation. The Federal Land Development Authority and its role in modernising the rural Malay.**
Colin MacAndrews. Yogyakarta, Indonesia: Gadjah Mada University Press, 1977. 212p. 4 maps. bibliog.
This book examines the origins, development, and organization of the Federal Land Development Authority (FELDA), and in particular the role which it has played in modernizing the rural Malay. Specifically it considers: the emergence of a cohesive land development strategy in Malaysia from 1957; the emergence, growth, organization and structure of FELDA from its inception in 1956; its role in modernizing the rural Malay, initially by inducing internal migration and then by actively modernizing the FELDA settlers in the schemes; the actual working of four specific FELDA schemes; the overall effectiveness of FELDA as a mechanism for inducing rapid change in Malaysia; and the applicability of the FELDA model to other countries.

603 **Farmer and village in West Malaysia.**
Tsutomu Ouchi, Naomi Saeki, Akira Takahashi, Kenzō Horii,
Manabu Tanaka. Tokyo: Faculty of Economics, University of
Tokyo, 1977. 198p. 11 maps. bibliog.

This study aims to analyse through field observations 'the economic consequences
of recent developments in paddy farming' in West Malaysia brought about by
technological innovation in food production from the later 1960s and by
government programmes. Particular attention is paid to: structural changes in
agricultural production and rural economy; changes in land relations; trends in
the labour situation; mobility in rural society; regional and stratified distribution
of agricultural changes; and the role of national policies in agricultural
development. Field research was conducted in two villages in Perlis, and one in
Pahang. In essence the project was designed to examine the causes and limits of
the diffusion of technological innovation in agriculture.

604 **FELDA. 21 years of land development.**
Tunku Shamsul Bahrin, P. D. A. Perera. Kuala Lumpur:
FELDA, 1977. 167p. 4 maps.

The Federal Land Development Authority (FELDA) was established in 1956 to
promote major land development and settlement projects in the Federation, in an
attempt to combat rural landlessness and rural poverty. Over the following two
decades, FELDA was instrumental in transforming nearly one million acres of
jungle land into holdings, chiefly of rubber and palm oil, and in providing its
resettled families with basic community services and amenities. This commemor-
ative publication considers in detail FELDA's achievements over its first twenty-
one years.

605 **The swamp-sago industry in West Malaysia. A study of the Sungei
Batu Pahat floodplain.**
Tan Koonlin. Singapore: Institute of Southeast Asian Studies,
1983. 174p. 8 maps. bibliog.

The principal chapters of this study provide: an introductory survey of the swamp-
sago industry in West Malaysia; an examination of sago farming in the Batu Pahat
floodplain in Johor; a discussion of the system of sago production; and an outline
of recommendations for government action to secure the future development of
the sago industry.

606 **Oil palm cultivation in Malaya. Technical and economic aspects.**
C. N. Williams, Y. C. Hsu. Kuala Lumpur: University of Malaya
Press, 1970. 205p. 3 maps. bibliog.

The purpose of this book is to provide 'some practical guidance to estate
managers in the cultivation of oil palm in Malaya', although the book will also be
of interest to development economists and agriculture students. It is divided into
two parts. The first part deals with technical aspects, and considers the botany of
the oil palm, the climate and soils best suited to oil palm growing, various
technical problems related to its cultivation, the selection of planting material,
and the harvesting of the fruit produced. The second part deals with economic

aspects, and considers the techniques of management of an oil palm business; and 'ways to calculate profit and market prospects of oil palm products'. There is a very large number of photographs and line drawings.

The tobacco industry of North Borneo: a distinctive form of plantation agriculture.
See item no. 135.

Planters and speculators. Chinese and European agricultural enterprise in Malaya, 1786-1921.
See item no. 208.

Further readings on Malaysian economic development.
See item no. 516.

Readings on Malaysian economic development.
See item no. 517.

Changing planning perspectives of agricultural development in Malaysia.
See item no. 522.

Malaysia. Growth and equity in a multiracial society.
See item no. 531.

Bureaucracy and rural development in Malaysia. A study of complex organizations in stimulating economic development in new states.
See item no. 556.

Rubber

607 **The natural rubber industry. Its development, technology, and economy in Malaysia.**
Colin Barlow.   Kuala Lumpur: Oxford University Press, 1978.
500p. 5 maps. bibliog.

This volume analyses the development of the rubber industry in Peninsular Malaysia, exploring its historical, technological, social, political and, in particular, economic aspects. This last aspect includes discussion of: the structure of the industry; the economics of production; the rubber market; and wage arrangements, ownership, taxation, and the organization of production, each as at the early 1970s. The study also considers some international issues in the development of natural rubber as they relate to Malaysia. Finally Barlow suggests adjustments which might 'improve the situation of the natural rubber industry in the 1970s and 1980s'.

608 **Development policies and patterns of agrarian dominance in the Malaysian rubber export economy.**
Martin Rudner. *Modern Asian Studies*, vol. 15, part 1 (Feb. 1981), p. 83-105.

Rudner is concerned with Malaysian rubber policy since independence, but particularly in the 1970s. He argues that in the mid-1950s, changing world market conditions for the export of natural rubber and the political transition to independence, prompted a government rubber policy which encouraged large-scale replanting and new planting with high-yielding rubber, as well as an expansion of peasant participation in rubber cultivation. By the mid-1970s this policy of 'favouring technological *cum* entrepreneurial innovation appears to have altered direction'. Indeed the policy goal now is to protect 'the newly established economic and social order in the Malaysian rubber planting [sector] against further pressures for developmental change'. Rudner argues that the International Natural Rubber Agreement on Price Stabilization of 1976, like its predecessors of the 1920s and 1930s, 'threatens the Malaysian rubber economy with structural stagnation and eventual competitive decay'.

609 **Malayan rubber policy: development and anti-development during the 1950s.**
Martin Rudner. *Journal of Southeast Asian Studies*, vol. 7, no. 2 (Sept. 1976), p. 235-59.

The 1950s constituted a turning point in the history of Malayan rubber. Internationally, the creation of a large synthetic rubber industry in the main consuming country, the United States, 'posed a challenge to the competitive position and long-run prospects of Malayan plantation rubber'. Domestically, the rubber industry was required to consider not only 'its own internal development towards more efficient forms of production' but also the provision of 'a resource base for the development of other economic and social sectors'. Rudner considers 'the predominant economic issues and policy dilemmas that beset Malayan rubber during the first half of the 1950s, and examines the later policy and institutional changes that set in motion a development revolution in Malayan rubber during the second half of that decade'.

610 **Rubber strategy for post-war Malaya, 1945-48.**
Martin Rudner. *Journal of Southeast Asian Studies*, vol. 1, no. 1 (March 1970), p. 23-36.

The prospects for the Malayan rubber industry in the immediate post-war years were threatened by two considerations: 1. the restriction schemes of the inter-war decades had led to the virtual stagnation of Malayan rubber acreage, whilst acreage and output in the Dutch East Indies had expanded markedly; and 2. the emergence of a major synthetic rubber industry in the United States. Rudner examines the strategy developed by the Malayan authorities to meet these two challenges, but he concludes that the strategy led 'to the virtual decay of Malaya's rubber industry by the mid-1950s'.

191

611 **The state and peasant innovation in rural development: the case of Malaysian rubber.**
Martin Rudner. *Asian and African Studies*, vol. 6 (1970), p. 75-96.

Rudner provides a survey of the development of the smallholder sector of the Malaysian rubber industry, from the beginnings of the industry in the early 20th century, although with particular emphasis on the period from the early 1950s. He draws out the strong discrimination practised by the colonial administration against the smallholder sector; and he contrasts this with the favourable treatment of the peasant rubber producer from the mid-1950s. He gives considerable emphasis to the changes in the relationship between the peasant and the state that followed upon *Merdeka*. His central theme is that 'contemporary Malaysian rural development has been rooted in a smallholding peasantry able and willing to innovate, so that the progressive removal of legal-institutional obstacles, coupled to the provision of critical supports by government, resulted [from the mid-1950s] in real gains in rubber productivity'. Reprinted in: *Readings on Malaysian Economic Development*, edited by David Lim, (Kuala Lumpur, 1975, p. 321-31).

The rubber industry. A study in competition and monopoly.
See item no. 190.

Investment in the rubber industry in Malaya c.1900-1922.
See item no. 199.

Peasant smallholders in the Malayan economy: an historical study with special reference to the rubber industry.
See item no. 200.

Rubber in Malaya 1876-1922. The genesis of the industry.
See item no. 201.

Western rubber planting enterprise in Southeast Asia 1876-1921.
See item no. 234.

Rice

612 **Rice processing in Peninsular Malaysia. An economic and technical analysis.**
L. J. Fredericks, R. J. G. Wells. Kuala Lumpur: Oxford University Press, 1983. 200p. map. bibliog.

This study is intended primarily for undergraduate students of economics, agriculture, and agricultural economics. There are chapters on the rice processing industry; milling; storage; drying; choice of techniques; and government rice policy and the rice processing industry.

613   **The effects of farming techniques on rice yields: a case study in Kelantan, Malaysia.**
Akimi Fujimoto.   *Kajian Ekonomi Malaysia* (Malaysian Economic Studies), vol. 14, no. 1 (June 1977), p. 51-8.

Kelantan is one of the most important rice-producing areas in Peninsular Malaysia. However the average yield per acre in the state remains below the national average. This paper seeks to determine the extent to which farmers in Kelantan can raise their level of productivity 'within the context of available resources (mainly labour) and prevailing technology, [and] with little additional cash resources'. In other words it is concerned with the effects of farming techniques on the level of rice yield, as observed among Malay peasants in Kelantan. Fieldwork was conducted in 1973-74. The conclusion is that particular farming techniques 'could increase rice yield without further cash expenditure'.

614   **Rice in Malaya. A study in historical geography.**
R. D. Hill.   Kuala Lumpur: Oxford University Press, 1977. 234p. 19 maps. bibliog.

This volume is primarily concerned with the cultivation of rice in Peninsular Malaya from the beginning of the 19th century through to the first decade of the 20th century. There is analysis of, for example: the processes by which the area under rice expanded during this period; the concentration of rice-growing in Malaya in the north-west of the country; and the technical aspects of rice cultivation in this period.

615   **Rice economy and land tenure in West Malaysia. A comparative study of eight villages.**
Kenzō Horii.   Tokyo: Institute of Developing Economies, produced by East West Publications, 1981. 217p. 6 maps. bibliog.

This work is concerned with the socio-economic structure of Malay rice-growing villages in the late 1960s. It considers in particular: the land tenure system; village society and kinship; the labour utilization system; irrigation and drainage organization; the role of Islam in the village, including the effects on Malay rice farmers of the Islamic law of inheritance and the *zakat* (religious tithe) system; and agricultural policy. Data is drawn mainly from fieldwork conducted in two villages in the coastal area of Krian District, Perak, in 1968-69.

616   **Three Malay villages: a sociology of paddy growers in West Malaysia.**
Edited by Masuo Kuchiba, Yoshihiro Tsubouchi, Narifumi Maeda.   Honolulu: The University Press of Hawaii, 1979. 356p. 12 maps. bibliog. (Monograph of the Center for Southeast Asian Studies, Kyoto University, no. 14).

The three villages studied are in Kedah, Kelantan, and Melaka. The sociological features analysed include: family and kinship; paddy growing and the farm economy; religion and social structure in the village; land and residence; marriage, divorce and the family; income and social strata; village organization and leadership; social networks; and religion and leadership. Two final chapters consider the environment and technology of paddy growing. The fieldwork was carried out mainly between 1968 and 1972.

617 **Income distribution among farm households in the Muda irrigation scheme: a developmental perspective.**
K. C. Lai. *Kajian Ekonomi Malaysia* (Malaysian Economic Studies), vol. 15, no. 1 (June 1978), p. 38-57.

In the broadest terms, Lai is concerned with the commonly held view that agricultural development increases income inequalities within the traditional sector. His paper presents some results of an empirical study (conducted in 1972-73) on income distribution among rice farmers recently brought into double-cropping through the implementation of the Muda irrigation scheme in north-west Malaysia. In aggregate terms, the scheme is a successful one but little is known of the manner in which the income increases are distributed. In detail Lai examines: income distribution by size and across various specified farm groups; and changes in income distribution over time. He also evaluates the distribution of income in the light of poverty levels and other income standards. He concludes that rapid economic growth in the Muda irrigation scheme 'has not engendered widened income inequalities'; but also that poverty and generally small farm sizes 'continue to pose important challenges to development policy there'.

618 **Rice economy employment and income in Malaysia.**
John T. Purcal. Honolulu: University Press of Hawaii, 1972.
248p. map. bibliog.

This work is the result of a study of four villages in Province Wellesley, designed to investigate economic conditions among padi farmers. The study was carried out in 1962-63. There is analysis of: labour utilization; income of padi farmers; and expenditure patterns of households, each with reference to double-cropping and single-cropping areas. Finally there is a consideration of the problems and methods of marketing padi in the four villages studied.

Mining

619 **International commodity control – the tin experience.**
Mohamed Ariff. In: *Mineral resources in the Pacific area. Papers and proceedings of the Ninth Pacific Trade and Development Conference; San Francisco, August 1977.* Edited by Lawrence B. Krause, Hugh Patrick. San Francisco: Federal Reserve Bank of San Francisco, 1978. p. 571-97.

As Mohamed Ariff notes in an opening paragraph, there were four international tin agreements in the pre-war period beginning in 1931, and there have been four in the post-war period from 1956; a fifth post-war international tin agreement was provisionally introduced in July 1976. This paper examines 'the nature and functions, scope and limitations, and practical difficulties and outcomes of these international tin control schemes'. It divides into three sections: a brief historical sketch of the tin agreements; an evaluation of the performance of tin control schemes; and an analysis of some of the issues associated with tin control, and some policy implications. The paper is followed [p. 598-610] by the discussant's comments, and by a report on the general discussion of Mohamed Ariff's paper.

620 **Tin: its production and marketing.**
William Robertson. London, Canberra: Croom Helm, 1982. 212p. bibliog.

This study of the contemporary world tin market includes consideration of: production methods and costs; consumption trends and fluctuations in the leading countries; smelting and the market system; the International Tin Agreement and problems of market intervention; forecasting market trends; and long-run market prospects. As Malaysia is by far the largest producer of tin in the world, the Malaysian industry receives considerable attention.

195

Mining

621 **The off-shore petroleum resources of South-East Asia. Potential conflict situations and related economic considerations.**
Corazón Morales Siddayao. Kuala Lumpur: Oxford University Press, under the auspices of the Institute of Southeast Asian Studies, Singapore, 1978. 205p. 6 maps. bibliog.

From the early 1970s there has been a very marked expansion in the prospecting for, and exploitation of, the offshore petroleum resources of South East Asia. This study examines the potential for conflict or cooperation among the nations of the region arising from the search for petroleum resources in the seabed. The chapters consider: the value of petroleum to the South East Asian economies; the offshore petroleum resource potential of the region; potential sources of conflict and the law of the sea issues; actual territorial disputes over potential offshore petroleum fields (including disputes with respect to the Gulf of Thailand; the South China Sea; and Sabah, which involved controversy between Malaysia and the Philippines); potential conflict situations arising from geological settings and environmental phenomena; and some economic factors bearing on the resolution of conflicts over oil resources. As indicated above, Malaysia features prominently in the discussion.

622 **Commodity prices and appropriate technology – some lessons from tin mining.**
John Thoburn. *Journal of Development Studies*, vol. 14, no. 1 (Oct. 1977), p. 35-52.

This paper compares the private and social profitabilities of different techniques of tin mining in Malaysia, the first group of techniques being labour-intensive, locally operated and locally developed, and the second group being more capital-intensive and worked mostly by foreign firms. Thoburn concludes that no one group of techniques has proved universally superior in Malaysia, and that 'the ranking of techniques has proved sensitive both to the discount rate chosen and to the product price'.

623 **Multinationals, mining and development. A study of the tin industry.**
John Thoburn. Farnborough, England: Gower Publishing, 1981. 183p. bibliog.

This study is concerned with the methods by which less developed countries can 'increase the contribution of mineral exports to their socio-economic development'. More specifically it is concerned mainly with the changing structure of the world tin industry in terms of foreign investment and its alternatives; with the development gains which have accrued to host countries through the operation of market forces; and with attempts by governments to shift the distribution of benefits from tin production by foreign companies in favour of the host country. It concentrates on the four largest producers – Malaysia, Bolivia, Thailand and Indonesia. Chapter six considers the effects of present government policies on new investment in the tin industry in South East Asia. The concluding chapter includes some policy recommendations.

The Malayan tin industry to 1914. With special reference to the states of Perak, Selangor, Negri Sembilan and Pahang.
See item no. 236.

Western enterprise and the development of the Malayan tin industry to 1914.
See item no. 238.

The development of the tin mining industry of Malaya.
See item no. 239.

Transport

624 Southeast Asian regional transport survey.
Asian Development Bank. Singapore: Straits Times Press, 1972-3. 5 vols. maps. bibliog.

An exhaustively detailed survey of the transport facilities of seven countries in South East Asia, undertaken by the Asian Development Bank at the end of the 1960s. The countries surveyed were: Laos, Indonesia, Malaysia, the Philippines, Singapore, Thailand, and South Vietnam. The survey was concerned with all modes of transport in the region; and the time horizon was the period 1970-90. The survey was primarily concerned with internationally-orientated transport facilities. 'Its scope transcends national boundaries, viewing the transportation facilities and services in the seven countries and in the international waters and air space of these countries as a system'.

625 Bridge and barrier. Transport and communications in colonial Malaya 1870-1957.
Amarjit Kaur. Singapore: Oxford University Press, 1985. 235p. 35 maps. bibliog.

The author is primarily concerned with the growth of the railway network (and to a lesser extent, the road system) in the peninsula during the colonial period, and with the impact of railways on the regions they traversed and on the general Malayan economy. She examines the role of transport against 'the background of foreign entrepreneurial activity in tin and rubber, government and private investment in transport, and colonial government policy'. There is also a brief discussion of the growth of postal, telegraphic and telephone communications, and of the more recent development of air services.

626 **The impact of railroads on the Malayan economy, 1874-1941.**
Amarjit Kaur. *Journal of Asian Studies*, vol. 39, no. 4 (Aug.
1980), p. 693-710.

Kaur is concerned with three aspects of railroad development in Malaya over the period 1874-1941: 'first, the railroad as both a consumer and a transport agency; second, the specific role of the railways in contributing to the emergence of an extractive-colonial economy; and finally, the ways in which the railroad system led to the uneven distribution of capitalistic development in Malaya'.

627 **Malaysia. Travel planner '86.**
Kuala Lumpur: Tourist Development Corporation of Malaysia,
1985. 84p. 15 maps.

This very attractively-produced guide, distributed without charge, is obviously aimed towards the tourist. It includes most useful information with respect to transportation within Malaysia, for example: a distance chart; domestic air fares; train fares; advice on the use of taxis, buses and trishaws; and advice to motorists visiting Malaysia. There is also precise, practical information on how to reach all the major places of tourist interest.

628 **Urban transport in South and Southeast Asia. An annotated bibliography.**
V. Setty Pendakur. Singapore: Institute of Southeast Asian
Studies, Library Bulletin no. 15, 1984. 107p.

This annotated bibliography contains 433 entries, arranged alphabetically. There is both a geographical and a subject index. There are 22 entries specifically for Malaysia.

Employment and Manpower

629 **Rural labour force and industrial conflict in West Malaysia.**
Fatimah Halim. *Journal of Contemporary Asia*, vol. 11, no. 3
(1981), p. 271-96.

This paper is concerned with structural changes in peasant agriculture in contemporary Malaysia, and the increasing participation of rural workers in the wage work sector. It considers: how the rural masses are being transformed, while 'remaining as share-croppers within the village economy and . . . [their] gradual re-location in the wage sector'; and the relations between labour and capital in three specific industrial enterprises – the contract workers in a state-owned sugar plantation; a rubber-processing plant; and a unionized assembly plant. The author concludes that in the struggle between labour and industrial capital, 'the despairing weakness of the working class remains the constant variable'.

630 **Women and work in West Malaysia.**
Hing Ai Yun. *Journal of Contemporary Asia*, vol. 14, no. 2
(1984), p. 204-18.

Discusses the structure of women's work (paid and unpaid) in contemporary Malaysia. It considers: structural changes in the Malaysian economy from 1955 to 1980; and Malaysian female labour force participation – which involves discussion of domestic and family farm work; the female wage worker; and domestic labour.

631 **A note on labour underutilization in Peninsular Malaysia, 1970.**
Charles Hirschman. *Malayan Economic Review*, vol. 24, no. 2
(Oct. 1979), p. 89-104.

Hirschman argues that as the conventional definition of the unemployment rate used in data collection in developing countries excludes discouraged workers as well as the under-employed, it seriously understates the magnitude of labour underutilization. His paper seeks to explore several alternative measures of

200

labour underutilization using the 1970 Population Census of Malaysia. The sections of the article consider: labour force concepts and measurement in the 1970 Malaysia Population Census; alternative measures of labour underutilization; correlates of labour underutilization; and marginal employment. Among his conclusions: labour underutilization in both 'the unemployed component and in the idle discouraged worker population is a significant problem among youth in Peninsular Malaysia . . . but the magnitude . . . is shown to be larger than that revealed by [official] unemployment rates'.

632 **Women's labour force participation and socioeconomic development: the case of Peninsular Malaysia, 1957-1970.**
Charles Hirschman, Akbar Aghajanian. *Journal of Southeast Asian Studies*, vol. 11, no. 1 (March 1980), p. 30-49.
This study analyses changes in labour force participation of women, in both the agricultural and non-agricultural sectors in Peninsular Malaysia, based upon 1957 and 1970 census data. The article includes comparative analysis of female labour force participation for the three major ethnic communities; and concludes that for this period there were gradual increases in women's labour force participation rates in Peninsular Malaysia, which resulted from a combination of a decline in agricultural employment and sizable growth in non-agricultural employment, especially among younger women. It is also argued that 'within levels of education, residence, and marital/family status, the differences between Malay and Indian [female] employment in the modern sector were minimal. But Chinese women did have higher proportions in the modern sector, especially for those with a secondary education and among single women'.

633 **Growth and utilization of Malaysian labor supply.**
Donald R. Snodgrass. *Philippine Economic Journal*, no. 30, vol. 15, no. 1-2 (1976), p. 273-313.
The main part of this paper examines the principal labour force and employment trends in Peninsular Malaysia from 1947 mainly to the late 1960s. Specifically, it provides a detailed consideration of the supply of labour, labour absorption, and the emergence of a marked labour surplus (unemployment), first measured in the 1960s. There is also a very brief discussion of labour force and employment trends in East Malaysia. The remaining major section of the paper examines the employment-creation strategy pursued in Malaysia. This involves a consideration of the relationships between employment and the growth of output; between employment and income distribution; and between employment and the ownership and control of the economy. There is also an analysis of policy instruments relevant to the expansion of employment: relative prices and incentives; supply-side policies; rural development; and special labour-intensive activities. Snodgrass concludes that, as of the mid-1970s, Malaysia has been experiencing a serious employment problem. Its only basic solution is 'structural economic change of a kind which will absorb much more labour outside agriculture'.

Urbanization and the urban population in Peninsular Malaysia, 1970.
See item no. 58.

Employment and Manpower

Industrial and occupational change in Peninsular Malaysia, 1947-70.
See item no. 509.

Further readings on Malaysian economic development.
See item no. 516.

Readings on Malaysian economic development.
See item no. 517.

The urban labor market and income distribution. A study of Malaysia.
See item no. 519.

Malaysia. Growth and equity in a multiracial society.
See item no. 531.

Labour Movement and Trade Unions

634 The National Union of Plantation Workers. The history of the plantation workers of Malaya 1946-1958.
Charles Gamba. Singapore: Donald Moore for Eastern Universities Press, 1962. 292p. map. bibliog.

The National Union of Plantation Workers was formed in 1954 by an amalgamation of a number of small labour unions which had their origins in the immediate post-war period. This history is concerned primarily with the work of the National Union of Plantation Workers (NUPW) in the negotiation of plantation wages and working conditions in the mid-1950s.

635 The origins of trade unionism in Malaya. A study in colonial labour unrest.
Charles Gamba. Singapore: Donald Moore for Eastern Universities Press, 1962. 511p. map.

During the 1950s the author was, for several years, the only European representative of Asian-organized industrial labour on the Labour Arbitration Boards and the Labour Courts of Inquiry, in negotiations with the Governments of the Federation of Malaya and Singapore. In 1960 he became the first president of the Industrial Arbitration Court in Singapore. His study of the origins of trade unionism in Malaya covers the period 1945-50. It therefore considers, for example: the work of the British trade union adviser; labour unrest in Malaya and Singapore in the immediate post-war years; labour and the declaration of the Emergency in 1948; and the establishment of the Malayan Trade Union Council and the Singapore Trade Unions Congress at the end of the 1940s. A lengthy appendix reproduces eighteen documents concerned with the trade union movement in that period.

636 **Workers' resistance and management control: a comparative case study of male and female workers in West Malaysia.**
Fatimah Halim. *Journal of Contemporary Asia*, vol. 13, no. 2 (1983), p. 131-50.

This study is concerned with the severe conflict between labour and capital, characteristic (Fatimah Halim argues) of the industrial sector in West Malaysia. Arguing from detailed case studies of a shoe factory and a textile factory, and from a general analysis of 'social and economic dynamics outside of the two firms studied', she suggests that manifestations of conflict were obvious and numerous. They were located in: the policies of the state towards labour, including the use of the Internal Security Act to limit expression, and the introduction of legislation to control labour organizations; employer strategies towards labour, which sought to divide the workforce by sex and race; and worker resistance in the form of wildcat strikes, high rates of labour turnover and absenteeism, and a marked degree of stealing, wastage, dawdling and time-watching.

637 **Malayan labor in transition. Labor policy and trade unionism, 1955-63.**
Martin Rudner. *Modern Asian Studies*, vol. 7, part 1 (Jan. 1973), p. 21-45.

Following the breaking of the communist domination of the Malayan labour movement in 1948, and the reconstruction of a more compliant and docile trade union movement under the tutelage of the colonial government from the end of the 1940s, there arose in the early summer of 1955 'a better organized, more experienced, more confident trade union leadership reflecting the crest of national self-awareness accompanying the advent of self-government'. Rudner considers the activities and policies of this new leadership – essentially the Malayan Trade Union Congress – as it sought, with only very limited success, to define the role of trade unionism in an independent Malaya. Indeed in the early 1960s, the Malayan trade union movement had an insufficient authority and wider political base to resist the introduction of restrictive legislation, consolidated in the Industrial Relations Act of 1967.

638 **Malaysian Trades Union Congress 1949-1974.**
S. J. H. Zaidi. Petaling Jaya: Malaysian Trades Union Congress, 1975. 535p. bibliog.

This volume provides a detailed factual account of the first twenty-five years of the Malaysian Trades Union Congress, written by its Secretary-General from January 1964.

Malaya. The making of a neo-colony.
See item no. 110.

Industrial conflict in Malaya. Prelude to the communist revolt of 1948.
See item no. 273.

Rural labour force and industrial conflict in West Malaysia.
See item no. 629.

Statistics

639 **Banci penduduk dan perumahan Malaysia, 1970. (1970 Population
and housing census of Malaysia.)**
Kuala Lumpur: Jabatan Perangkaan Malaysia.
Volume 1: Basic population tables. This volume appears in thirteen separate (and
substantial) parts. Each part is devoted in turn to one of the states of the
Federation, with separate additional parts for Penang and Melaka. They were
published at various times in the mid-1970s, and therefore constitute the most
recently published basic population census data for Malaysia. Earlier censuses: 1.
'Report on the census of the Federated Malay States, 1901' (Kuala Lumpur,
1901); 2. 'The census of the Federated Malay States, 1911', compiled by A. M.
Pountney (Kuala Lumpur, 1912); 3. 'Census of British Malaya, 1921', compiled
by J. E. Nathan (London, 1922); 4. 'British Malaya: a report on the 1931 census',
compiled by C. A. Vlieland (London, 1932); 5. 'Malaya: a report on the 1947
census of population', compiled by M. V. del Tufo (London, 1949); 6. 'The 1957
census: a preliminary report based on "first count" total returns', T. E. Smith
(Kuala Lumpur, 1957).

640 **Bank Negara Malaysia. Quarterly Economic Bulletin.**
Kuala Lumpur: Bank Negara Malaysia, 1968-. quarterly.
This quarterly bulletin, the first issue of which appeared in March 1968, divides
into three sections: a review of financial and economic conditions; notes, articles,
and speeches; and an extensive statistical section, which presents the principal
financial and economic indicators.

641 **Ministry of Finance, Malaysia. Economic Report.**
Kuala Lumpur: Ministry of Finance Malaysia, 1972-. annual.
This annual economic report, the first issue of which appeared in 1972, is
published on Budget Day as a supplement to the Minister of Finance's Budget
Speech. The report contains a comprehensive analysis of economic, fiscal and

205

monetary developments and prospects in Malaysia. There is a substantial statistical appendix which includes the principal economic and financial indicators.

642 **Perangkaan perdagangan luar Sarawak. Statistics of external trade Sarawak.**
Kuching, Malaysia: Department of Statistics Malaysia (Sarawak Branch). annual.

A publication which provides, in exhaustive detail, the external trade statistics of Sarawak year-by-year. The publication details above are for the issues for the early 1980s: minor variations are to be anticipated for earlier issues.

643 **National accounts of West Malaysia 1947-1971.**
V. V. Bhanoji Rao. Singapore: Heinemann Educational Books (Asia), 1976. 109p. bibliog.

The major portion of this study represents an attempt to compile, for 1947-71, 'West Malaysian national accounts data by demand aggregates at current and constant prices, and the gross domestic product data at constant factor cost by industry of origin'. The results are distilled in a relatively substantial statistical appendix. Drawing on the data in that appendix, one concluding chapter offers some observations on the economic performance of West Malaysia, 1947-71.

644 **Siaran Perangkaan Bulanan Semenanjung Malaysia. Monthly statistical bulletin: Peninsular Malaysia.**
Kuala Lumpur: Jabatan Perangkaan, Department of Statistics.

These volumes provide statistical information under the following headings: climate; population and vital statistics; agriculture, forestry and fishing; mining, manufacturing and electricity; transport and communications; external trade; banking and finance; prices; labour; and social statistics. Note: the statistics cover only West Malaysia. The title given above is that of 1979. In an earlier form this publication was titled, in English: *Monthly Statistical Bulletin of West Malaysia*; and prior to that, *Monthly Statistical Bulletin of the States of Malaya*.

645 **Siaran Perangkaan Tahunan. Annual Bulletin of Statistics, Sabah.**
Kota Kinabalu, Malaysia: Department of Statistics, 1964-. annual.

This publication, the first issue of which appeared for 1964, provides a wide range of important selected statistics for Sabah year-by-year.

Environment

646 **Solar radiation in Malaysia. A study on availability and distribution of solar energy in Malaysia.**
Donald G. S. Chuah, S. L. Lee. Singapore: Oxford University Press, 1984. 122p. 25 maps. bibliog.

A very detailed, technical-statistical study which seeks to document the availability and distribution of solar energy in West Malaysia, in order to establish the feasibility of solar power as an alternative source of energy in the peninsula. The broad conclusion from a wealth of statistical data is that 'the solar radiation in Malaysia is sufficient for the operation of solar powered devices'.

647 **Environment, development and natural resource crisis in Asia and the Pacific.**
Penang: Sahabat Alam Malaysia (Friends of the Earth Malaysia), 1984. 422p. 6 maps.

This volume brings together thirty-eight papers presented at a symposium organized by Friends of the Earth Malaysia, and held in Penang in October 1983. The papers are grouped: overview; forest, land, wildlife and national parks; fisheries and sea pollution; mineral and energy resources; human settlements, urban growth and effects of tourism; food and agriculture; pesticides, toxic wastes and the working environment; NGO's [Non-Governmental Organization] action; NGO experiences – environmental education and action. The majority of papers have an attached list of references. There are some seven papers specifically concerned with Malaysia.

648 **The state of Malaysian environment 1983/84. Towards greater environmental awareness.**
Friends of the Earth Malaysia.   Penang: Sahabat Alam Malaysia (Friends of the Earth Malaysia), 1983. 97p.

This slim book (the third in the series) seeks to create environmental awareness in Malaysia. Chapters include: agriculture and pesticides; fishery resources; urban environmental impacts; occupational health and the working environment; Sarawak – timber, environment and the tribal communities; environment campaigns; environment quality in Malaysia; the environment – access to information and education.

649 **Man and nature in Malaysia. Attitudes to wildlife and conservation.**
Adrian G. Marshall. In: *Nature and man in South East Asia.*
Edited by P. A. Stott.   London: School of Oriental and African Studies, 1978. p. 23-33.

This paper considers not *methods* of conservation but rather attitudes towards it. It asks the question 'How do Malaysians view their environment and, in the context of their cultural, technological, political, economic situation, what hope is there that they will manage to conserve their splendid forests?' A list of references is attached.

Development and environment in Peninsular Malaysia.
See item no. 50.

Education

650 **Key questions on Malaysian education.**
Penang: Consumers' Association of Penang, 1984. 176p.
This volume contains summaries – in the form of press reports – of the almost seventy papers delivered at a seminar on 'Education and Development', held in Penang in November 1983. Among the comprehensive range of themes considered: the distribution of benefits in Malaysian education; education as cultural colonization; management of schools; education and the underprivileged; training and manpower planning; reading habits, literacy and textbooks; alternative and innovative education. Many of the summaries are too brief to be of much value.

651 **Handbook. Southeast Asian institutions of higher learning, 1983-1985.**
Bangkok: Association of Southeast Asian Institutions of Higher Learning [Thammasat University], 1982. 643p. maps.
This handbook, which is divided by country, includes five entries for Malaysia: Universiti Kebangsaan Malaysia; Universiti Malaya; Universiti Pertanian Malaysia; Universiti Teknologi Malaysia; Universiti Sains Malaysia. Each entry contains such information as: brief history of the institution; teaching staff; constitution; library; courses of study.

Education

652 **Educational policy and occupational structures in Peninsular Malaysia.**
Christine Inglis. In: *Issues in Malaysian development.* Edited by James C. Jackson, Martin Rudner. Singapore: Heinemann Educational Books (Asia), for the Asian Studies Association of Australia, 1979. p. 205-31.

The first section of this paper argues that in Malaysia the relationship between education and occupation cannot be discussed merely in terms of 'level of schooling attained'. This is because of the development during the colonial period of four separate education streams based on different languages of instruction. However, since independence, Malaysia has moved towards a uniform mass education system; and these changes in the educational structure have had potentially important implications for the relationship between education and occupation – which are examined in the second section of the paper.

653 **Studies on Malaysian education. An annotated bibliography.**
Edited by S. Kanagasabai, Chew Sing Buan, Koh Boh Boon, Leong Yin Ching. Kuala Lumpur: Faculty of Education, University of Malaya, 1980. 97p.

A selective (129 entries) bibliography of research studies conducted on all levels of Malaysian education. It includes a large number of references to unpublished theses and academic exercises submitted to Malaysian and foreign universities. The annotations are, in general, extremely full, such that this volume, in its own right, provides a very valuable account of the state of research in this field. It includes studies published/presented upto and including 1978.

654 **Higher education in Malaysia: a bibliography.**
Co-ordinator Khoo Siew Mun. Singapore: Regional Institute of Higher Education and Development, December 1983. 198p.

This bibliography contains 1,573 items in English and Bahasa Malaysia divided under the following 13 headings: educational policy and higher education in Malaysia; colleges and college-type education; universities and university education; financing colleges and universities; legislating colleges and universities; governance of colleges and universities; staff in colleges and universities; courses of study, curriculum development and evaluation; teaching methods; students in colleges and universities; the graduates; university research; higher education information and statistics. There is an introductory essay on higher education in Malaysia; a list of sources; and three indices.

655 **Educational planning in West Malaysia.**
Eddy Lee. Kuala Lumpur: Oxford University Press, 1972. 63p. bibliog.

This is a critical analysis of the 1967 'Report of the Higher Education Planning Committee' which was to serve as the guidelines for the expansion of educational facilities in West Malaysia over the period 1967-85. The study assesses the recommendations of the report against Malaysia's trained manpower requirements, as well as the financial implications of the report.

656 **A review of the educational developments in the Federated Malay States to 1939.**

Philip Loh Fook Seng. *Journal of Southeast Asian Studies*, vol. 5, no. 2 (Sept. 1974), p. 225-38.

Loh considers the development and character of the four separate school systems (Malay, Chinese, Tamil, and English language) in the Federated Malay States from around 1900 to the outbreak of the Second World War. Particular attention is paid to the role of the British colonial administration in this sphere. Loh concludes that a shared system of 'civic values and western knowledge made available to the different ethnic groups through English education tended to reduce ethnic separateness and, in retrospect, may be viewed as the most constructive British contribution to the educational development of the Federated Malay States'.

657 **Seeds of separatism: educational policy in Malaya 1874-1940.**

Philip Loh Fook Seng. Kuala Lumpur: Oxford University Press, 1975. 165p. bibliog.

This volume is concerned with the origins and development to 1940 of the four school systems which were established in Malaya during the colonial period – education in the vernacular for the mass of the Malays, Chinese and Indians, and education in English for the Malayan élites. Loh's study aims to show the manner in which 'the exigencies of British rule and the attitudes of their officials influenced the development of the four school systems'.

658 **Educational planning and expenditure decisions in developing countries. With a Malaysian case study.**

Robert W. McMeekin, Jr. New York, London: Praeger Publishers, 1975. 195p. bibliog.

This study in the orientation and application of economic analysis to educational planning in developing countries contains two chapters which draw on the Malaysian experience. The first considers a policy question that arose around 1970, as to the proportion of candidates that would be permitted to proceed from the lower secondary to the upper secondary level of school education, that is, how rapidly the upper secondary level should be permitted to expand in relation to other levels. The second Malaysia chapter considers the expansion of vocational school enrolment as a proportion of total upper secondary enrolment – as a means to improve the employment opportunities and earning power of school graduates. Four lengthy appendixes are also concerned with planning and research in the Malaysian educational system.

659 **Student development in Malaysian universities.**

Thangavelu Marimuthu. Singapore: Regional Institute of Higher Education and Development, 1984. 89p. bibliog. (RIHED Occasional Paper no. 19).

The main focus of this study is on the influence exercised by Malaysian universities on their students, in terms of changes in their attitudes, aspirations, values and norms. Consideration is given to: Malaysian students' perceptions and expectations of university education; learning practices and examination procedures; the quality and frequency of student-staff interaction. Data for the study was collected from 693 final-year students drawn from the five Malaysian universities. This is one of a considerable number of studies on aspects of higher education in Malaysia published by RIHED.

660   **Cultivators and administrators. British educational policy towards the Malays 1875-1906.**
Rex Stevenson.   Kuala Lumpur: Oxford University Press, 1975. 240p. bibliog.

Stevenson's study of British educational policy towards the Malays covers the period from the opening of the first Malay vernacular school in 1875 through to the amalgamation of the education departments of the SS and FMS in 1906. The year 1906 was also the first year of work for the Malay College at Kuala Kangsar. It examines separately for the entire period the growth of 'a system of vernacular education for the broad mass of the Malay peasantry on one hand, and the successive attempts to provide a select number of Malays, for the most part the sons of Rajas and chiefs, with an education in English on the other'. Consideration is also given to Malay attitudes and reactions 'to modern secular education'.

661   **Issues in Malaysian education: past, present, and future.**
Tham Seong Chee.   *Journal of Southeast Asian Studies*, vol. 10, no. 2 (Sept. 1979), p. 321-50.

Tham provides a brief survey of the history of Malaysian education from the final years of colonial rule to the end of the 1960s; an examination of educational issues in the 1970s, in the context of the Constitutional Amendment Act of 1971, the New Economic Policy, and the *Rukunegara*; and a consideration of the future prospects of education in Malaysia, in the context of the search for national unity and the attainment of communal parity in economic status.

662   **Education in Malaysia.**
Francis Wong Hoy Kee, Ee Tiang Hong.   Kuala Lumpur: Heinemann Educational Books (Asia), 1975. 2nd ed. 190p. map. bibliog.

This volume is divided into three parts. The first provides a brief account of education in Malaya during the colonial period through to the Japanese occupation. The second part considers educational changes in the period from 1945 through to 1963, with particular attention paid to post-war educational reconstruction and to the educational problems which arose with independence – with respect to nationalism, Malayanization, language, and university education. The final (and most substantial) part considers educational developments and problems from 1963, and discusses such aspects as: the provision of education to promote national unity; the administration of education; teacher training; the federal inspectorate; and the economy and educational diversification.

663   **Perspectives: the development of education in Malaysia and Singapore.**
Francis Wong Hoy Kee, Gwee Yee Hean.   Kuala Lumpur:
Heinemann Educational Books (Asia), 1972. 177p. bibliog.

This study of the development of education in Malaysia and Singapore considers: the historical development of education from 1786-1965; the structure of education (primary, secondary, university, technical, teacher-training, adult and further, and special education); the administration of education (including discussion of the inspectorate of schools, and examinations); and the curriculum (including analysis of the responsible authorities, structure, composition and emphasis, and teaching methods and materials). A lengthy final chapter examines 'the educational challenge ahead for Malaysia and Singapore in terms of goals and problems'.

Malay society, 1874-1920s.
See item no. 209.

Multi-ethnic politics: the case of Malaysia.
See item no. 421.

Ethnicity, class and development. Malaysia.
See item no. 551.

Literature

General

664 **MA-RAI-EE.**
Chin Kee Onn. Singapore: Eastern Universities Press, 1981.
302p.

'Maraiee' was the name given to Malaya by the Japanese during their occupation of 1941-45. This novel, drawn from the author's own experiences and observations during that period, provides a most powerful, violent account of Malaya under Japanese rule. It was first published in 1952 by George Harrap and Company.

665 **Dossier: littérature Malaysienne.** (Dossier: Malaysian literature.)
Archipel, no. 19 (1980), p. 169-296.

This collection of fifteen articles and short notes (of which thirteen are in French) provides a critical survey of modern Malaysian literature. It includes contributions on: the literary and intellectual life of Kuala Lumpur since 1970; Malay literature from the early 19th century; the evolution of Tamil literature; Chinese poetry; English-language poetry; the evocation of rural life in the novels of Shahnon Ahmad; and a selective bibliography of books and articles relating to modern Malay literature.

666 **Scorpion orchid.**
Lloyd Fernando. Kuala Lumpur: Heinemann Educational Books
(Asia), 1976. 147p.

This novel is set in the Malaya of the early 1950s. Against a background of social upheaval as Malaya moves towards independence, it explores a crisis of self-awareness faced by four young Malayan men, members of the last colonial generation.

214

667 **Twenty-two Malaysian stories. An anthology of writing in English.**
Selected and edited by Lloyd Fernando. Singapore: Heinemann
Educational Books (Asia), 1968. 238p.

According to Fernando, the short stories 'collected here represent exhaustively
the best writing in English in this form by Malaysian and Singapore writers over
the dozen years or so up to 1966'.

668 **. . . And the rain my drink.**
Han Suyin. Frogmore, England: Panther Books, 1973. 238p.
map.

Han Suyin was born in Beijing of a European mother and a Chinese father. This
novel, which was first published (by Jonathan Cape) in 1956, provides a most
penetrating and vivid account of life in Malaya during the Emergency.

669 **Singapore and Malaysian writing.**
Edited by Kirpal Singh. *Pacific Quarterly Moana*, vol. 4, no. 1
(Jan. 1979), 104p.

This special issue on contemporary writing in Singapore and Malaysia contains
three critical articles (including one by Ee Tiang Hong on Malaysian poetry in
English), two short stories and an extract from a novel, twenty-five poems, and a
number of book reviews.

670 **The second tongue. An anthology of poetry from Malaysia and
Singapore.**
Selected and with an introduction by Edwin Thumboo.
Singapore: Heinemann Educational Books (Asia), 1976. 198p.

This anthology brings together the most significant poetry in English from
Malaysia and Singapore written over the period from the early 1950s. A lengthy
introductory essay by Edwin Thumboo provides an account and analysis of the
development of poetry writing in English in the two countries in that period.

671 **Bunga Emas. An anthology of contemporary Malaysian literature
(1930-1963).**
Edited by T. Wignesan. London, Kuala Lumpur: Anthony Blond
with Rayirath (Raybooks) Publications Malaysia, 1964. 272p.
bibliog.

This compilation contains fifty-seven examples from the work (poems, short-
stories, one-act plays, novella) of twenty-two Malaysian writers, writing in English
(44), Chinese (7) and Tamil (6). There are, for copyright reasons, no examples of
the work of Malay writers. A postscript includes articles on: the Malayan short
story in English; the origins and scope of Tamil literature in Malaysia; a brief
survey of contemporary Malay literature; and, by Wang Gung-wu, a short
introduction to Chinese writing in Malaya. There are brief biographical notes on
each of the writers.

Malay

672 The hikayat Abdullah.
Abdullah bin Abdul Kadir, an annotated translation by A. H.
Hill. Kuala Lumpur: Oxford University Press, 1970. 353p.
7 maps. bibliog.

Abdullah bin Abdul Kadir (1797-1854) was a prominent Malay writer,
interpreter, and teacher of Malay to many of the most notable Europeans in the
peninsula in the first half of the 19th century. His autobiography, published in
Malay in 1849, provides a record of his times, 'intimate pen-pictures' of major
personalities of that period (including Raffles, Farquhar, and Butterworth), and
well-observed descriptions of the events of everyday life. An introduction to this
translation includes: a sketch of the political background to 19th-century Malaya;
a survey of Abdullah's life; and a discussion of Abdullah's literary works.

673 The origin of the Malay sha'ir.
Syed Naguib Al-Attas. Kuala Lumpur: Dewan Bahasa dan
Pustaka, 1968. 64p.

A detailed examination of the origin of the Malay *sha'ir* (a verse-form composed
of four lines to a verse having the same end-rhyme). The author identifies the
originator of this verse-form as the 16th-century Malay Ṣūfī poet and writer on
doctrine, Ḥamzah Fansūrī. This study is a contribution not only to research on
classical Malay literature but also to an understanding of the Islamization of the
Malay world. See also: *Concluding postscript to the origin of the Malay sha'ir*, by
Syed Naguib Al-Attas (Kuala Lumpur: Dewan Bahasa dan Pustaka, 1971. 58p.).

674 Crisis.
Alias Ali, translated by Barclay M. Newman. Kuala Lumpur:
Dewan Bahasa dan Pustaka, Ministry of Education, Malaysia,
1980. 245p.

First published in Malay in 1966, this novel offers a humorous view of a Malaysian
political election and of the individuals who contest it. The humour is whimsical
rather than cynical.

675 The Prince of Mount Tahan.
Ishak Haji Muhammad, translated by Harry Aveling. Kuala
Lumpur: Heinemann Educational Books (Asia), 1980. 68p.

This novel, first published in Malay in 1937, was written by a prominent Malay
nationalist who was imprisoned by the British both before and after the Japanese
occupation. It is concerned with the attempts of two British scientific explorers to
steal Mount Tahan (on the Pahang/Kelantan border) from its ruler so that the
British administration could turn it into a hill station. It is a highly satirical work,
in which the British are portrayed as exasperatingly silly.

676 **The Malay Islāmic Ḥikāyat.**
Ismail Hamid. Bangi, Malaysia: Penerbit Universiti Kebangsaan
Malaysia, 1983. 228p. bibliog. (Institut Bahasa Kesusasteraan dan
Kebudayaan Melayu Monograph no. 1).

Malay Islamic hikayats deal mostly with historical narratives about the Prophet
Muhammad and other Muslim personages in the history of Islam, although they
are accounts with pronounced legendary elements. This study considers, for
example: the introduction of Islam to the Malay archipelago; the influence of
Islam on the Malay language and on Malay literature; the hikayats of the Prophet
Muhammad; the hikayats of the companions; the romances of Muslim heroes;
and the religious meaning of the Malay Islamic hikayats.

677 **The study of traditional Malay literature, with a selected**
bibliography.
Ismail Hussein. Kuala Lumpur: Dewan Bahasa dan Pustaka,
Kementerian Pelajaran Malaysia, 1974. 75p.

Ismail Hussein provides a critical, historical, account of the study of traditional
Malay literature, paying particular attention to the work of Winstedt and
Hooykaas. This account is followed by a selected bibliography of works,
translations, and articles (mostly in European languages), on Malay traditional
literature. The text was published earlier in *Journal of the Malaysian Branch of
the Royal Asiatic Society*, vol. 39, part 2 (1966), p. 1-22. *Asian Studies*
(Philippines), vol. 4, no. 1 (1968), p. 66-89. The bibliography was originally
published in *Tenggara*, no. 4 (1969), p. 94-115.

678 **Malay myths and legends.**
Jan Knappert. Kuala Lumpur: Heinemann Educational Books
(Asia), 1980. 294p.

Knappert provides a collection of myths and legends from the Malay world,
drawn from the three main sources for Malay literature – the Islamic tradition
from the Middle East; the Hindu and Buddhist traditions from India; and the
ancient heritage of original Malay stories. There is a lengthy introductory essay
which considers such themes as: the Malay oral tradition; the coming of Islam to
the Malay world; and cosmology, myths, and legends. But the sole objective of
the collection is to give enjoyment 'to readers who love tales of magic and
imagination'.

679 **Blood and tears.**
Keris Mas, translated from the Malay by Harry Aveling, with an
introduction by S. Husin Ali. Petaling Jaya: Oxford University
Press, 1984. 158p.

Keris Mas is arguably the most prominent contemporary Malay short story writer.
This volume brings together twenty stories, originally published in Malay between
1946 and 1960. Keris Mas is primarily concerned with the ordinary people, and
with their reaction to the exuberant nationalism and bewildering social change of
the years in which he wrote.

680 **A bird's-eye view of the development of modern Malay literature,
1921-1941.**
Li Chuan Siu.   Kuala Lumpur: Penerbitan Pustaka Antara, 1970.
58p. bibliog.

After a very brief introductory chapter which considers the promotion of modern
Malay literature over the period 1921-41, this study provides an account and
analysis of twelve prominent Malay writers from that period and of their work.

681 **An introduction to the promotion and development of modern
Malay literature 1942-1962.**
Li Chuan Siu.   Yogyakarta, Indonesia: Penerbitan Yayasan
Kanisius, 1975. 269p. bibliog.

This book divides into two main parts. The first provides a relatively brief account
of the institutional promotion and development of Malay literature between 1942
and 1962. The second (and major) part considers twenty-five prominent Malay
writers from that period and their work.

682 **Concepts of Malay ethos in indigenous Malay writings.**
Virginia Matheson.   *Journal of Southeast Asian Studies*, vol. 10,
no. 2 (Sept. 1979), p. 351-71.

The aim of this study is to examine indigenous Malay writings in an attempt to
discover how Malays expressed their identity as a people. 'In what context was
the term *Melayu* used; in what types of documents did it appear; and did the
concept of "Malayness" vary with time and place?' Matheson uses mainly court-
sponsored documents, probably the earliest being the 17th-century *Sejarah
Melayu*.

683 **Modern Malaysian stories II.**
Kuala Lumpur: Dewan Bahasa dan Pustaka, Kementerian
Pelajaran Malaysia, 1983. 176p.

This anthology contains fifteen short stories (translated from Malay) which were
originally published between 1969 and 1979. Two frequent themes in the
collection are rural poverty, and the adverse effects of modernization. A brief
introduction examines historically the development of the short story in modern
Malay literature. There are brief biographical notes on each author.

684 **Trends in modern Malay literature.**
Mohd. Taib Osman. In: *Malaysia: a survey*. Edited by Wang
Gungwu. Singapore: Donald Moore Books, 1964. p. 210-24.

A valuable, if brief, introduction to modern Malay literature, from its emergence
in the mid-1920s through to the early 1960s.

685 **The travel journals of Si Tenggang II.**
Muhammad Haji Salleh, translated by the poet. Kuala Lumpur:
Dewan Bahasa dan Pustaka, Ministry of Education, Malaysia,
1979. 72p.

A collection of poems by one of the most prominent of contemporary Malay poets. First published in Malay in 1975, it was awarded the ASEAN Literary Award for 1977.

686 **Modern Malaysian poetry.**
Translated by Barclay M. Newman. Kuala Lumpur: Dewan
Bahasa dan Pustaka, Ministry of Education, Malaysia, 1980. 155p.

This is an anthology of 105 poems (in translation from Malay) which have been awarded the annual Malaysian National Literary Award between 1971 and 1976.

687 **Modern Malaysian stories.**
Translated by Barclay M. Newman. Kuala Lumpur: Dewan
Bahasa dan Pustaka, Ministry of Education, Malaysia, 1977. 152p.

An anthology of thirteen short stories (in translation from Malay) by a number of prominent Malay writers.

688 **Salina.**
A. Samad Said, translated from the Malay by Harry
Aveling. Kuala Lumpur: Dewan Bahasa dan Pustaka,
Kementerian Pelajaran Malaysia, 1975. 278p.

This controversial novel, first published in Malay in 1961, has as a central character Salina, a prostitute. The strength of the novel lies in its atmosphere rather than in its plot. It provides an invaluable insight into Malay social values and behaviour – through the extended passages of dialogue which are to be found throughout almost all the book.

689 **No harvest but a thorn.**
Shahnon Ahmad, translated and introduced by Adibah
Amin. Kuala Lumpur: Oxford University Press, 1972. 168p.

Shahnon Ahmad is the outstanding Malay novelist of his generation. This work, first published in Malay in 1966, is set in the remote village of Banggul Derdap where the author himself was born. It is concerned with a family's bitter struggle for existence – against both the forces of nature and human parasites – and of the religious faith which sustains them in adversity.

690 **Srengenge. A novel from Malaysia.**
Shahnon Ahmad, translated from the Malay by Harry
Aveling. Kuala Lumpur: Heinemann Educational Books (Asia),
1979. 212p.

This novel, first published in Malay in 1973, is set in a small, rice-growing Malay village in Kedah, at the foot of a wild, uncultivated mountain, Srengenge. It focuses on the contrasting relationships of a number of men in the village with the mountain: two who love it for the sport it affords them (snaring doves, trapping porcupines, and setting lime for humming birds); a man who hates it, is defiant of its very existence, and wants to destroy it, turn it into dry rice fields; and the *Imam* who worships Srengenge, because it is the place where his love, the wild spotted doves, gather. According to Aveling, this novel 'evokes the myths, beliefs and traditions which control every aspect of rural [Malay] life'.

691 Authors and audiences in traditional Malay literature.

Amin Sweeney.   Berkeley, California: University of California, Center for South and Southeast Asia Studies, 1980. 83p. bibliog. (Monograph Series no. 20).

Sweeney examines three aspects of traditional Malay literature (that corpus of manuscript literature of the palaces generally referred to as 'classical', as well as oral literature). Those aspects are: its presentation; its consumption by audiences; and methods of composition. For Sweeney argues that 'a prerequisite for the fruitful study of traditional Malay literature as literature is some understanding of the presentation, consumption and methods of composition of that literature'. With that understanding, the Western reader will come to accept that traditional Malay literature is 'neither a poor cousin of Western literature nor an unfathomable creation by alien beings operating by entirely different rules from our own'.

692 The voyages of Mohamed Ibrahim Munshi.

Translated, with an introduction and notes by Amin Sweeney, Nigel Phillips.   Kuala Lumpur: Oxford University Press, 1975. 145p. 2 maps. bibliog.

In 1871-72, the sultan of Johor sent Mohamed Ibrahim, a court writer and a son of Abdullah bin Abdul Kadir (the author of the *Hikayat Abdullah*), on five voyages to various parts of the west coast of the Malay peninsula. This book comprises his account of four of those voyages. A lengthy introduction sketches in the historical background, and considers the author and his work.

693 Shahnon Ahmad's *No harvest but a thorn.*

Edwin Thumboo.   *Journal of Southeast Asian Studies*, vol. 10, no. 1 (March 1979), p. 89-103.

This article provides a detailed literary appreciation of Shahnon Ahmad's major novel.

694 A history of classical Malay literature.

Sir Richard Winstedt. Kuala Lumpur: Oxford University Press, 1969. 2nd ed. 323p. bibliog.

This is a classic introduction to the subject, written by arguably the most noted scholar of Malay literature and culture of the colonial period. There is consideration of: Malay folk literature; Hindu, Javanese and, most notably, Islamic influences and elements in classical Malay literature; Malay histories; Malay poetry. An appendix provides relatively extensive summaries of thirteen *hikayat.* This work first appeared as vol. 17, part 3 (January 1940) of the *Journal of the Malayan Branch of the Royal Asiatic Society* when it included a chapter on 19th and early 20th century Malay literature by Zain al'abidin. This chapter is omitted from the edition noted above.

695 **The evolution of the Malay short story: from its origins to the present day.**
Monique Zaini-Lajoubert. In: *The short story in South East Asia. Aspects of a genre.* Edited by J. H. C. S. Davidson, Helen Cordell. London: School of Oriental and African Studies, 1982. p. 185-201.
This brief introductory essay considers the influences which have shaped the content of the Malay short story from its first appearance in 1920, but more particularly from the early 1950s. There is also an extensive bibliography (p. 253-58) divided into: bibliographies; serials; literature related to the Malay short story; short stories in the vernacular; and translated Malay short stories.

696 **The Rāma saga in Malaysia. Its origin and development.**
Alexander Zieseniss, translated by P. W. Burch. Singapore: Malaysian Sociological Research Institute, 1963. 202p. bibliog.
This study, first published in German in 1928, is concerned with the acculturation of the Indian epic, the *Ramayana*, when it was introduced into Malay. Zieseniss first provides a summary of the Malay *Hikāyat Srī Rāma*; and then a comparison (in note form) of the Malay epic with the Indian Rama sagas.

The Malays. A cultural history.
See item no. 39.

Sĕjarah Mĕlayu, Malay Annals.
See item no. 120.

Studies in Malaysian oral and musical traditions.
See item no. 718.

Chinese

697 **Notes on the history of Malayan Chinese new literature 1920-1942.**
Fang Xiu, translated by Angus W. McDonald. Tokyo: Centre for East Asian Cultural Studies, 1977. 423p. 3 maps. (East Asian Cultural Studies Series, no. 18).
A most detailed account of Malayan Chinese literature in the two decades prior to the Japanese invasion. Particular attention is paid to literary movements and controversies, as well as to individual writers and their work.

698 **An anthology of modern Malaysian Chinese stories.**
Collected and translated by Ly Singko, in collaboration with Leon
Comber. Hong Kong: Heinemann Educational Books (Asia),
1967. 202p.

This anthology of thirteen short stories (in translation) by modern Malaysian
Chinese writers is preceded by a lengthy essay by Han Suyin in which she mainly
considers the historical origin and the evolution of a distinct Malaysian Chinese
literature from around 1920.

699 **Reunion and other stories.**
Translated by Ly Singko. Singapore: Heinemann Educational
Books (Asia), 1980. 183p.

This collection of thirteen short stories by eight Malaysian Chinese writers is seen
as a successor to *An anthology of modern Malaysian Chinese stories* translated by
Ly Singko with Leon Comber, in 1967. The majority of the stories here were
written in the later 1960s and early 1970s; but there are also a number from the
pre-war decades.

Western fiction set in Malaysia

700 **The Malayan trilogy.**
Anthony Burgess. Harmondsworth, England: Penguin Books,
1972. 624p.

This volume comprises three novels: *Time for a tiger*, *The enemy in the blanket*,
and *Beds in the East*. They were originally published by William Heinemann in
the later 1950s. At that time Anthony Burgess was an education officer in the
Malayan colonial service. These novels, which 'wittily dissect the racial and social
prejudices of post-war Malaya', clearly draw on that experience.

701 **Maugham's Malaysian stories.**
Selected and with an introduction by Anthony Burgess. Kuala
Lumpur: Heinemann Educational Books (Asia), 1969. 186p.

This volume contains six W. Somerset Maugham stories: 'The vessel of wrath';
'The force of circumstance'; 'The door of opportunity'; 'The four Dutchmen';
'P. & O.'; and 'A casual affair'.

702 **Lord Jim.**
Joseph Conrad. Harmondsworth, England: Penguin Books, 1957.
313p.

Jim, the young first mate of the *Patna*, loses his nerve during a storm at sea and
abandons ship. Driven by guilt he wanders through the ports of the East until he
finally settles in a remote corner of the Malay archipelago where he reclaims his

courage and integrity. First published in 1900, this is among the most powerful Western novels set in the Eastern seas.

703 **The soul of Malaya.**
Henri Fauconnier. Kuala Lumpur: Oxford University Press, 1965. 247p.

Fauconnier was a rubber planter in Malaya in the later colonial period. This autobiographical novel, first published in English in 1931, provides in its early part a particularly well-observed account of Tamil and European life on a Malayan rubber estate of that period. The more important part of the book, 'leading finally to the inevitable tragedy of an *amok*, is concerned with two Malay brothers, . . . in all their charm and superstition, and the relationship that develops between them, the narrator, and the planter, Rolain'.

704 **Maugham's Borneo stories.**
Selected and with an introduction by G. V. de Freitas. Hong Kong, Singapore, Kuala Lumpur: Heinemann Educational Books (Asia), 1976. 287p.

This is a collection of six Borneo-related stories by W. Somerset Maugham: 'The yellow streak'; 'The outstation'; 'Before the party'; 'Flotsam and Jetsam'; 'Neil MacAdam'; and 'Virtue'.

705 **English-language fiction relating to Malaysia, Singapore and Brunei: a check-list.**
William R. Roff. *Journal of the Malaysian Branch of the Royal Asiatic Society*, vol. 55, part 1 (July 1982), p. 62-77.

This check-list contains 368 items. Readers should be advised that there are a considerable number of inaccuracies.

706 **Stories and sketches by Sir Frank Swettenham.**
Selected and introduced by William R. Roff. Kuala Lumpur: Oxford University Press, 1967. 216p.

Sir Frank Swettenham served in Malaya from 1871 until 1904, the last three years as Governor of the Straits Settlements and High Commissioner for the Malay States. Approximately half the twenty-one stories in this volume are taken from Swettenham's first major collection of stories, *Malay sketches*, which was originally published in 1895. Many of the stories are directly autobiographical.

707 **Stories by Sir Hugh Clifford.**
Selected and introduced by William R. Roff. Kuala Lumpur: Oxford University Press, 1966. 225p.

Sir Hugh Clifford served in the Malayan administration from 1883-1903 and from 1927-29, in the latter period as Governor of the Straits Settlements and High Commissioner for the Malay States. The majority of the thirteen stories collected here first appeared at the end of the 1890s. All are set in Malaya, and each draws closely on Clifford's long experience as a British administrator living among the

Malays. They demonstrate the author's sympathy with and understanding of Malay society in the period prior to major Western intrusion.

708 **The consul's file.**
Paul Theroux. Harmondsworth, England: Penguin Books, 1978. 202p.

This collection of twenty short stories provides an evocative and entertaining insight into the contemporary life of 'Ayer Hitam', a small town in West Malaysia, as seen through the eyes of the resident American consul.

709 **The virgin soldiers.**
Leslie Thomas. London: Pan Books, 1967. 205p.

This racy novel recounts the experiences, in brothels and bars as much as in the jungle, of British soldiers conscripted to fight the communist insurrection in Malaya in the early 1950s.

The Arts

710 **Brandon's guide to theatre in Asia.**
James R. Brandon. Honolulu: University Press of Hawaii, 1976. 178p. bibliog.
The purpose of this guide is to help the traveller in Asia 'find and enjoy exciting living theater'. It offers practical guidance as to where to go, how to get there, and what to expect. The guide is organized on a country-by-country basis. The Malaysian section (p. 122-31) offers a brief introduction to the main forms of theatre to be seen (including the shadow play, folk-dance dramas, Chinese opera, and modern drama), and a guide to where they may be seen (principally in Kuala Lumpur and Penang).

711 **Theatre in Southeast Asia.**
James R. Brandon. Cambridge, Massachusetts: Harvard University Press, 1967. 370p. 6 maps. bibliog.
Brandon seeks to present some of the basic facts about theatre in Southeast Asia 'as it exists and functions today' (mid-1960s). The book is based primarily on the author's observations and interviews. The study is organized not on a country-to-country basis, but thematically: origins and background; theatre as art; theatre as a social institution; and theatre as communication. There are a considerable number of references to the theatre in Malaysia, although it should be added that the main focus of the study is Indonesian theatre.

712 **Cultural heritage of Sarawak.**
Lucas Chin. Kuching, Malaysia: Sarawak Museum, 1980. 105p. map. bibliog.
A lavishly produced and illustrated introduction to the material culture of the indigenous peoples of Sarawak. It includes consideration of: prehistoric artefacts; excavated trade ceramics; rock-carvings and megaliths; brass artefacts and their

uses; costumes, jewelleries and ornaments; woodcarvings; historical buildings; and preservation and trade in cultural objects.

713   **New drama one.**
Selected, edited and introduced by Lloyd Fernando.   Kuala Lumpur: Oxford University Press, 1972. 147p.
This volume brings together the texts of three plays (by Edward Dorall, K. Das, and Lee Joo For), as representatives of a major growth of Malaysian drama in English from the mid-1960s. Fernando's introduction considers developments in English-language drama in Malaysia during the decades before and after independence, and assesses critically the plays included here. Each play is preceded by an author's note. There is a concluding list of Malaysian plays in English, as well as biographical notes on the playwrights represented here. There is also a companion volume which includes plays by Patrick Yeoh, Lee Joo For and Edward Dorall entitled *New drama two*, selected, edited and introduced by Lloyd Fernando (Kuala Lumpur: Oxford University Press, 1972. 153p.).

714   **Silat Melayu. The Malay art of attack and defence.**
Ku Ahmad bin Ku Mustaffa, Wong Kiew Kit.   Kuala Lumpur: Oxford University Press, 1978. 76p.
This study provides: a brief outline of the historical, social and cultural aspects of *silat*; a discussion of some of its major styles; an exposition of a basic set of *silat* movements 'which the reader can readily follow and practice on his own'; a detailed explanation of *silat* stances, counters, combat sequences, holds, and locks; an examination of *silat* weapons; and a comparative study of *silat* and other forms of martial arts. There are a very large number of instructional photographs.

715   **Living crafts of Malaysia.**
Mubin Sheppard.   Singapore: Times Books International, 1978. 118p.
A lavishly illustrated book which describes ten individual craftsmen at work in Malaysia and their indigenous, traditional crafts: wood-carver; silversmith; ironsmith; silk-weaver; Sarawak potter; maker of shadow puppets; Sarawak beadworker; maker of screw-pine mats; kite-maker; and maker of bird cage-traps.

716   **Taman indera. A royal pleasure ground. Malay decorative arts and pastimes.**
Mubin Sheppard.   Kuala Lumpur: Oxford University Press, 1972. 207p. 3 maps. bibliog.
This lavishly produced and illustrated study on Malay decorative arts and pastimes includes chapters on: palaces and wood carving; musical instruments; *ma'yong* – the Malay dance drama; the Malay shadow play; dancing; dress; weapons; *silat* – the Malay art of self-defence; metal work; kites and kite flying; spinning tops; and decorative art and the spirit world.

717 **Taman saujana. Dance, drama, music and magic in Malaya long and not-so-long ago.**
Mubin Sheppard. Petaling Jaya: International Book Service, 1983. 114p. bibliog.

Essentially a popular introduction to Malay arts which includes consideration of: *joget gamelan* – a form of court dance with *gamelan* accompaniment; *nobat* – a royal orchestra; *ma'yong* – the Malay dance drama; *wayang kulit* – the Malay shadow play; magic stones, and other examples of the occult in Peninsular Malaysia; and *silat* – the Malay art of self-defence. There are some thirty-five black-and-white photographs.

718 **Studies in Malaysian oral and musical traditions.**
Ann Arbor, Michigan: University of Michigan, Center for South and Southeast Asian Studies, 1974. 99p. bibliog. (Michigan Papers on South and Southeast Asia, no. 8).

This volume contains two papers: William P. Malm, 'Music in Kelantan, Malaysia and some of its cultural implications'; and Amin Sweeney, 'Professional Malay story-telling: some questions of style and presentation'. The Sweeney paper is reprinted from the *Journal of the Malaysian Branch of the Royal Asiatic Society*, vol. 46, part 2 (Dec. 1973), p. 1-53.

719 **Malay shadow puppets. The Wayang Siam of Kelantan.**
Amin Sweeney. London: Trustees of the British Museum, 1972. 83p. map. bibliog.

The shadow play – in which the shadows of puppets (usually made from cow hide) are projected onto a screen – is among the most prominent forms of traditional entertainment in large areas of South East Asia. Sweeney provides a brief introduction to the Malay variation of this genre, the *Wayang Siam*, found predominantly in Kelantan. He examines: the social context of the shadow play; the types, appearance and construction of the puppets; the performance; a brief survey of the repertoire; and the chief characters and the basic tale. There are thirty-six plates, mainly of the puppets themselves.

720 **The *Ramayana* and the Malay shadow-play.**
P. L. Amin Sweeney. Kuala Lumpur: Penerbit Universiti Kebangsaan Malaysia, 1972. 464p. 2 maps. bibliog.

This study divides into three parts. The first examines the Malay shadow-theatre, particular attention being given to the delivery, presentation and language of the repertoire; and to the cultural context of the genre, including its socio-economic aspects, the teacher-pupil relationship, and the role of the *dalang* (puppeteer). The second part primarily examines the oral Malay version of the Indian epic-tale, the *Ramayana*, which forms the basic repertoire of the shadow theatre. An English-language summary of the key text is provided; and there is also comparison of a number of versions of that text, and comparison with local literary versions of the *Rama* saga. The third part provides two excerpts in Malay from the key text; and a transcription of two actual performances of the same part of the story. This is an extremely detailed and authoritative study.

227

721 **Traditional drama and music of Southeast Asia.**
Edited by Mohd. Taib Osman.   Kuala Lumpur: Dewan Bahasa
dan Pustaka, Kementerian Pelajaran Malaysia, 1974. 354p.

This volume consists of papers presented at the International Conference on
Traditional Drama and Music of Southeast Asia, held in Kuala Lumpur in August
1969. The papers are grouped into three sections: the shadow play in Southeast
Asia; traditional theatre in Southeast Asia; and music and musical instruments in
Southeast Asia. There are some ten papers, distributed across the three sections,
which focus on Malaysia. A number of the papers have a list of references.

The Malays. A cultural history.
See item no. 39.

Jah-hĕt of Malaysia, art and culture.
See item no. 303.

Recreation

722　**Gambling games of Malaya.**
　　C. T. Dobree. Kuala Lumpur: Caxton Press, 1955. 146p.
Provides very detailed descriptions of the majority of gambling games played in Malaya as of the mid-1950s, divided by the following headings: documentary betting and lottery games; games with cards; games with dominoes; dice games; and miscellaneous games. At the time of writing the author was Assistant Commissioner of Police in Malaya, and the book was primarily intended as a reference work for magistrates hearing contested gambling cases. There are a large number of plates and illustrations.

723　**Some Kelantan games and entertainments.**
　　A. H. Hill　*Journal of the Malayan Branch of the Royal Asiatic Society*, vol. 25, part 1 (Aug. 1952), p. 20-34.
This brief paper describes four forms of recreation enjoyed by the Kelantan Malays, at least in the early 1950s: bull-fighting; kite-flying; the 'tiger game' [a board game]; and the shadow play. The *Journal of the Malayan/Malaysian Branch of the Royal Asiatic Society* frequently includes articles on Malay pastimes, entertainments, and games. For further references see the subject index of *Index Malaysiana* [735].

Taman indera. A royal pleasure ground. Malay decorative arts and pastimes.
See item no. 716.

Libraries

724 **Libraries in West Malaysia and Singapore. A short history.**
Edward Lim Huck Tee. Kuala Lumpur: University of Malaya
Library, 1970. 161p. bibliog.

Lim seeks to trace the history of every major library in West Malaysia and
Singapore (omitting only the libraries of social and recreational clubs). The
chapter headings are: books and libraries in Malaysia before the coming of the
West; a survey of developments in libraries and librarianship in Malaya, 1817-
1961; public library services in Malaya; a history of public library services in
Singapore; special libraries in Malaya and Singapore; educational libraries in
Malaya and Singapore; problems of library provision in West Malaysia and
Singapore; and recent developments in West Malaysia.

725 **Panduan Perpustakaan di Malaysia. Directory of Libraries in
Malaysia.**
Compiled and edited by Ch'ng Kin See, Ahmad Bakeri bin Abu
Bakar. Kuala Lumpur: National Library of Malaysia, 1978. 324p.

A directory which includes information on: opening hours; access; staff; the
collection; library services; catalogue arrangement; classification system; and
publications, for 177 national, academic, public, and special libraries in Malaysia.
There is a subject index to the special collections.

Mass Media

726 **Broadcasting in Peninsular Malaysia.**
Ronny Adhikarya, with Woon Ai Leng, Wong Hock Seng, Khor Yoke Lim.   London: Routledge & Kegan Paul, in association with the International Institute of Communications, 1977. 102p. 2 maps. bibliog.
After an introductory chapter which examines the structure of the mass media in Malaysia, the telecommunications system, and the national education system, this study considers: the historical development of radio and television in Malaysia; the regulations and policies which govern broadcasting operations; and the organization and processes of the Department of Broadcasting (Radio and Television Malaysia), of the Radio Royal Australian Air Force at Butterworth, of the Educational Media Service (a division of the Ministry of Education), and of Rediffusion (a cable broadcasting station). Two brief concluding chapters examine evolution in the future, and communication policies.

727 **Switch on: switch off. Mass media audiences in Malaysia.**
Newell Grenfell.   Kuala Lumpur: Oxford University Press, 1979. 260p. 2 maps. bibliog.
Grenfell's study of mass media audiences in Peninsular Malaysia considers the following forms of mass communication: radio; private-enterprise wired broadcasting; television; cinema; mobile-unit film shows; and the print media (daily papers, weekly publications, and journals). For each of these media there is first an outline of the medium and its audience; this is followed by an analysis of the demographic patterns of the audience (by sex, age, location, ethnic group); and thirdly there is consideration of the profile of the audience. The analysis is drawn from surveys undertaken in the mid-1970s. An opening chapter traces the development of audience research in Malaysia from 1959-75.

Professional
Periodicals

728 Asian Survey.
Berkeley, California: University of California Press, 1961- .
monthly.

The February issue each year contains a brief survey of the major, mainly political developments in Malaysia in the previous year. In addition, articles relating to Malaysia frequently appear in the remaining issues of each volume. This is a useful source of political-economic analysis of contemporary Asia.

729 Contemporary Southeast Asia.
Singapore: Institute of Southeast Asian Studies, 1979- . quarterly.

This journal carries articles on political, economic, social and technological developments in contemporary South East Asia. It appears to be aimed not solely at an academic audience but also at the senior business and diplomatic communities. Each issue contains a brief documentation section which usually reproduces important policy statements by senior officials or politicians from within or outside the region.

730 Far Eastern Economic Review.
Hong Kong: Far Eastern Economic Review, 1946- . weekly.

Informed, thorough and perceptive, this weekly publication is an essential source for those who wish to keep abreast of political, economic and commercial developments throughout Asia. The coverage of Malaysia is notably fine.

731 Journal of Asian Studies.
Ann Arbor, Michigan: Association for Asian Studies, 1956-
quarterly.

The premier American journal in Asian studies which occasionally carries articles on Malaysia. It has an excellent, and relatively comprehensive, book review section. This journal succeeds the *Far Eastern Quarterly*, published November 1941 to September 1956.

732 **Journal of Contemporary Asia.**

Stockholm: Journal of Contemporary Asia, 1970- . quarterly.

A scholarly journal which has a pronounced radical stance. It is devoted to the analysis of economic, political and social conditions throughout contemporary Asia. There are frequent contributions on Malaysia.

733 **Journal of Southeast Asian History.**

Singapore: Department of History, University of Singapore, 1960-1969. semi-annual.

This was the principal historical journal for the region during the 1960s, a decade in which there was a dramatic expansion in scholarly interest in South East Asian history. *JSEAH* carried a high proportion of articles on the history of Malaya/Malaysia. There was a reasonably strong book review section.

734 **Journal of Southeast Asian Studies.**

Singapore: McGraw-Hill Far Eastern Publishers (1970-1977); Singapore University Press (1978-), 1970- . semi-annual.

This is the successor to *JSEAH*, now including articles in the social sciences (perhaps most notably economics and politics), as well as history. As with *JSEAH*, Malaysia is well-represented: and there is a reasonably strong book review section.

735 **Journal of the Malaysian Branch of the Royal Asiatic Society.**

Kuala Lumpur: Malaysian Branch of the Royal Asiatic Society, 1923- . semi-annual.

From 1923-63 inclusive, this journal was known as the *Journal of the Malayan Branch of the Royal Asiatic Society*. It formed the continuation of the *Journal of the Straits Branch, Royal Asiatic Society*, published 1878-1922. The Malaysian Branch of the Royal Asiatic Society has published three indices: *Index Malaysiana. An index to the Journal of the Straits Branch Royal Asiatic Society and the Journal of the Malayan Branch Royal Asiatic Society, 1878-1963*, by Lim Huck Tee and D. E. K. Wijasuriya (Kuala Lumpur, 1970. 395p.); *Index Malaysiana. Supplement I. An index to the Journal of the Malaysian Branch of the Royal Asiatic Society and the JMBRAS monographs, 1964-1973*, by D. E. K. Wijasuriya and Lim Huck Tee, (Kuala Lumpur, 1974. 66p.); and *Index Malaysiana. Supplement no. 2, 1974-1983*, by D. E. K. Wijasuriya, Lim Huck Tee (Petaling Jaya, 1985. 72p.). A long-established journal which is simply the essential source for the study of Malaya/Malaysia. Over the decades its particular strengths have been in history, archaeology, natural history, literature and culture, and anthropology.

736 **Journal of Tropical Geography.**
Kuala Lumpur, Singapore: Departments of Geography, The
University of Singapore and The University of Malaya, 1953-79.
semi-annual.

Upto and including vol. 10 (June 1957) this journal was called *The Malayan
Journal of Tropical Geography*. Although this journal was concerned with the
geography (in all its aspects) of the tropical world, it carried a notably high
proportion of articles on that of Malaysia.

737 **Kajian Ekonomi Malaysia.** (Malaysian Economic Studies.)
Kuala Lumpur: Persatuan Ekonomi Malaysia [Malaysian
Economic Association], 1964- . semi-annual.

This journal of the Malaysian Economic Association is devoted mainly to articles
on the contemporary economy of Malaysia, and is thus an essential source for
economists. Articles are in English.

738 **Kajian Malaysia.** (Journal of Malaysian Studies.)
Penang: Universiti Sains Malaysia, 1983- . semi-annual.

Recently established, this journal has yet to develop a distinctive character. But it
invites scholarly articles in the social sciences and humanities relating to Malaysia,
and to judge by its opening issues it promises to be an important source for the
study of Malaysia. Some articles are in English, some in Bahasa Malaysia.

739 **Malaya Law Review.**
Singapore: Faculty of Law, The National University of Singapore,
1959- . semi-annual.

From 1959-61 inclusive, this journal was titled: *University of Malaya Law Review*.
This is an international academic law journal which quite frequently carries
articles on legal developments in Malaysia.

740 **Malayan Economic Review.**
Singapore: Economic Society of Singapore and the Department of
Economics and Statistics, The National University of Singapore,
1956-82. semi-annual.

Continued as: *The Singapore Economic Review*, 1983- . An international journal
of economics which quite frequently carries articles on the contemporary
economy of Malaysia.

741 **Malayan Law Journal.**
Singapore, Kuala Lumpur: Malayan Law Journal Pte. Ltd.,
1932- . semi-annual.

A journal which consists mainly of law reports, and is therefore intended
primarily for the legal practitioner.

742 Modern Asian Studies.

Cambridge, England: Cambridge University Press, 1967-
quarterly.

This is the British counterpart to the *Journal of Asian Studies* (q.v.), although it allows notably less space for book reviews. There are frequent articles on Malaysia, perhaps most notably in history, economics and politics.

743 Pacific Affairs.

Vancouver, British Columbia: University of British Columbia,
1928- . quarterly.

This journal of the contemporary social, economic and political affairs of Asia and the Pacific frequently carries articles on Malaysia. There is an excellent book review section.

744 Sarawak Museum Journal.

Kuching, Malaysia: The Museum, Kuching, Sarawak.

The first issue was produced in 1911; but by 1937 only 15 issues had appeared. The journal was re-established in 1949. By the early 1980s there was one, occasionally two, issues each year. Index for all issues 1911-1979, vol. 28, no. 49 (Dec. 1980). This is an essential source for studies on the natural history, archaeology, and anthropology of Borneo. Reference should also be made to: *The Brunei Museum Journal* (Brunei: The Brunei Museum, 1969- .); *Sabah Society Journal* (Kota Kinabalu: The Sabah Society, 1961- .); *Federation Museums Journal [New Series]* (Kuala Lumpur: Museums Department, Peninsular Malaysia, 1954/55-).

745 Southeast Asian Affairs.

Singapore: Institute of Southeast Asian Studies, 1974- . annually.

Each issue of this annual publication usually carries two (occasionally three) articles on Malaysia. One provides an annual review of major political, economic, social, and strategic developments; one (or two) is of a more specialized nature, focusing on an important aspect of contemporary Malaysia, and not necessarily concerning itself solely with the year under review. This is an essential source.

746 Southeast Asian Journal of Social Science.

Singapore: Institute of Southeast Asian Studies and the
Department of Sociology of the National University of Singapore,
1973- . semi-annual.

Although containing articles from across the social sciences, this journal is perhaps most noted for its contributions in sociology. It carries a high proportion of articles on Malaysia. It was founded, in 1973, by the amalgamation of the *Southeast Asian Journal of Sociology* and the *Southeast Asian Journal of Economic Development and Social Change.*

Directories

747 A dictionary of the economic products of the Malay peninsula.
I. H. Burkill.   Kuala Lumpur: Ministry of Agriculture &
Co-operatives, Malaysia, 1966. 2nd ed. 2 vols.

The first edition of this dictionary was published in 1935 by the Crown Agents for
the Colonies. This second edition involves only minor corrections. Running to
almost 2,500 pages, it remains the authoritative reference to the animal,
vegetable, and mineral products of the Malay peninsula.

748 Who's who in Malaysia and Singapore 1983-84.
Petaling Jaya: Who's Who Publications, 1983. 2 vols.

This is the fifteenth edition of a directory which was first published in 1955. The
first volume [477p.] is devoted to Malaysia, the second to Singapore. This edition
contains a subject index, that is an index to prominent Malaysians divided by
occupation or by form of organization: for example, economists; legal profession;
religious organizations; trade unions. This directory is an invaluable guide to 'top'
Malaysians.

General
Bibliographies

749 A bibliography of bibliographies on Malaysia.
Ding Choo Ming. Petaling Jaya: Hexagon Elite Publications, 1981.
184p.
This bibliography contains 507 fully annotated entries organized into 22 subject
divisions. There is both an author index and a title index.

750 A bibliography of bibliographies on Malaysia: supplement I.
Ding Choo Ming. *Southeast Asian Research Materials Group:
Newsletter*, no. 23 (Dec. 1982), p. 1-14.
This supplement to Ding Choo Ming's *A bibliography of bibliographies on
Malaysia*, (Petaling Jaya: Hexagon Elite Publications, 1981. 184p.) contains
thirty-one annotated entries. A second supplement is 'A bibliography of
bibliographies on Malaysia: supplement II', by Ding Choo Ming. *Southeast Asian
Research Materials Group: Newsletter*, no. 26 (March 1984), p. 1-13. This
supplement contains a further forty-nine annotated entries.

751 Bibliography of Malaysia and Singapore.
R. S. Karni. Kuala Lumpur: Penerbit Universiti Malaya, 1980.
649p.
This work is a development of the *Bibliography of Malaya* compiled by H. A. R.
Cheeseman (London: Longmans & Green for the British Association of Malaya,
1959). It is an apparently exhaustive bibliography of works relating to Peninsular
Malaysia and Singapore in English, Dutch, French and Portuguese, published
upto and including 1966. The bibliography is divided into the following main
subject headings: generalities; religion; social science, economics, government,
education; natural science; applied science, medicine, technology; architecture;
linguistics, languages, literature; and geography, biography, history. There is no
index by author or by title.

237

752 **Malaysian studies: present knowledge and research trends.**
Edited by John A. Lent.   DeKalb, Illinois: Northern Illinois
University, Center for Southeast Asian Studies, 1979. 466p.
bibliogs. (Occasional Paper no. 7).

This volume examines the state of Malaysian studies as of the late 1970s, and
suggests further areas for research in this field. The examination is restricted to
the following disciplines: sociology; anthropology; political science; mass
communications; and education. For each discipline there is an extensive
bibliography. A major part (40 per cent) of the volume is taken up by a chapter
titled 'Doctoral research on Malaya and Malaysia, 1895-1977: a comprehensive
bibliography and statistical overview'.

753 **West Malaysia and Singapore: a selected bibliography.**
Karl J. Pelzer.   New Haven, Connecticut: Human Relations Area
Files Press, Behavior Science Bibliographies, 1971. 394p.

The entries in this bibliography are divided under the following headings:
periodicals and conference proceedings cited (in this bibliography); bibliographies; serials devoted exclusively to West Malaysia and Singapore; description
– popular and scientific; general; history; physical geography; economic, political,
and regional geography; man and culture; economy; the state; Singapore. Over
half the entries are in the categories: man and culture; economy. There is an
author index.

754 **University of Singapore Library. Catalogue of the
Singapore/Malaysia collection.**
Boston, Massachusetts: G. K. Hall, 1968. 757p.

At the time of publication of this catalogue, the University of Singapore Library
held approximately 7,500 catalogued items relating to Malaysia and Singapore.
The collection is particularly strong in source material for the history of the
peninsular Malay states, Singapore, and the Borneo territories, from their
founding, through the colonial period, to independence and after. It also
included, at that time, over 1,000 theses and academic exercises mostly submitted
to the universities of Singapore and Malaya; press cuttings; company reports;
directories. Excluded from this catalogue are: Chinese titles; legal and medical
literature. This is an invaluable guide. See also: *University of Singapore Library.
Catalogue of the Singapore/Malaysia collection. Supplement, 1968-1972.* (Singapore: Singapore University Press, 1974. 324p.). This supplement includes
approximately 3,100 catalogued items.

Index

The index is a single alphabetical sequence of authors (personal and corporate), titles of publications and subjects. Index entries refer both to the main items and to other works mentioned in the notes to each item. Title entries are in italics. Numeration refers to the items as numbered.

239

241

Bauer, P. T. 190, 525
BBC – British Broadcasting
    Corporation 188
Beadworking
    Sarawak 715
Beaglehole, J. H. 480
Bedlington, S. 379
Beds in the East 700
Bees 92
Before the party 704
Beijing 668
    influence on communist activity
        391
Beliefs
    Berawan 304
    Borneo 325
    Dayak 312
    Dusun 307, 330
    traditional 362
    see also Animistic beliefs; Religion
Benham, F. C. 525
Berawan peoples
    afterlife beliefs and rituals 304
    death rituals 321
Berry, P. Y. 69
Bertam Valley
    settlement history 545
Betting 722
Bibliographies 174, 749-754
    anthropology 752
    applied science 751
    archaeology 99, 101
    architecture 751
    biography 751
    British Malaya (1867-1942) 156
    climate 47
    demography 288
    drug abuse 369
    economics 516-517, 751, 753
    education 653-654, 751-752
    geography 751, 753
    geology 46
    government 751
    history 751, 753
        economic 235
    Kelantan 445
    Kinabalu 82
    languages 751
    linguistics 751
    literature 751, 677, 695
        modern Malay 665
    Malaysian studies 749-752

man and culture 753
mass communications 752
medicine 751
Melaka studies 34
natural science 751
political science 752-753
population and development 286
religion 751
Singapore 751, 753
social science 751
sociology 752
technology 751
urban transport 628
West Malaysia 753
women in Malaysia 366
Bibliography of bibliographies on
    Malaysia 749
    : *supplement I* 750
    : *supplement II* 750
Bibliography of the demography of
    Malaysia and Brunei 288
Bibliography of Malaya 751
Bibliography of Malaysia and
    Singapore 751
Bidayuh people 313
Bilek family 308, 310
Biography
    bibliography 751
Bird cage-traps 715
Bird, I. L. 64, 207
Bird's-eye view of the development of
    modern Malay literature,
    1921-1941 680
Birds *see* Fauna
Birds of Borneo 90
Birds of the Malay peninsula. A general
    account . . . 87
Birds of the Malay peninsula,
    Singapore and Penang. An
    account of all the Malayan species,
    with a note of their occurrence in
    Sumatra, Borneo, and Java and a
    list of the birds of those islands 72
Birth *see* Childbirth
Birth-spirits 363
Bisch, J. 305
Black, I. 133
Blagden, C. O. 302
Blood and tears 679
Blythe, W. 191
Boat People 397
Boh, M. 571

246

247

259

FELDA. 21 years of land development
604
Fernandez, D. 516
Fernando, L. 666-667, 713
Fertility, human
Iban people 323
impact of economic and social
development 286
Festivals
Borneo under British rule 324
religious 326
Indian 351
Fiction
set in Malaysia 700-709
Filipinos
alleged indolence 187
Finance 517
external 505
federal 268, 505
for education 655
investment by MCA 534
local government 505
private 518
public 9, 504-505, 518, 539
national accounts data 643
state 505
statistics 644
Finance and banking 215-216, 518,
571-575
*Financial development in Malaya and
Singapore* 572
*Financial institutions and markets in
Malaysia* 575
*Financial institutions and markets in
Southeast Asia. A study of Brunei,
Indonesia, Malaysia, Philippines,
Singapore and Thailand* 575
Firth, Raymond 358, 547, 561
Firth, Rosemary 525, 548
Fiscal policy 513, 516, 531
redistribution 526
Fiscal prospects 641
Fiscal system *see* Taxation
Fish
poisonous 93, 359
Fisher, C. A. 40
Fisheries 504
in school syllabus 41
resources 648
sea pollution 647
statistics 644
Fishermen

income 528
ownership 562
social structure of a fishing village
community 544, 547, 552
Fisk, E. K. 9, 524
Five-Year Plans 517
First (1956-60) 523
Second (1961-5) 523
Fleming, W. A. 71
Fletcher, N. McH. 489
Floering, I. 593
Flora
forest flowers 77
garden flowers 78
Kinabalu 82
mosses 80
palms 97
roadside flowers 77
seashore flowers 77
seed plants 80
waste spaces 77
wild flowers 76-77
see also Botany
Flora and fauna 69-97
Flotsam and jetsam 704
*Flourish for the bishop. Brooke's friend
Grant. Two studies in Sarawak
history, 1848-1868* 141
Fodor's Southeast Asia 1985 65
Folk literature 694
Folklore
British North Borneo 32
Dusun people 307, 325
Murut people 325
Orang Asli 301
superstition in folk-tales 361
Food 647
beliefs and behaviour 368
Borneo under British 324
marketing 510
production 588
new techniques 600, 603
Food and agriculture Malaysia 2000
588
Force of circumstance 701
Foreign correspondents
hear speech on Federation (1961)
412
Foreign exchange
rate policy 503
reserves 503
Foreign investment 31, 516, 578

GDP – gross domestic product 643
Geddes, W. R. 312
Geography 9, 40-68
  bibliography 751, 753
  British North Borneo 32
  economic 50-51, 55
  historical 55, 107
  human settlement 52-63
  North Borneo 55
  physical 8, 44-49, 55
  political 107
  Sabah 132
  Sarawak 43
  social 8, 57
  travellers' accounts 64-68
  tropical
    periodicals 736
Geology 46
  in school syllabus 41
  Kinabalu 82
  Peninsular Malaysia 44
*Geology of the Malay Peninsula (West
  Malaysia and Singapore)* 46
Geomorphology
  Kinabalu 82
  Mulu rain forest 73
George Town
  race and the man in the street 426
  social structure 24
  Town Council suspended (1966) 483
Gerakan 383
Gerakan Rakyat Malaysia 416
German intervention
  feared by British 154, 160
  not feared 170
Ghosh, K. K. 183
Ghosts 364
Gimlette, J. D. 359
Gladstone
  replaced by Disraeli (1874) 166
Glenister, A. G. 72
Global economic crisis 518
GNP – gross national product 527, 559
Goa
  Portuguese administration 128
Gobbett, D. J. 46
Gods
  primitive 364
Goh Ban Lee 52
Goh Cheng Teik 422
Goh, K. C. 592
Golay, F. H. 28, 506

Golden chersonese and the way thither
  64, 207
Golden khersonese 106–108
*Golden khersonese. Studies in the
  historical geography of the Malay
  peninsula before A.D. 1500* 107
Goody, J. 308
Gordon, S. 27
Gosling, L. A. P. 18
Gould, J. W. 10
*Government and economic
  development* 527
Government 10, 31, 38, 204, 264, 403,
  414, 533
  Alliance (1957-69) 227, 400
    (1971-5) 532
  annual budget 512
  available resources 512-513
  Barisan Nasional coalition 383
  bibliography 751
  Chinese businessmen as revenue
    farmers 194
  coalition in Sarawak 458
  conflict with organized labour
    (1945-8) 273
  economic planning 522
  expenditure 512-513, 520
  federal
  general election (1982) 431
  institutions 469
  left-wing politics restricted [in
    Singapore] 278
  life of government servants and
    families 188
  National Front 468
    (1945-65) 402
  officials 552
  parliamentary 268
    suspended after May 1969 riots 437
  programmes for development 546
  records 191, 267
  Singapore 150
  state
    election (1982) 431
  see also Local government
Government agencies 507
  land distribution 52
    in Cameron Highlands 545
  Multi-Purpose Holdings Berhad 534
  NEP targets 535
Government and politics in Malaysia
  402-403

265

269

271

Manpower
  planning 502
  trained 655
Manufacturing 51, 189, 502, 506, 539
  capital utilization 516
  control 516
  expansion of exports 580
  foreign investment 582
  growth in Peninsular Malaysia 580
  in school syllabus 41
  need for investment 531
  ownership 516
  problems of women workers 367
  profit–wage ratio 516
  statistics 644
  West Malaysia 517
Manuscript literature 691
Manuscript sources 126
Maps
  historical
    Melaka 34
Marcos
  President of Philippines 494
Marimuthu, T. 551, 659
Marital status
  ethnic differences 289
  people of Borneo 284
  religious differences 289
Marketing 548
  fish 547
  food 510
  local 529
  role of cooperatives 564
Marriage 300, 319, 324
  Bidayuh people 313
  Iban people 308, 319
  inter-speech group 13
  law reform (1972) 473
  legal systems affecting 339
  patterns 566
    impact of economic and social
      development 286
    Kelantan 371
    trends 289
  rural women 37
  Semai people 293
  village 616
  see also Wedding customs
Marsden, W. 334
Marshall, A. G. 649
Mas, K. 679
Masked comrades. A study of the

Communist United Front in
  Malaya, 1945-48 248
Mason, M. 188
Mass communications
  bibliography 752
Mass media 726-727
  impact on village community 566
Mat Salleh revolts 133
Mat-making 715
Matheson, V. 126-127, 682
Matrilineal kinship system
  in Jelebu 563
Maugham, W. Somerset 701, 704
Maugham's Borneo stories 704
Maugham's Malaysian stories 701
Mauzy, D. K. 398-399, 403
Maxwell, G.
  decentralization proposals (1920)
    183
Ma'yong [Malay dance drama] 716-717
May 13: before and after 419
May 13 tragedy. A report 425
May thirteenth incident and democracy
  in Malaysia 422
Mayerchak, P. M. 423
Mazumdar, D. 519
MCA – Malaysian Chinese Association
  244, 257, 265, 278, 383, 451
  electoral results (1969) 421
  investment arm
    Multi-Purpose Holdings Berhad
      534
  part of Barisan Nasional coalition
    383
  Perak 452
  portfolios acquired 423
MCP – Malayan Communist Party 27,
  162, 248, 250-251, 254, 256, 267,
  272, 384, 418
Means, G. P. 342-343, 400, 403, 424
Mecca
  pilgrimage 224, 448
  social and health hazards 180
Medicine
  bibliography 751
  medical research 196
  practice of *bomoh* or *pawang* 359
  Semai people
    diagnosis and treatment of disease
      293
  see also Healers
Medway, Lord 85-87, 90

279

281

287

288

297

Social organization *contd.*
Malays 332
in Sarawak 14
Murut people 325
Negeri Sembilan
Jelebu district 563
New Villages 27
Orang Asli 292
*Social organization. Essays presented
to Raymond Firth* 562
*Social organization of Islam in
Kelantan* 449
Social prejudices 700
*Social relations – the ethnic and class
factors* 551
*Social relations of dependence in a
Malay state: nineteenth century
Perak*
Social science
bibliography 751
British Malaya 156
intersection of class and race 380
periodicals 746
research in Sarawak 304
theories of inequality 526
Social services 504
Sabah 132
Social statistics 644
Social stratification 563
on rubber plantation 15
under British rule 226
Social structure 9-10, 16, 38
effect of occupational status 544, 547
effect of urbanization 50
European community 193
Kedah 24
Kelantan 554
New Economic Policy 501
Penang 24
under British rule 226
villages 616
Social structure in Southeast Asia 309
Social traditions
based on kinship 4
Social values
portrayed in literature 688
Social welfare 504
provision
population changes 283
see also Health and welfare
Socialist Front 584
Society 116, 210

Kelantan 147
Kuala Lumpur (1885-1912) 195
traditional Malay 448
*Society and cosmos. Chewong of
Peninsular Malaysia* 298
*Socio-economic basis of ethnic
consciousness – the Chinese in the
1970s* 551
Sociology 746
bibliography 752
*Sociology of production in rural Malay
society* 544
*Sociology of secret societies. A study of
Chinese secret societies in
Singapore and Peninsular
Malaysia* 21
*Sociology of South-East Asia. Readings
on social change and development*
25
SOE – Special Operations Executive 255
Force 136   280
SOE in the Far East 255
Soenarno, R. 173
Soh Eng Lim 270
Soil 588
erosion 42
in school syllabus 41
local god of the soil 350
Peninsular Malaysia 44
suited to oil palms 606
Solar radiation 47 *see also* Energy
*Solar radiation in Malaysia. A study on
availability and distribution of
solar energy in Malaysia* 646
*Some aspects of Ṣūfism as understood
and practised among the Malays*
338
*Some development implications of
political integration and
disintegration in Malaysia* 527
*Some reflections on padi
double-cropping in West Malaysia*
517
*Some trends in the Peninsular Malaysia
plantation sector 1963-1973* 591
Somerset Maugham, W. 701, 704
Soothsaying 359
Sopiee, M. N. 31, 271, 412
Sothi Rachagan 551
Soul of Malaya 703
South China Sea
offshore petroleum 621

298

301

304

Maps of Malaysia

These maps show the more important towns and other features.

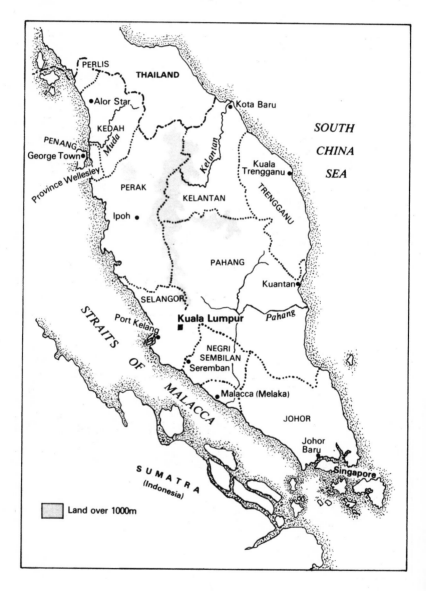

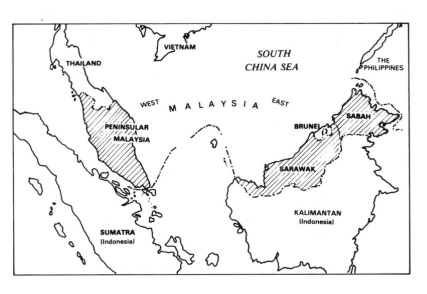

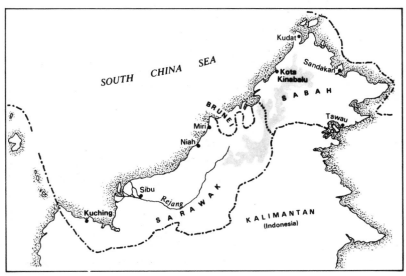